The Knights Templars
In England

The Knights Templars In England

Thomas W. Parker

The University of Arizona Press

Tucson   1963

J.A.H.

Discipulo et Amico

Preface

MUCH has been written about the Knights Templars as an international military order and about their trial and the dissolution of their order, but little has been done systematically or in detail on their organization and activities in individual countries. This work seeks to fill this gap for England by presenting a survey of the history of the Templars there from the time of their appearance in the third decade of the twelfth century to their dissolution in the early years of the fourteenth. In order to give balance and perspective to them and their activities, brief consideration is given to the Templars on the Continent and in the Holy Land as well; however, chief attention is directed to their organization, privileges, holdings, and political and economic activities in England. Because of the nature of the source materials, the particular activities the Templars engaged in, and the reliance of the order upon the crown for support, the treatment of the subject is oriented toward their relations with the English kings.

Except for the Inquest of 1185 and a few minor documents, primary source materials must be gleaned mainly from the miscellaneous references in the Public Records and in the various volumes of the Rolls Series. Secondary authorities are surprisingly few. There are only three general works of note: the lengthy and detailed essay on the Templars in England in the twelfth century written by Beatrice Lees as an introduction to her edition of the Inquest;[1] the doctoral dissertation of Clarence Perkins[2] which is chiefly concerned with a discussion of the privileges and the trial of the Templars in England; and the introductory chapters of J. Bruce Williamson's study of the Temple in London.[3]

Tucson, Arizona   T.W.P.
January, 1963

Contents

The Knights Templars
In England

chapter one

Introduction

THE KNIGHTS TEMPLARS were the most colorful, the most powerful, and the most widely known of the crusading orders of the Middle Ages. Accordingly, their history is to a large degree a part of the history of the Crusades; and in this sense, the struggle for the faith and the Holy Land receives major emphasis in any discussion of the order and its activities. But the Templars were concerned with political and economic as well as with religious and military matters. Indeed, their power and accomplishments as feudal lords and bankers seem as great as, if not greater than, their achievements and contributions as soldiers of Christ and His Church, as can be seen both in the general history and in the specific affairs of the order in the various areas where the Templars were active, whether in the states of the Holy Land or in the states of western Europe.[1]

Since the Templars have unfortunately left no specific or official history of their order, such information as we possess must be pieced together from the incomplete and not always impartial or accurate records and reports which have survived from the Middle Ages. All that the Templars themselves have left are copies of their Rule and a limited collection of charters. Several historical writers of the High Middle Ages, both in the Holy Land and in western Europe, provide valuable but not very extensive material. In addition, the public records of individual countries, especially England and France, furnish considerable but controversial political and financial data; and papal records abound with references to the order.

In England, the major concern of this study, information on the Templars has to be drawn chiefly from references in the public records, the accounts of contemporary historical writers, and such Templar records as still survive. Though most of the order's English records have disappeared, a few important charters and a number of miscellaneous documents do exist. The reason for the disappearance of the records is not wholly known. Especially on the local level, probably the mere passage of time accounts for the loss of many of them, while on the national level, destruction by fire seems the probable explanation. At the time of the dissolution of the order and the subsequent assignment of former Templar lands to the Knights Hospitallers, full records seem to have existed at New Temple in London, the central office and depository of the order, and at local preceptories. These records, at least in part, formed the basis for the claims and counter-claims of the king, individual nobles, and the Hospitallers.[2] Later, at the time of Wat Tyler's insurrection (summer, 1381), when the rebels attacked and destroyed much property in London, New Temple was among the buildings ravaged and burned.[3] There is no indication that either the Hospitallers, who were to hold the Temple for many years, or the Apprentices of the Law, who have occupied it since at least the last quarter of the fourteenth century, disposed of any of the Templar records.

Origins of the Templars

Of the precise origin of the Templars, little is known beyond brief mention by several medieval writers.[4] To this, modern historians have been able to add little, if anything.[5] Apparently, the origin of the Order of the Temple is to be found in the determination of two Frankish knights in the East — Hugh of Payens (in Champagne) and Geoffrey of St. Omer (in Artois) — who, being distressed by the sufferings of Christian pilgrims, decided to devote their lives to the protection and aid of these people as they made their way from Asia Minor and the sea ports of the eastern Mediterranean to the Holy City. It was in 1118 that these two men, renouncing all worldly ambition and choosing to live like monks, went to Arnulf, Patriarch of Jerusalem, and before him took vows of poverty, chastity, and obedience and formally announced their noble and useful purpose. Soon, however, another duty — which was to become their chief purpose — was added: to do battle against the infidel, whether or not Christian pilgrims were threatened.

From its dwelling place, the new order received its name; for, lacking a place to live, Hugh and Geoffrey, and the six or seven other men who had joined them, were given a residence within the precincts of his own palace area and near the church known as the Temple of Solomon, by Baldwin II, King of Jerusalem. From this, the Templars (*Templarii*) became known first as "the poor fellow soldiers of Christ and of the Temple of Solomon" (*Pauperes Commilitiones Christi et Templi Salomonis*) and later as the "Knights of the Temple of Solomon of Jerusalem" (*Fratres Militiae Templi Salomonis Ierusalem*).[6]

The first few years of their existence provided no indication of the importance the Templars were to assume. It was at the end of nine years, when there were still only nine members,[7] that the Templars turned to

Bernard, Abbot of Clairvaux, for aid and advice. Baldwin II, writing on behalf of this worthy new order and praising its cause (1127), begged the saintly and influential abbot to help by encouraging the pope to confirm the order and to approve a rule for it.[8] Responding favorably, the great Cistercian advocated the cause of the Templars and indicated a willingness to help them draw up a rule.[9] Meanwhile, Hugh, received by Honorius II, was assured of papal sympathy and instructed to present a petition to the church council which had been called to meet at Troyes in 1128. The Council approved the new order, entrusted the revision and amplification of its existing rule to Bernard, and decreed that their new constitution and rule should be put into effect after being finally sanctioned by the pope and the patriarch of Jerusalem.[10] When both Honorius and Stephen, pope and patriarch respectively, subsequently gave their approval, the Templars' fortune took a decided turn for the better.

Because of their fame arising from their soldierly skill which brought victory in battle and their religious enthusiasm which set an example of self-sacrifice, and in addition, because of Bernard's words of praise which were as unstinting as they were influential,[11] the Templars soon found themselves besieged by recruits and patronized by kings, popes, princes, and other lords, both lay and ecclesiastical. Both in the east and the west, these gifts and privileges, as well as recruits, now came to them in great number. William of Tyre gave testimony of this growth when he said: "There was not a prince in western Europe who did not contribute to their maintenance, and in wealth they were the equals of kings."[12] Later (1244) in a similar vein, Matthew Paris wrote, ". . . the Templars in Christendom [have] nine thousand manors . . . besides the emoluments and various revenues arising from their brotherhoods, and from procurations, all of which are increased by their privileges."[13]

Papal Privileges

Especially important among the many and extensive privileges bestowed upon the Templars over a period of more than a century and a half were those granted by the popes, practically all of whom from Celestine II to Clement V issued bulls — many of them still surviving — on their behalf.[14] Among the major privileges granted to the order as a whole by the various popes were the following: First an exemption from payment of clerical taxes of all sorts.[15] This meant that regular tithes, on the one hand, and special levies of twentieths, fifteenths, and the like, for the Crusades, on the other, were not to be collected from the Templars. Second, a requirement that the clergy urge Christians to contribute to the Templars.[16] This meant special encouragement to fund-

raising activities on behalf of the Templars and provision of funds
without effort on their part. Third, a reservation of offerings collected
on certain days in certain churches for the Templars.[17] This provided a
sort of compulsory support of the Templars in addition to the voluntary
contributions just mentioned. Fourth, an authority to open churches in
order to hold services and collect offerings even in places under the
interdict.[18] This somewhat surprising concession provided still more
revenue for the Templars. Fifth, a right to have their own chaplains, to
build their own chapels (*oratoria*), and to bury the dead in their own
churchyards.[19] These grants meant the Templars could go their own way
in religious matters irrespective of the regular and secular clergy and
helped to make the Templars practically independent of all churchmen
except the pope.[20] Sixth, an exemption from excommunication and interdict.[21] This meant that neither the Templars nor their vassals or tenants
could be proceeded against by the usual religious means and thus further
removed the order from dependence upon the ordinary religious groups.
Seventh, a requirement that all prelates uphold and protect the rights,
persons, and goods of the Templars.[22] This further strengthened the
Templars' immunity from unfriendly action by their critics and rivals
and promoted respect for their privileges. In addition to the grant of
other lesser privileges,[23] too numerous to mention here, papal grants and
confirmations of land, other property, and money were many and extensive.[24] The net effect of these papal privileges was to put the Templars
under the special protection of the popes and to render them practically
immune from all other jurisdiction, lay or ecclesiastical. Thus we note
that the order had been raised to a position of extraordinary power, influence, and privilege. To these papal gifts and privileges were added
those given by temporal rulers — for example, the specific and additional
privileges received by the Templars in England which will be considered
in the next chapter.

It is not in the least surprising to find that the rights and privileges
of the Templars were not always respected and that considerable resentment and opposition arose — as is clearly evident in the numerous papal
bulls which so often restated the provisions of earlier ones and which
repeatedly directed recognition and acceptance of the Templars' privileges.[25] Upon occasion, however, it was necessary for the popes to
check, or to seek to check, the Templars' tendencies toward excessive
greed, arrogance, and independence.[26] In short, the financial rights and
exemptions, the ecclesiastical privileges and immunities, and their own
actions and attitudes made the Templars powerful and independent and
aroused rivalry and hatred which would one day return to plague them.
Yet, in the early years, and indeed, throughout much of their history,

the Templars were well thought of, especially because of their very real achievements against the infidel.[27]

Organization

The organization and rule of the Templars had much in common with those of most western monastic orders of the Middle Ages, but it was the Cistercian order that the Templars used as their chief model,[28] a not unexpected choice in view of the prominence of the Cistercians in the early twelfth century and especially in view of the willingness of Bernard of Clairvaux to help the new group draw up its rule and to support its program. Quite naturally, the specific details of organization, especially those of a military nature, had to be worked out slowly on the basis of necessity and experience. Not until 1163, when Pope Alexander III issued *Omne datum optimum,* mentioned above, was a definite and centralized organization officially established. But this was in large part a confirmation of the system which had evolved in the preceding half-century during which the order had gained great power and risen to a level of wide influence both in the east and the west. The Templars' organization, as revealed in the papal bull and in the Rule of the order, must now be briefly examined.[29]

The chief official of the Templars, chosen by a complicated electoral procedure and serving for life, was the Grand Master whose headquarters were in Jerusalem and whose powers were extensive, including, as they did, leadership in battle, appointment and supervision of officials, administration of the order's property, and discipline of individual members. Though limited to some degree by the Council of the order, in which he had one vote and in which the principle of majority vote prevailed, he, nonetheless, by his power of appointment and of determining who should be called to sit in council, must often have dominated both the Council and the order.[30] Second in command was the Seneschal who was supreme in the absence of the Grand Master.[31] Below the Seneschal was the Marshall, a sort of minister of war and normally the immediate subordinate of the Grand Master on campaign.[32] Below these officers was the Commander of the Realm of Jerusalem who served as the Master of the Province of Jerusalem and also as the Grand Treasurer of the whole order.[33] Strictly limited in his spheres of activity and jurisdiction, but still one of the chief officials of the order, was the Commander of the City of Jerusalem whose task it was to defend Christian pilgrims and to provide them with food and horses in the Holy Land.[34]

Initially the organization and rule of the order pertained to Templars in the Holy Land alone; but in time, as the order expanded into Europe, the organization, somewhat modified, was applied there, too.[35]

At the head of each province, a large territorial area often coterminous with a state or kingdom, was a Provincial Master — also called Grand Preceptor or Grand Prior — who was to the province what the Grand Master was to the whole order. Though apparently appointed technically by the Grand Master — at least in the early years — the provincial master was probably to a large degree free of his actual or direct control. In turn, the provincial master was responsibile for the appointment and supervision of subordinate officials in his province and was expected to consult with his provincial council before deciding important matters or undertaking major activities. Each province was divided into preceptories which served as the basic administrative units and as the recruiting stations of the order. The individual preceptories were often local manors which had come into the hands of the Templars and had thereby been transformed into religious houses. The term preceptory, therefore, is used to refer both to the territory and to the office for the management of the territory. The powers and importance of any individual preceptor would vary according to the size and wealth of his preceptory as well as according to the ability and personality of the preceptor himself. Subordinate to the preceptors, but essential to the effective functioning of the preceptory, must have been the business agents and estate stewards as well as the serfs who worked the Templar lands.[36]

Alongside the officials of the order where the chapters which shared in the administration of the order and in the determination of policy. A general chapter, or chapter for business, was held, apparently at least once each year, usually at Jerusalem, except in the later years, after the capture of that city by the Moslems and the withdrawal of the Christians from the Holy Land, when it of necessity met elsewhere. This chapter, over which the Grand Master presided, served as the supreme assembly of the order; and it was expected that its advice and counsel would be followed by the Grand Master.[37] Its specific membership, apart from the chief officials of the order, was left to the discretion of the Grand Master who was to admit only those he knew "to be worthy and profitable to give advice."[38] This general chapter was to be concerned with such matters as these: the admission of new brothers; the grant, confirmation, or sale of Templar land; decision on matters of war and military activities; the dispatch of envoys to foreign powers; the request for aid for the order and for the Holy Land; administration during the absence of the Grand Master; and the discussion of matters of general interest and importance to the order.[39]

There was another type of chapter, too — one concerned with discipline primarily — which met frequently, perhaps weekly, and which all Templars in a given preceptory were to attend.[40] At these meetings, the brothers were expected to confess their sins voluntarily, but if they did not, the other brothers were expected to denounce them; and at these meetings, the proper penance for offenses was to be assigned.[41] At first, the penance seems to have been largely left to the discretion of the Master; but in time, the most usual offenses, together with their penalties, were listed in the Rule.[42]

In addition to the general and disciplinary chapters meeting in Jerusalem, there were provincial chapters and local chapters[43] — the former dealing with the business of the order in the province, and the latter dealing with local matters in each preceptory and especially with matters of discipline.[44] Unfortunately, practically nothing is known about these provincial and local chapters.

Classes of Membership

There were at least five classes of brothers recognized by the Templars in their Rule. The first and highest class was that of the knights *(fratres milites, frères chevaliers)* who could be distinguished by their garment, a white mantle with a red cross.[45] Upon joining the order, the knight surrendered his property, took the monastic vows,[46] and agreed never to leave unless to join another religious order having a stricter rule.[47] Few in number[48] and necessarily of noble and legitimate lineage,[49] the knights served as mounted warriors and as officials of the order. The sergeants or esquires *(clientes, frères sergens; armigeri, écuyers),* who made up a second class, were required to be of free birth.[50] Prohibited from wearing the white mantle, they instead wore black or brown robes.[51] Some of these men served as light-armed troops, and the younger of them were often assigned as squires to older knights. In addition to military service, however, the sergeants might serve as minor officials, supervisors of local administration, and attendants or assistants of the great dignitaries of the order.[52] With this group may be associated the *frères casaliers* who managed and protected the smaller Templar houses and farms *(casaux).*[53] A third class was composed of chaplains *fratres capellani, frères chapelains).* In the beginning, the order relied upon outside priests to render spiritual services — especially confession and the mass — to them;[54] but not too many years had passed before the Templars were authorized to have their own priests who in time became full members of the order and were wholly independent of diocesan authority.[55] A group of manual laborers, artisans, domestic servants, and workers of the soil who performed the countless obvious and necessary tasks and services required within the order formed a fourth class of craftsmen and menials *(frères de métier).*[56] No doubt, the great majority of persons calling themselves Templars fell into this category — in modern terms, they might be referred to as "lay brothers." A number of men of rather uncertain position formed the fifth class, a group of associates of the order *(affiliés)* or temporary members. For example, married men *(frères mariés, confrères)* were permitted to join under certain conditions; crusaders in the Holy Land were allowed to join for a time only *(fratres ad terminum, frères à termine);* and men might, for the salvation of their souls, be received into the order at the point of death.[57] Women, of course, were denied membership though they might be associated with the order as wives of associate members.[58] These classes of membership existed throughout the order, both in the east and in the west.

The life of the Templars was both religious and military. Indeed, the union of these two spheres of activity was the reason for the existence of the order; and the degree to which the Templars adhered to this life was to be, in large measure, the degree to which they succeed or failed. As a religious and military group, the Templar order admitted neither children nor women.[59] As a religious group, its members lived the communal and restricted life of monks bound by vows of poverty, chastity, and obedience, and emphasizing prayer, silence, and moderation in food and drink as well.[60] As a military group, it emphasized constant training, rigid discipline, mastery of tactics and strategy, careful maintenance of equipment, and victory in battle.[61] For support, since charity was not enough, the Templars were permitted by their Rule, as well as by the heads of the church and the state, to possess property,[62] institutional rather than personal, and to receive tithes.[63]

The Templars and the Crusades

This is not the place for any lengthy discussion of the history of the Templars in the east or of the Crusades,[64] but it is necessary to refer briefly to the Templars outside of England and to their participation in the Crusades in order to give some balance and perspective and a fuller meaning to the activities and position of the English Templars.

The First Crusade and the establishment of the Christian states in the east — Jerusalem, Edessa, Tripoli, and Antioch — in a sense necessited the existence of a military order. After Jerusalem had been captured (July, 1099) and Ascalon had fallen (August, 1099), many crusaders assumed their purpose had been achieved and their aid was no longer needed. The departure of many of them for their homes in Europe left scarcely enough troops to garrison the few towns held by the Christians and left almost defenseless against recurring Arab raids the weak Kingdom of Jerusalem, over which Godfrey of Bouillon and then, within a year, Baldwin I, ruled. Fortunately for themselves, the Christians had found the Moslem world upon which they had descended disunited after the death (1092) of the powerful sultan Malik Shah. But since the rivalry of the Moslem leaders and the disunity of the Moslem states could not be counted upon as being permanent, there was an urgent need for large numbers of Christian recruits and pilgrims. Unfortunately, the needed aid and services were not forthcoming. It was in this setting and under these conditions that the Templars came into being.

The Order of the Temple was not exactly the first, nor was it the last, of the crusading orders to come into existence. The Knights Hospitallers, who had been formed some years earlier in the Holy Land as a group to aid the sick and the needy, soon became a military organization. Their first wholly military action — and the Templars' as well — seems to have been the assistance given in the 1130's to Baldwin II, King of Jerusalem, against his daughter, Alice of Antioch.[65] Like the Templars, who became their chief rivals, the Hospitallers received privileges and gifts from popes, kings, and others. Later, in 1197, a third military crusading order, the Teutonic Knights, appeared in the Holy Land.

The chief concern of the Templars in the east was military — to wage war against the infidel. For many years, their bravery, tenacity, and achievements were a constant example to their fellow Christians and a terror to their enemies. As time passed, the Templars assumed other interests as well — possession of large estates, accumulation of portable forms of wealth, participation in trade, and rivalry with the Hospitallers and the Patriarch of Jerusalem. Though individual activities of the Templars and the motivation behind certain of these activities may have been justifiably suspect upon occasion, nonetheless, the Templars in the east remained throughout basically faithful to their original purpose and repeatedly appear in the front rank, with their Grand Master as one of the chief leaders, in the many campaigns against and battles with the Moslems.

As early as 1136, at the Battle of Aleppo, the Templars, not yet the great military power they were soon to become, fought valiantly under the command of Fulk of Anjou in his unsuccessful contest with Zengi, Atabeg of Mosul, a new and powerful Moslem leader. Real impetus to the increase in power and numbers of the Templars came after Zengi's capture of Edessa in 1144 — an event which called forth the preaching of the Second Crusade by St. Bernard and others, led Pope Eugenius III to authorize the Templars to wear the red cross on their garments, and brought numerous men and gifts to the order. Though much had been hoped for, nothing of note came of the Second Crusade.

Louis VII of France and Conrad III of the Holy Roman Empire, failing in the seige of Damascus (1148), abandoned plans to beseige the key city of Ascalon and returned to Europe instead. Although some persons blamed the Templars for the Christian defeat at Damascus,[66] Louis, writing to Suger, Abbot of St. Denis, spoke well of the Templars, saying he could not have "existed even for the shortest time" without their assistance.[67] With the departure of the French and German kings and their armies, the task of securing fortresses and of guarding the frontiers was more and more assigned to the Templars who successfully seized control of Ascalon and Gaza (1149), fortress cities along the coast, which they were to hold for some years.

The rise to power of Saladin, a Moslem of great talent and fame, and a man dedicated to the expulsion of the Christians from the east, was a most portentous development. In 1177, the Christians, with the Templars in the forefront, had temporarily checked the Moslem forces at Ascalon. The next year, Saladin's attack on Jacob's Ford, an important Templar fortress on the northern frontier of the Latin Kingdom of Jerusalem, was unsuccessful; but shortly thereafter (1179), Saladin was victorious in an open battle near the Ford. For the next several years, there existed an uneasy truce between the Moslems and Christians. This ended in 1187, when Saladin launched a new and decisive campaign against the Christians and their holdings after the repeated violations of the truce by Reginald of Chatillon, one of the prominent Christian lords whose hatred of the Moslems knew no bounds and whose political ambitions had not been satisfied. The key battle (July 4) was fought outside Hattin,[68] west of the Sea of Galilee, after the Master of the Temple had unwisely convinced Guy, King of Jerusalem, to take the offensive on the sun-scorched, waterless plain. The Christians were overwhelmingly defeated, and the king, the Masters of the Templars and Hospitallers, together with many of their men, as well as numerous lords and nobles, were captured. Most of his captives Saladin generously released, but his hatred of the crusading orders was so intense that all Templar and Hospitaller prisoners, perhaps two hundred in number, were executed forthwith. Following up his victory, Saladin proceeded immediately to further attacks, capturing many Christian cities along the coast, including Acre, and finally, on October 3, 1187, Jerusalem itself. Only Tyre, Antioch, Tripoli, and a few other Latin possessions remained in Christian hands.

The fall of Jerusalem called forth the Third Crusade so familiarly associated with the colorful English king, Richard, the Lion-Hearted. In June of 1191, several months after the arrival of Philip Augustus of France and many months after his departure from England, Richard finally reached the Holy Land. Despite the rivalry of the two kings and their failure to cooperate in the seige of the city, Acre surrendered to the Christian forces in July. This favorable event gave Philip, who pleaded ill health, reason to hasten back to France while Richard, still desiring to regain control of Jerusalem, stayed on for another year. Not much attention was given to the Holy City, however. For, the Templars and Hospitallers, envious of the able and popular English leader and concerned with strengthening their own positions and regaining control of lands they had lost to Saladin, convinced Richard to direct chief attention to Ascalon and Jaffa — cities which fell to the Christians in 1192. Seizing the opportunity offered by the fall of Jaffa, Richard made a truce with Saladin (September 2, 1192), which permitted Christians to visit the Holy City, and then set out for Europe and further adventure, making his way initially in the guise of a Templar.

The crusade sent by Henry VI, Holy Roman Emperor, (1197) was of little importance. Some minor successes were achieved with the aid of the Templars and others, but the early death of the emperor ended western interest in the campaign. Even less successful for the Holy Land was the Fourth Crusade (1202-04) so avidly promoted by Pope Innocent III. Instead of proceeding to the proposed attack on Egypt, which might have checked Moslem power and thereby made easier the recovery of the Holy Land, the crusaders launched an attack on Constantinople, which served to bring advantages not to the Holy Land but to Venice. Nor was the Fifth Crusade (1218-19) successful. Directed against Egypt, this crusade, in which the Templars played a key role, resulted in the capture of Damietta, an important Egyptian frontier outpost, which was promptly lost when the flooding of the Nile necessitated withdrawal.

The crusade of Emperor Frederick II (1228-29) improved the Christian position in the east despite the bitter opposition of the Templars and Hospitallers.[69] After initially refusing to fight under the command of the emperor, who had been excommunicated by Pope Gregory IX, the two military orders finally did render some degree of cooperation and assistance. Though facing great odds, Frederick fought effectively and was able to conclude a ten-year treaty with Al Kamil, the Sultan of Egypt. According to the treaty terms, the Christians were to regain Nazareth, Bethlehem, Jaffa, and all of Jerusalem except the Temple and Mosque of Omar; and Frederick was to see to it that no Christian disturbed any of Al Kamil's possessions. This favorable treaty, along with the emperor's success where the Templars had failed and his open contempt and disrespect for them, was strongly resented by the Templars who must have seen in Frederick an immediate threat to the maintenance of their own power and influence in the east. In anger, they informed the Sultan of Frederick's proposed visit to the alleged place of Christ's baptism. Al Kamil, however, rejected the treachery intended and sent their letter to Frederick, thus giving the emperor additional reason for wanting to humble the proud Templars. Frederick, however, was unable to do anything about the Templars because the crusade which Pope Gregory IX was preaching against him required his immediate return to Europe. The Holy City remained in Christian hands for a decade before it again fell to the Moslems.

Louis IX of France, a devoted and eager if not very successful crusader, undertook two campaigns which he hoped would regain control of the Holy Land for the Christians. His first crusade (1248-54), warmly supported by the Templars, was directed against the Moslem ruler in Egypt. After capturing Damietta, in the Nile delta, the French king moved southward, unsuccessfully beseiging the stronghold of Mansourah. In the retreat from there, Louis himself was captured and was briefly held prisoner by Baibars, Sultan of Egypt; and Damietta was again taken by the Moslems. Louis remained in the east for several more years and was aided by the Templars financially as well as militarily.[70] After his departure, the rivalry between the Templars and Hospitallers broke out into open warfare, thereby further weakening the Christian position in the east. Indeed, by 1268 the Christians retained control of little more than Tyre, Acre, and Tripoli. In 1270, because of the Christian losses in the east, Louis IX again took the cross. But his attention this time was turned to North Africa where he had been erroneously informed the Bey of Tunis was willing to be converted to Christianity. Prince Edward of England joined in the proposed crusade, and after the death of Louis, proceeded to the Holy Land where, with the cooperation of the Templars and others, he made several raids into the area around Acre.

Participation in the major crusades does not represent the only military activity of the Templars. An important — perhaps the most important — part of their activity involved garrison duty in the fortresses and frequent skirmishes with the enemy along the frontiers of the Christian kingdoms in the east.[71] It certainly would be no exaggeration to say that the Templars, aided by the Hospitallers and Teutonic Knights, apart from being the first line of defense in time of war, rendered their most valuable service as defenders of the persons, lands, and possessions of the eastern Christians in the years when the religious fervor and military spirit of their fellow Christians waned. Had it not been for the constant vigilance of the military orders, the loss of Christian holdings in the east would have occurred long before the end of the thirteenth century.

The final struggle in the Holy Land was soon to come. The Moslems, determined to drive the Christians out of the east, continued their campaign with vigor during the 1280's. When Acre, the last Christian stronghold in the east was attacked, the Christians, led by the Master of the Temple, resisted as best they could. During the last hours of the seige, eleven Templars, under cover of darkness, escaped by sea with the wealth of the order to Cyprus while a small band of determined Templars remained behind and fought to the death.[72] With the fall of Acre (May 28, 1291), Christian possession of territory in the Near East ended and the Crusades as such were over. In the long run, the purpose of the Templars had not been achieved; and without persons and property to protect in the east, the need for the military orders was no longer urgent — especially was this true inasmuch as no organized or sustained effort to regain the Holy Land was undertaken. Though there was much talk about campaigns against the Turks, and though this talk increased when the Turks soon began extending their power into Europe, the idea and fervor of the crusades were not to revive, and projects of reconquest never really got beyond words.[73]

While the Templars were active in the east, they were busy in Europe as well, seeking recruits and amassing wealth, supposedly for the campaign against the infidel. Many Templar houses had been established in France, England, Germany, Italy, and Spain;[74] and as the houses and wealth of the order increased, the provincial organization, referred to above, was worked out for the practical supervision of these areas and the effective utilization of their men and resources. France seems to have been the chief area; and Paris, the chief center in the west. Indeed, as time passed, the Templars tended to concentrate increasingly in the west where individual members not only achieved positions of great political influence as diplomats and as counsellors to kings and princes but also successfully engaged in economic activities as brokers of international exchange and lenders of money as well as supervisors of agricultural production. With power and wealth came abuses which were probably greater in number and seriousness in the west than in the east. It will not prove wholly surprising to find the Templars, after having been driven from the Holy Land, ultimately attacked, tried, and convicted by their rivals and former supporters in the west.

chapter two

The Templars in England

Origins

OF THE INTRODUCTION and settlement of the Templars in England little is known.[1] After attending the Council of Troyes (1128), which had formally recognized his new order, Hugh de Payens, the first Grand Master, journeyed to Normandy. There Henry I, the English monarch, received him with honor, and after presenting him with gifts of gold and silver, sent him to England and Scotland where, besides being given additional treasures of gold and silver for the Holy Land, it is said, he enlisted an undetermined number of men for service in Jerusalem.[2] Whether or not a Templar unit was actually established in England and whether or not grants of land were made at this time to the new order cannot be known for certain though it seems probable. All that can be ascertained is that grants of land, both royal and private, were made to the Templars in England during the reign of King Stephen, the earliest being that of Temple Cressing in Essex, made in 1137 by Matilda, his wife, in a charter issued at Évreux in northern France.[3] From this time on, grants and confirmation of grants of land and privileges to the Templars appear with increasing frequency. Stephen, as well as Matilda, was generous to the Templars. Generous, too, were the rivals of Stephen in the contest for the control of England following the death of Henry I. Thus, from approximately 1135 on, it can be said that the rise of the Templars to power and wealth in England proceeded in rapid fashion.

At least two reasons for the success of the Templars during this period of civil strife may be cited. One the one hand, the Templars profited from the crusading sympathies of the time. Stephen of England was a member of a distinguished crusading family, being the son of that Stephen of Blois who had been an important leader on the First Crusade; and Matilda, his wife, was a member of a Boulogne family closely associated with the crusading movement. Interestingly enough, Hugh de Payens was from Champagne, an area controlled by Stephen's family;

and Godfrey of St. Omer, another of the original founders of the Templars, was a vassal of the Count of Boulogne. In England, as elsewhere, enthusiasm for the crusades and generosity to crusaders existed among the various groups in society. On the other hand, the Templars seem to have played shrewd politics during the period of civil turmoil, serving both parties and winning rewards from both sides, as charters and documents favoring the Templars, about sixty of which have survived, attest.[4] Unfortunately, just what the Templars did in the wars cannot be ascertained. Nor can their donors, be they of Stephen's party or of his rival's party, even be determined with certainty in many instances. It was not the Templars alone, however, who profited from the troubles of the reign of Stephen. William of Newburgh stated that more religious houses were founded in the troubled reign of Stephen than during the one hundred preceding years.[5] Though his statement may not be literally true, his emphasis is well taken.

About two years after her original grant of Temple Cressing, Matilda gave the Templars Temple Cowley in Oxfordshire; and another two years later, in 1141, Uphall in Essex.[6] Stephen not only subsequently confirmed these grants[7] but himself made grants to the order — for example, land and mills at Dinsley in Hertfordshire (*ca.* 1142).[8] His rival, the Empress Matilda, daughter of Henry I and wife of Geoffrey of Anjou — whose family had also long been associated with the crusades — at this same time granted pasture in Shotover Forest to the Cowley Templars.[9] The Sandford Cartulary and documents in the Inquest of 1185 record a number of additional grants by various persons in this period.[10] Hence, by 1142, when Stephen had won out in the contest for the control of England, the Templars had acquired a goodly number of holdings in southeastern and south-central England. The next decade witnessed a marked increase in Templar holdings — and privileges — in England. The record reveals Stephen confirming grants to the Templars — for example, grants of land by Gilbert, Earl of Pembroke, in Berkshire;[11] the grant by Matilda of the manor and half-hundred of Witham in Essex;[12] the grant by William Marci of lands within London;[13] and the grant of Robert of Ferrer of the manor of Bisham in Berkshire.[14] Finally, shortly before his death (1154), Stephen issued a general charter to the Templars confirming to them all their liberties and gifts which they had been in seisin of at the previous Easter.[15] All this shows that, though the details are incomplete and often imprecise, the Templars were firmly established in England by 1154 and that they must already have obtained lands, privileges, and exemptions of importance. This was the foundation on which the Templars were to build their great edifice of power, wealth, and influence.

Organization

The general organization of the Templars in the East and in the provinces, as it is revealed in their Rule and as it gradually evolved, was discussed in the preceding chapter. Here the concern is with the provincial and local organization in England — a subject about which little is known.[16] This lack of information is partly due to the small number of Templar records in England; but it may also in part be due to the fact that there is relatively little to know. After all, England was a remote province which developed later than and was less involved in the crusading movement than many of those on the continent.[17] Precise details on the Templar organization in England, then, cannot be given.

The same five classes that existed elsewhere among the Templars also existed in England.[18] Most important, though fewest in number, were the knights who had to be of noble lineage; more numerous than the knights were the sergeants, or serving brothers, who were free-born men; and fewest in number were the chaplains, or priests, of the order. At the bottom of the social scale were the manual workers and craftsmen, a numerous group without whose practical skills the Templar organization could not function. Also recognized as part of the Templar order were the associates who might join the order on a temporary basis, usually during the last years of their lives.

The total membership of the Templars can be estimated only at the time of their dissolution when presumably their number was greatest. If Perkins, who has carefully examined the records dealing with their imprisonment and trial, is right, their number was remarkably small and certainly far smaller than many another religious group in England. After eliminating duplication in names, he concludes there were 144 Templars in England in their last years, including 15 to 20 knights, 8 to 16 priests, and 108 to 121 sergeants or serving brothers.[19] These figures omit, however, associate members whose status is not wholly clear and whose numbers cannot possibly be determined. Regardless of the accuracy, or inaccuracy, of these figures, the point is clearly made that one must avoid any notion of the Templars as a numerous group. For the sake of clarity, it should be pointed out that the many tenants of the Templars, who were in no sense members of the order — although they were quite willing to claim and exercise Templar privileges — are properly excluded from consideration here.

With time, definite units, offices, and officials emerged in the provinces; their exact evolution, however, cannot be traced. Indeed, whether England was always a separate province *(ballia)* or whether it was in the earliest years appended to the French province is unclear. Most of the time, however, England, including Scotland and Ireland, formed a

separate province[20] under a master or grand preceptor whose usual title
was *Magister Militiae Templi in Anglia.* Whether the Master served on
a temporary basis or held office for life is not always clear; and for the
early years, not even the names of the men who held the mastership
can be determined. But with the coming of the thirteenth century, some
degree of consistency in organization is to be found, and a satisfactory
list of masters can be drawn up.[21] There is some uncertainty about the
manner of appointment of the Master in England. Initially he may well
have been named by the Grand Master of the order;[22] but the brief
tenure and rapid turnover of the Grand Mastership during the years of
warfare in the east, the many other urgent problems the Grand Master
had to deal with, and the slowness and difficulty of communication
between Jerusalem and England, make it doubtful that this was consistently or effectively done. Inasmuch as the Master in England frequently came from distinguished noble families associated with the
administration of the king — for example, Richard de Hastings and
Geoffrey Fitz Stephen — and since the Templars themselves stood to
profit if their masters were on good terms with the crown, the possibility
of royal appointment or intervention must be considered. However,
there is no evidence to suggest that the king was ever directly responsible
for or even ever actively intervened in the selection of a master. Most
likely, the Master in England came to be chosen by the English Templars, probably by the knights and officials only,[23] who were wise enough
to select a person not apt to be disapproved of by either the Grand
Master or the king. If, as is likely, the Master in England had to take
the same oath as did the provincial masters on the continent, he had to:

> . . . promise to Jesus Christ . . . and to His Vicar, the Sovereign Pontiff
> and his successors, perpetual obedience and fidelity; . . . defend . . .
> the mysteries of faith; . . . be submissive and obedient to the Master-
> general of the Order in conformity with the statutes prescribed by . . .
> St. Bernard; . . . at all times in case of need pass the seas to go and
> fight; . . . not sell the property of the Order, nor consent that it be sold
> or alienated; . . . always preserve chastity; . . . be faithful to the king
> of [England]; . . . never surrender to the enemy the towns and places
> belonging to the Order; [and] aid and defend [the religious] by words,
> by arms, and by all sorts of good offices. . . .[24]

From the central headquarters of the order at the preceptory in London, where the annual chapters were held,[25] the master exercised general
supervisory powers over the officials, members, and property of the
order. Being, like other great feudal lords, an itinerant rather than a
sedentary ruler, he frequently travelled from preceptory to preceptory
with his staff and attendants, supervising his subordinates, attending to
the business of the order, and living off the proceeds of the order's

estates.[26] It was the master also, who, on behalf of the order, often through one of his agents, accepted the many donations which were usually given "magistro et fratribus Milicie Templi in Anglia."[27]

Below the master, directly responsible to him, and evidently appointed by him, were the preceptors *(preceptores)* or commanders, each of whom was charged with the discipline and training of the Templars and with the supervision and administration of Templar properties in his preceptory *(preceptoria)*.[28] The most important of these officials were the preceptors of Ireland and Scotland who, though often referred to as master in their respective areas, were actually subordinate to the master at London.[29] The miscellaneous information which survives pertains to preceptories more than to preceptors and does not permit accurate lists of preceptories (or of preceptors) to be compiled for most of the period. By the time of the dissolution, however, the number of preceptories had reached approximately forty;[30] but the number of preceptors was considerably less, due apparently to the fact that one perceptor might simultaneously exercise jurisdiction over more than one preceptory.[31] Though specific information is lacking on the point, it would seem reasonable to assume that a major preceptory was run by a knight and that the great majority of preceptories were headed by a sergeant, or serving brother.

The Templars also had procurators *(procuratores)* — men serving as business agents or lawyers — whose task it was to represent the order, or individuals in the order, in such matters as the receipt and acceptance of donations of all kinds, the transfer and sale of land and goods of all sorts, and in the defense or prosecution of cases involving the Templars. In such references as can be found, the procurators were always themselves members of the order.[32]

In addition to the officials mentioned thus far, the Templars must have maintained a large, trained clerical staff, at least at their central headquarters in London. Though no specific indication of such is given in the records, the composition of documents, the attestations of clerks and chaplains, the use of seals, and the like, make this assumption necessary since most of the Templars were illiterate.[33] There may of course have been some Templars who could read and write, in addition to their priests, but it is impossible to ascertain if any of these clerks employed at New Temple or elsewhere were themselves members of the order.[34]

Like many other religious organizations, the English Templars met together in chapter, sometimes at London, and sometimes in local areas. Since the composition and dates of the chapters are not specified in the source materials, one can only speculate on the membership and frequency of the meetings. When, upon occasion, the "whole chapter" *(totum capitulum)* is mentioned as meeting in London,[35] it is conceivable that all the Templars in the English province were summoned. For the most part, however, it would seem more likely that the London chapter was normally attended by the master and the preceptors only. Addison[36] suggests that there were two types of chapters — one general and the other particular. The general chapter, he says, was composed of the master and preceptors, met once a year at London, dealt with matters pertaining to the Holy Land, received accounts of their stewardship from the various officials, and framed rules and regulations for the management of Templar properties. The particular chapter, he says, met irregularly at the different preceptories which the master visited; admitted new members; made appointments to vacant benefices; dealt with the purchase, sale, or exchange of land; and imposed penalties on erring brothers. Addison's distinction is reasonable and helpful, but is perhaps an over-simplification. Only in part can what he says about the activities of the chapters be verified by historical references,[37] and the point that a distinction was made between the two types of chapters cannot be documented. Most references to the chapters simply use the term "capitulum" without a preceding adjective. Hence, what is known of the chapter in England must be based upon the assumption, which is in general acceptable, that the English chapters, both in composition and business, were modelled after those discussed in the Rule.

Little is known about the preceptory *(preceptoria* or *domus),* the basic unit of organization in England, or about the manner in which it functioned. Chief among the preceptories was the Temple at London,[38] the central headquarters which administratively set the pattern, policies, and procedures for the other preceptories to follow. In a sense, the London center was the mother house; and the other preceptories were cells.[39] Economically, the Templar organization was overwhelmingly based on the manorial system, many preceptories being in fact manors transformed by the grant of their donors into religious houses — e.g., Temple Cressing in Essex, Temple Cowley in Oxfordshire, and Temple Guiting in Gloucestershire. Beginning in the twelfth century and fully emerging in the thirteenth, the preceptory became the acknowledged local center through which the Templars administered their many holdings and rendered their obligations as feudal landlords. In addition to the preceptors, who supervised the Templar properties, there were obviously estate stewards and other officials who were directly concerned with the actual production of crops. Lees suggests that many of these men may have been members of middle-class Anglo-Norman families and knights of the order able to deal as equals with the clergy and with the squires and gentry of the countryside.[40] Forming the great bulk of the persons on the Templar lands and doing the actual work were the manorial specialists and peasants — men who had no direct ties to the Templar order.

The lands constituting these preceptories, probably from the beginning, represented many types of rural economy — the small manors,[41] the large honors,[42] the great fiefs,[43] the lesser fiefs,[44] ecclesiastical states,[45] and scattered manorial holdings.[46] But the bulk of Templar possessions was composed of grants of small units of land and small sums of rent made by persons or groups of humble status — units ranging from one-half acre to two acres, to ten or more acres,[47] and rents ranging from twelve pence to forty shillings.[48] Kosminsky in his recent studies, based primarily on the Hundred Rolls for 1278-79, groups the manors of England into large (over 1,000 acres of arable land), medium (between 500 and 1,000 acres), and small (less than 500 acres)[49] and finds that the church held manors in each of these categories.[50] However, his research — agreeing with the data presented here — further shows that the lands of the Templars (and Hospitallers) consisted for the most part of small manors and countless petty holdings and rental rights on the manors of other lords.[51] To illustrate, he found the Templars had four medium, twelve small, and no large manors in the area covered by the 1278-79 survey.[52] Specifically, in Duxford (Cambridgeshire), the Master of the Temple in England held his demesne from seven different persons in differing proportions.[53]

Both with respect to the lands and crops and the manner of production, it would seem that what had been before continued under and after the Templars[54] — another instance of the persistence and relative imperviousness to change of the manorial system. The type of economic activity engaged in depended upon the resources and customs of the area. Accordingly, some areas produced grain and legumes; some areas were used mostly for pasturage of cattle or sheep; and on most estates were forests which provided wood and game animals. On the Templar manors and other holdings were laborers in the fields, herdsmen, gardeners, millers, artisans of various sorts, and others.[55] Over all, regardless of specialization, was imposed a degree of centralized control aiming at a common goal — the increase of revenue for financing the Holy War.

The tenants of the Templars as seen in the Inquest of 1185, like the tenants seen in the Extents and Hundred Rolls, fell into three main groups:[56] those who rendered services only *(opera et servitia)*; those who rendered services and/or paid a money rent *(opera vel redditus)*; and those who paid a money rent only *(reditus assissae)*. In most counties examples for each of the three groups can be cited. Generally speaking, however, it can be said that services were most consistently demanded and were most common in such areas as Yorkshire,[57] that money payments were common in areas around London,[58] and that the payment of service and/or money was found in all areas where the Templars had holdings.[59] A tendency toward and preference for money can be seen in such areas as Essex, Kent, Warwickshire, Oxfordshire, and Hertfordshire where such statements as these are found in the Inquest: ". . . *et si non dederit den [arios] faciet quolibet ebdomeda tocius anni ij opera [ciones]* . . .;"[60] ". . . *pro xxx d. vel predictam operacionem* . . .;"[61] ". . . *pro virgata terre x sol. et quieti sunt de omnibus aliis consuetudinibus ville* . . .;"[62] ". . . *ij d. vel iiij galli [nas] ad electionem illorum* . . .;"[63] ". . . *quiete ab omnibus serviciis pro iiij sol.* . . .;"[64] or ". . . *tenet pro xviij d. pro omni servicio.* . . ."[65]

This matter of commutation of payments from services to money is one of the most significant and controversial subjects in the economic history of the Middle Ages. Some writers, such as Lipson, Cunningham, and Ashley, are quite conservative in their views when they hold that commutation was often temporary and irregular and was not very extensive, and that, though it may have begun before the Norman Conquest, it did not become very noticeable till the thirteenth century, and did not become widespread till the fourteenth and fifteenth centuries.[66] Kosminsky in his studies of the agrarian history of England in the thirteenth century has come to a more positive conclusion, holding that commutation had increased — more rapidly and more easily on the small than on the large manors — until by the thirteenth century money rent had become the predominant form of rent in England.[67] Furthermore, he maintains that the lord could often demand money payment instead of service and that part of the dues shown as services were actually levied in money so that "the actual role of money rents was greater, perhaps much greater, than the sources indicate."[68] This is not to deny, however, that there was also a trend away from commutation back to the exaction of labor services apparent in the thirteenth century and later, especially on the large manors and on ecclesiastical estates.[69] Current research also suggests that the view expressed by such men as Nabholz[70] that the rise of a money economy played a major role in breaking down or altering the manorial system is a simplification which must be extensively qualified.

The records of the Templars, primarily the Inquest, provide us with no wholly decisive evidence on commutation, but they do indicate that commutation was definitely going on as early as the last part of the twelfth century in all the areas in which the Templars held land, and

they do suggest that the Templars showed a preference for money payments in many instances, a wholly reasonable preference in view of
their need for cash or other portable wealth for the support of their
activities in the Holy Land.

In addition to their ordinary feudal tenants, who no doubt held the
great bulk of their lands, the Templars came, increasingly as time
passed, to depend for the performance of many needed services upon
corrodaries, who in return received pensions (or corrodies) from the
Templars. These corrodaries might include clerics[71] who would perform
religious services for the Templars or laymen[72] who would render various
types of manual labor — such as carpentry, work in the fields, care of
animals, and odd jobs around the manor or Templar buildings. Corrodaries might also be persons or institutions, lay or ecclesiastical, who
transferred land to the Templars[73] — sometimes for their lifetime, sometimes for a stated period of years, and sometimes for an indefinite period
— or who gave to the Templars a sum of money[74] and in return were to
receive pensions or annual payments. In the case of an individual, a
corrody might involve the guarantee that the donor and his wife could
remain on their former property, or on a specific estate, for the remainder of their lives and that they would receive certain stated neces-
saries — e.g., 2 or 3d. per days for food, 10s. yearly for a robe, 40d. per
year for shoe leather, 5d. annually for miscellaneous items, a tallow
candle nightly, firewood as needed, and a groom assigned by the preceptor to serve them.[75] In case of an institution, a corrody commonly
involved the payment of a specified sum yearly.[76] Monastaries and nunneries apparently found it convenient upon occasion to transfer to the
Templars lands, tithes, or rents in return for an assured yearly payment.
For the Templars, the grants by individuals and by institutions offered
the opportunity, through efficient management, to increase their holdings and revenue. Thus, as the terms of the agreements and the great
popularity of the corrodies suggest, the system proved attractive for both
parties concerned. Most of the data on the Templar corrodaries comes
from the last years of the Templars' existence, but the complexity and
universality of the system indicate a development dating far back in
Templar history. The great document on this subject is the "corrodia
petita de domibus Templariorum"[77] which was drawn up at the time
of the dissolution of the order, when the Templars' property was in the
King's hands, so that Edward II would know which claims to corrodies
were valid and which were not.

So far the preceptorial organization in England, to the degree that
it can be known from the incomplete and miscellaneous nature of surviving evidence, has been briefly examined. Despite the fact that more

problems are raised than solved by existing records, it seems justifiable to suggest that, on the one hand, local variation was a dominant characteristic of Templar tenure and of their agricultural productivity and that, on the other hand, where some degree of similarity in tenure and productivity existed it may have been partly due to such administrative uniformity as the Templars were able to impose.

Before leaving the Templar organization in England, one must give some attention to the London center. Though the London holdings in one sense formed just another preceptory, the fact that the central headquarters were there made the London unit in fact far more important than the other preceptories. It may well be, as some suggest, that the origins of the London holdings are to be traced back to grants made to Hugh de Payens when he visited England in 1128.[78] The first area in the city held by the Templars was at Holborn where were built, in the parish of St. Andrew, their house and their church — the latter being constructed of stone brought from Caen in Normandy, and being circular in form like the Church of the Holy Sepulchre at Jerusalem.[79] When, shortly, their growing wealth and numbers made the Holborn holdings inadequate, the Templars sold these holdings, sometime between 1155 and 1162, to Robert de Chesney, Bishop of London, for one hundred marks and a small annual rent.[80] They then proceeded to establish themselves on a new site on the north bank of the Thames River where new and elaborate buildings were constructed.[81] To distinguish between the two centers, the Holborn unit was referred to as Old Temple *(Vetus Templum)* and the Thames unit as New Temple *(Novum Templum)*. Whether these new holdings were obtained by gift or by purchase and whether or not any buildings already existed on the Thames site are unknown. Desiring to make their London headquarters impressive and indicative of their growing wealth and power, the Templars began the construction of New Temple, a large and magnificent Gothic church, round in shape, with simple pointed arches and large window areas.[82] Dedicated on February 10, 1185, by Heraclius, Patriarch of Jerusalem,[83] probably in the presence of King Henry II, who was then in London and held the Templars in high esteem,[84] New Temple provided a fitting structure for the honor of God and St. Mary and the glory of the Templars, dominating as it did its immediate environs. In time, several small chapels were built nearby and two large halls — a "hall of priests," connected with the Temple by a cloister, and, a short distance away, a "hall of knights."[85] The former was probably where the Templars' business was conducted; and the latter, where the knights resided. Across the river, on the south side of the Thames, was a large field, approximately fifteen acres in size, known as Fickettscroft,[86] which may well have been used by the Templars for their military exercises. Associated with the London house also were mills, ponds, roads, gates, forges, and piers[87]— all of which provided needed services or revenues — and offices and clerks for the transaction and recording of matters of all kinds. This importance of New Temple as a political, administrative, and financial center, not only for the Templars, but for the crown and laymen as well, will be shown in detail in the next chapter.

Privileges

It is with much truth that Sir Edward Coke, writing in the sixteenth century, said the Templars had "so great and so large privileges, liberties, and immunities for themselves, their tenants, and farmers, etc., as no other Order had the like."[88] In examining these privileges, it will be convenient to divide them into groups — political, economic, jurisdictional, and religious — and to make an effort to specify what they consisted of, from whom they were obtained, how effectively they were maintained, and how unique or widespread they were.

The religious privileges, since they were mostly granted by the papacy, applied throughout Christendom and, as seen in the preceding chapter, included, among other things, the right of the Templars to have their own priests and to receive special collections or offerings, and exemption of the Templars from ecclesiastical taxation of all sorts and from all but papal excommunication and interdict. In addition, the popes supported most of the activities of the Templars, granted indulgences for aid to the order and its cause, and used their influence with both the clergy and laity on the Templars' behalf. As also seen above, these extensive privileges did not go unresented by the clergy and were not always maintained unimpaired as papal orders directing recognition of and compliance with them indicate. Many other religious groups, including the Knights Hospitallers, the rivals of the Templars, also received comprehensive privileges; but probably no group received quite so many or quite such extensive ones.

The Templars were equally favored by laymen, including first and foremost the kings of England and secondarily the great and lesser lords. Since the privileges granted by the king were the more important and since the lay lords were in many instances only following the lead of the king, the concern here will be largely limited to the grant of privileges by the crown. The first charter granting the Templars privileges and liberties, as well as confirming the grants of land and gifts already made, was issued by King Stephen in 1154[89] and was later confirmed by Henry II, his successor.[90] The first really comprehensive grant of privileges by the crown was that of Richard I (1189) who went well beyond the mere confirmation of the charters of Stephen and Henry II.[91] A decade later (1199), John issued his own charter of privileges to the Templars,[92] but it was essentially the same as that of Richard. Two charters (1227 and 1253) were issued by Henry III.[93] The first one, in large part a reissuance of John's charter, confirmed all donations made to the Templars by his predecessors and by other benefactors and added new privileges of his own. The second charter, known only from Edward II's confirmation of it (1280),[94] was an extension of the first and was maintained, with reservations, throughout the reign of Edward I and in the early years of the reign of Edward II.

Any of a number of reasons can be given for the grant of privileges to the Templars — piety, favoritism, and mutual advantage; but the most fundamental reason would seem to be an effort by the crown to preserve the strength and revenues of the Templars for the cause of the Holy Land.[95] Indeed, while the Templars were concerned primarily with the Holy Land, their troubles in England, and elsewhere, were not insuperable; but after the Holy Land had been lost, their difficulties increased and the reason not only for their privileges but even for the continued existence of the order itself was questioned.

The royal privileges granted to the Templars were political, economic, judicial, and jurisdictional in nature and scope. Since they tend to overlap the one with the other, no effort will be made to fit any one privilege, or set of privileges, into a single category. However, for the sake of convenience and clarity, six privileges — or sets of privileges — will be discussed here.

First, the Templars were exempt from secular taxation. This exemption was at certain times national, at other times local, and sometimes both.[96] Exemption from taxes on land, such as Danegeld,[97] carucage,[98] and tallage,[99] was repeatedly given. The right to maintain in each community one free guest *(hospes)*— i.e., a tenant of their choice — immune from tallage was common.[100] Exemption from special assessments made on behalf of the Holy Land[101] and from levies on movable property — e.g., tenths,[102] fifteenths,[103] twentieths,[104] and thirtieths[105]— was repeatedly granted, as was exemption from scutage[106] and from military service.[107] Second, the Templars were excused from payment of tolls in markets, at fairs, on bridges, and on highways.[108] In addition, they were at times permitted to import and export wine without payment of customs duties[109] and, similarly in time of peace, were not required to pay the export duty on wool going to Flanders.[110] Third, the Templars tended to be exempted from many ordinary feudal burdens and to be given special privileges instead. For example, they were granted freedom from amercements and fines for themselves[111] and free warren in their demesne lands.[112] Furthermore, they were granted freedom from assarts,[113] from waste and regard in the forests,[114] from murage,[115] from frankpledge,[116] and from *corvées*[117] — such as work on parks, castles, bridges, and buildings. Fourth, the Templars were exempted in time of war from seizure of their agricultural produce — such as grain and hay — by royal officials.[118] Fifth, the Templars received widespread judicial and jurisdictional privileges. They were permitted to hold their own courts with full jurisdiction over their tenants and other persons on their estates,[119] including specifically the power not only to try and punish their own vassals and villeins, but also to try and punish thieves, trespassers, breakers of the peace, and other malefactors found on their properties.[120] In addition, the Templars were permitted to retain the chattels of felons and fugitives, to exact fines and amercements on their vassals and tenants, to receive back from the Exchequer any amercements collected by royal officials from their vassals, and to impose drowning and hanging ("pit and gallows") upon wrongdoers.[121] They were also exempted from attendance at and responsibility to the courts of the shires and hundreds[122] and were granted quittance of summons of the courts of eyre and common pleas.[123] Finally, as chief of these judicial and jurisdictional privileges, they could be impleaded only before the king or his chief justice.[124] Sixth, all the rights given to the Templars, including those mentioned above and many others of less importance, were to be maintained even if they were not utilized.[125]

For practical purposes, since these many rights and privileges granted to the Templars applied to their vassals and tenants as well,[126] a very considerable group and number of people were involved. To indicate possession of these rights, the Templar houses, and those of their tenants, were marked with a cross.[127] Needless to say, when persons not legally entitled to the Templar privileges erected crosses on their property, special royal action had to be taken to check the practice.[128]

Having indicated some of the privileges granted to the Templars by royal charters and noted in contemporary documents and realizing the extent of these privileges, one must ask whether or not they were maintained and exercised unimpaired. The answer to this question, as the following paragraphs will show, must be a qualified one. At times, the privileges were in large measure held intact; but at other times, they were not. What is more, the Templars sometimes had to pay dearly for recognition of their privileges; and most of the time, they could maintain them only by constant vigilance and frequent resort to legal action. The degree to which the king — and the pope — supported the Templars was, in large measure, the degree to which the Templars were able to maintain their rights and privileges.

The Templars repeatedly found it necessary to appeal for support to the king and to the pope in order to gain and maintain their privileges.[129] Both the king[130] and the pope[131] directed that the rights and privileges of the Templars be respected, but the repetition of the appeals and of the orders for compliance suggests that the royal officials and the clergy did not always obey. Moreover, the king himself was inconsistent on the matter and upon occasion, especially when money was involved, followed the course most advantageous to the crown. Similarly, the popes, as in the struggle between Innocent III and King John over the appointment of Stephen Langton as Archbishop of Canterbury (1207), might limit Templar privileges when advantageous.[132] In addition, legal suits, the outcome of which are often unknown, were instituted by the Templars and others over claims and counterclaims of rights and privileges.[133]

Public records — especially the Pipe Rolls in which there are literally over a thousand references — abound with data alluding to the status of Templar privileges.[134] Though many of the entries are unclear or indefinite, others are obvious and significant. It is clear that the Templars were frequently pardoned by the king from payment of taxes and fines (a voluntary payment to the king for the grant of charters of rights, privileges, exemptions, land transfers, and the like). For example, they were pardoned from payments of fines for amercements,[135] essarts,[136] frankpledge,[137] disseisin,[138] murder,[139] hunting,[140] waste and regard in the forest,[141] false presentation,[142] and the like. They were also pardoned from the payment of such taxes as scutage and tallage.[143] Perhaps as frequently as they were pardoned, however, the Templars were compelled to pay fines and taxes to the crown. For example, they were called upon to make fine with the king for amercements,[144] essarts,[145] frankpledge,[146] murder,[147] waste and regard in the forest,[148] hunting,[149] default,[150] and the like, and were also compelled to pay scutage and tallage.[151] In addition to these payments, and highly indicative of the uncertain status of their privileges, the Templars repeatedly found it necessary to give the kings — especially John — large sums of money in order to maintain and to guarantee their privileges. For example, in 1199-1200, the Templars paid 400 marks to John, gave him a palfrey, and were listed as owing £1,000 for confirmations of their charters and for quittance of amercements due at the Exchequer.[152] In 1201, they again gave him a palfrey, this time for royal protection and the right to be impleaded only before the king or his chief justice.[153] In 1209, for an unknown reason, they paid him 4,000 marks.[154] In 1210, John exacted money from the Templars, as well as from other religious groups, apparently for reinstatement of their privileges or for contribution to the recovery of Normandy.[155] Again, in 1216, for some unspecified reason, the Templars gave John 200 marks and two horses.[156] Later, under Henry III, in 1226 and 1244, the Templars paid still other fines to the king.[157] From this information, it would appear that, on the one hand, the Templars probably contributed their share of the "voluntary" payments expected by the king; and on the other, that they found it necessary to make additional contributions in order to retain royal support.

Exemption from[158] and payment of[159] taxes varied from time to time. Henry III, on one occasion, having allowed his sheriffs to demand and take carucage from the Templars, ordered them to return the amounts collected or to leave the matter for later settlement.[160] At the same time, however, he wrote the Master of the Templars to consult with his brethren on how they should answer the king on this matter.[161] Though the outcome is not known, it would not be without precedent to find that the Templars decided to make a monetary gift to the king in order to encourage him to support the principle of their exemption from such exactions. Scutage and tallage were sometimes paid by the Templars,[162] and sometimes were not.[163] Upon occasion, when either had been exacted unjustifiably, the money was returned.[164] The issue involved, which never was settled, seems to have been a dual one — whether or not the tenants of the Templars were liable for scutage and whether or not all the lands of the Templars and their tenants, or only certain of them, were exempted from tallage. Interestingly enough, evidence exists to indicate that, at least upon occasion, the Templars were permitted to exact tallage from their tenants whenever the king levied tallage upon his subjects.[165] As a rule, the Templars' exemption from aids for the Holy Land seems to have been fairly consistently maintained. In one case, when an aid had been collected, it was ordered returned;[166] and in another case, when a proposal to levy such an aid on the Templars (and Hospitallers) was made,[167] nothing came of it except that the Templars were authorized to collect such an aid from their own tenants.[168] The special levies authorized by the popes in the form of tenths, fifteenths, twentieths, thirtieths, and the like, did not usually apply to the Templars or to several other religious orders.[169] A goodly number of times, however, at least on certain of their holdings, the Templars were compelled to pay these special levies,[170] at least until such time as the matter could be brought to the attention of the king who might order the amount paid refunded.[171] Under Henry III and Edward I, it appears that the Templars' exemption was often most effectively recognized and upheld after making fine with the king.[172] The resentment against the violation of the privilege of having a free guest *(hospes)* in each community proved an especially troublesome matter as will be indicated below in Chapter IV.

Since the public records and other source materials provide little direct evidence on the subject, it is necessary to show great caution in making any statements regarding the maintenance of or infringement upon the commercial privileges of the Templars. The absence of information to the contrary suggests that the exemption of the Templars from payment of tolls levied by the king and his officials must have been quite universally maintained. When it came to the payment of local tolls, however, it would seem that the Templars, like all other persons, were excused only if exempted by the proper local authorities. The only violations of the grant of royal commercial privileges which have been found deal with the improper collection of stallage[173] from the Templars and the improper exaction of money from the perquisites of a market.[174] Only after the dissolution of the order, are the king's officials found collecting the tolls and revenues of a Templar fair.[175] In the delicate field of foreign trade, the privileges regarding customs duties and the amount of goods which could be exchanged were temporary and localized from the start. When the Templars engaged in trade which the king considered proper, they experienced no difficulties; but when they engaged in trade which he considered unauthorized, their special privileges were cancelled.[176] Though royal officials frequently seized the goods of private individuals, if those goods were needed by the king, there survives a record of only one instance in which they unjustly seized Templar goods — specifically wool.[177]

The exemption of the Templars from ordinary feudal burdens and their independence from royal and other courts were not clear-cut. As has been indicated above, the Templars were sometimes pardoned from feudal burdens; but as often they seem to have been required to assume their share of them. In addition to the burdens already discussed, the exemption, on the one hand, and the requirement, on the other, for work on *corvées* by Templar tenants might be mentioned.[178] The right of the Templars to maintain their own courts and to be immune from all prosecution except before the king and his chief justice was often enough maintained.[179] But, nonetheless, the Templars were upon occasion brought before the assize courts, the courts of eyre, and the county courts, as the king's grant of pardon of fines imposed by such courts reveals.[180]

Of considerable importance and frequent use were royal letters of protection and safe-conduct issued for periods ranging from several months to three years. These letters were obtained by the Templars for their security in England as well as abroad and pertained in some instances to the individual Templar, usually the Master in England,[181] and in other instances to all the Templars and their lands and possessions.[182] The value and need for these letters was made especially obvious during the contest between Pope Boniface VIII and King Edward I over royal taxation of the clergy. Because of the issuance of the bull *Clericis laicos* (1296) and the subsequent refusal of the English clergy to contribute to the national tax levy, Edward withdrew the English clergy from the protection of the king's law and ordered the lay fees of the clergy, together with their goods and chattels, seized by the sheriffs. This meant that the clergy, including the Templars, could be proceeded against with impunity and that their lands and chattels were temporarily lost to them. The Templars soon came to terms with the king (February 22, 1297) and were received back into his protection, and their goods were returned to them.[183] The other religious groups likewise bowed to the royal will, and Boniface found it necessary to alter his instructions to the English clergy.

In summary, regarding the privileges of the Templars, it may be said that they were varied in nature; that they were not uniformly maintained; that such maintenance of them as was obtained was due to papal, and especially to royal support; that, though the kings made lavish grants of privileges and repeatedly ordered compliance with them, the actual enforcement of them was sporadic; that the kings demanded much in return for their grants and assistance; that the maintenance of the Templar privileges probably reached its height in the first half of the reign of Henry III; and that from the latter half of Henry III's reign on, and especially during the reign of Edward I, who was seeking to centralize the royal administration and to curtail privileges of both lay and clerical magnates and groups, the maintenance of their privileges proved increasingly more difficult to achieve.

Holdings

Starting with the limited holdings represented by such grants as those of Stephen and Matilda, discussed above, the English Templars consistently and quite rapidly expanded their property until they became numbered among the great landlords of the realm. An accurate survey of their holdings, however, cannot be given. The content and chronological coverage of surviving sources are too incomplete; the identification of place names cannot always be made with certainty; the multiplicity of land units and the local variation in size of the same basic unit hinders precision; and the indefiniteness and miscellaneous character of the documentary data prevent a comprehensive treatment. Furthermore, since the Templars were constantly acquiring, selling, and transferring land, it is frequently impossible to determine whether a particular estate belonging to the order in the period was actually still in their possession at another time. Yet some sort of survey must be attempted.

The sources for such a survey are limited. The earliest comprehensive material is to be gotten from the Inquest of 1185 which Geoffrey Fitz Stephen, then Master of the Temple in England, wisely had made. His reason, according to the opening statement of the Inquest was to make a record of Templar lands, possessions, and income so that no harm or disadvantage might befall the order.[184] Actually, this meant he was taking precautions in anticipation of trouble arising from the envy of the secular clergy — especially of the bishops — at the growing power and wealth and increasing prominence of the Templars.[185] The Inquest shows that Templar holdings were already, by 1185, extensive; that their greatest concentration was in Yorkshire and Lincolnshire; that they were let out in units ranging from less than an acre to eighty acres for varying rents and services; that they were given over to the production of grain, cattle, sheep, and the like; and that they were rented for cash whenever possible. The Inquest, however, is not complete as it lacks data on holdings in and around London and in Cambridgeshire. These two omissions can be compensated for, however — the former, by references in the Public Records, and the latter, by the Sandford Cartulary, drawn up between 1265 and 1274, which deals in detail with Templar holdings in Cambridgeshire. Unfortuntely, demesne land, which was not always rented out and which may have amounted to about one-half of the arable land, was not reported in the Inquest.[186] There are other difficulties too. Except for the convenient use of acres in some cases — but even acres may vary in size from area to area — it is very hard to make sense out of the land units. Messuages are repeatedly referred to, evidently meaning a house and the small plot of land on which it was located. Especially troublesome are the units which vary in size from region to region — for example, carucates may be 120, 160, or 240 acres in size; hides, 64, 96, or 120; virgates, 15, 24, or 30; and bovates, 20, 24, or 30.[187] Tofts, however, appear to be regularly units of twelve acres. In addition, indefinite units such as crofts, cotlands, meadows, gardens, woodlands, vills, and pastures are widely used. To add further to the confusion, it is sometimes unclear whether or not certain areas are being counted twice in the returns from the counties. Despite these deficiencies and difficulties, the Inquest is a most useful and revealing document.

Equally as important as a source for Templar possessions in England is the Hospitaller Report of 1338, one section of which deals with former Templar lands currently in the hands of the Knights of the Hospital of St. John of Jerusalem.[188] This report to the Grand Prior of the order was drawn up by Prior Philip de Thame, an efficient manager and supervisor, who had been sent from Italy to straighten out the financial difficulties which the English Hospitallers had fallen into under the priorship of Thomas Larcher. The change in the financial condition from a debit to a credit status was not due solely to the able leadership of de Thame, however. Perhaps equally important was the actual transfer of many of the former Templar estates to the Hospitallers — a goal toward which the prior's predecessor had worked long and diligently.[189] Like the Templar Inquest, the Hospitaller Report records the lands, possessions, and income of the order. In some respects, it is clearer than the Inquest — for example, the lands are carefully listed by county; and the areas, many of which are expressed in acres, are given. But the Report is much less detailed than the Inquest, and like the Inquest, is also incomplete. Though certain Templar lands which the Hospitallers claimed but had not yet obtained are specifically indicated,[190] there are still additional holdings known to have been in their possession at this date which were omitted.[191] Nonetheless, the survey of 1338 was reasonably complete and accurate.

In addition to these two primary sources, valuable information on Templar holdings can be obtained from the Public Record collection and from Dugdale's *Monasticon*. The data in the Public Records tend to be miscellaneous, being references to gifts and/or confirmations of gifts, transfers of land, and court cases involving the Templars. Insofar as the Templars in twelfth century England are concerned, the *Monasticon* has been in large measure superseded by Miss Lees' edition of the Inquest together with other documents pertaining to that century; but it remains of some value for the twelfth century and is indispensable for the thirteenth. Yet another source of information on Templar goods, lands, and income, is the survey made by the king's officials in 1308. Because this document still exists in manuscript form only, references to it here must be made on the basis of secondary works.[192]

The following survey of Templar holdings in England represents a combination of material gained from the above sources. To attempt to be complete would be folly — the surviving data and the limits of space and interest prevent it. It is deemed important here not to list every known area held by the Templars but only to indicate the major holdings in the various counties. Furthermore, it should be remembered that for the most part the Templars' holdings were small and irregular rather than large and consolidated units. In making this survey, special emphasis will be placed on the preceptories which, though varying in size, wealth, and importance, regularly consisted of at least a manor, a manor house, a chapel, and a number of outbuildings and formed the basic administrative units of the Templars. Since the Templars were most active and numerous in Yorkshire and Lincolnshire, it is fitting to start with these two counties.

In Yorkshire there were ten preceptories and several houses of almost equal importance. Indeed, Templar interests were so concentrated in this county that it was early found necessary to appoint a Chief Preceptor in Yorkshire[193] to supervise the vast estates, the varied activities, and the large income of the order there. The oldest preceptory in Yorkshire was Temple Hirst, the origins of which are to be found in Ralph de Hastings' grant of the manor of Hirst to the Templars in 1152.[194] Penhill and Temple Cowton, growing out of initial gifts of land by Roger Mowbray (*ca.* 1142) and greatly enlarged by grants of subsequent donors, became preceptories sometime after 1185.[195] The origin of the preceptory of Temple Newsam is to be found in a grant of land made by William de Villiers — a leading noble of the realm like Hastings and Mowbray — sometime before his death in 1181.[196] The grant of Westerdale, which early became a preceptory, was confirmed by King John in 1203 and included a moiety of the advowson of Beeford Church as well as its own estates and chapel.[197] The preceptory of Ribston and Wetherby seems to have started with a grant by Robert de Ros, a noble, of the manor, vill and mills of Ribston, along with the advowson of the church of Walshford. To this was later added the vill and church of Hunsingore, the vill of Wetherby, and a number of smaller areas[198] which made Ribston and Wetherby one of the wealthiest Templar units. Sometime prior to 1258, the Templars were given the manor and church of Copmanthorp which were added to the castle mills below York, which had earlier (before 1185) been donated to the order by Roger Mowbray. Another church and additional lands were subsequently obtained and were attached to the above units to form the preceptory of Copmanthorp.[199] The origin of the Faxfleet unit, a wealthy one, and the areas under its jurisdiction are unknown.[200] Nor is much known about two other wealthy preceptories, Foulbridge and Whitley.[201] On the basis of their average net income expressed in pounds for the years 1308 to 1338, when Templar possessions were in the king's hands, the Yorkshire preceptories would be ranked in the following order:[202] Ribston and Wetherby (£270), Foulbridge (£208), Faxfleet (£115), Temple Hirst (£111), Temple Newsam (£108), Temple Cowton (£97), Westerdale (£55), Copmanthorp (£43), Whitley (£27) and Penhill (£24). In addition to these units, there were several Templar houses — e.g., Alveston, Cave, and Etton, worth £19, £31, and £19 respectively, each of which possessed extensive lands and had its own church—which never became preceptories but were more important than many a preceptory in another county.[203] All of these estates with the exception of Faxfleet, Temple Hirst, and Temple Newsam, passed ultimately to the Hospitallers.[204]

In Lincolnshire, there were five preceptories, four of them among the richer and more powerful houses of the English Templars. Eagle, supposedly founded by a grant of King Stephen, included lands and churches in adjacent areas as well as the manor and church of Eagle[205] and in 1308 was listed as worth £125. Willoughton, founded by a noble in the reign of Stephen, and enlarged greatly by subsequent grants by other lords, included nearly the whole vill of Willoughton with a moiety of the advowson of the church there and churches in five and lands in eight other communities[206] and brought in £261 in 1308. Aslackby, established apparently in 1164, included lands, subsequently increased, and the church of the area[207] and was valued at £78. Temple Bruer, founded late in the reign of Henry II,[208] in an area then considered wasteland, became, thanks to subsequent gifts and hard work, one of the largest, richest, and most prominent Templar houses in England including several churches, at least one market, extensive arable lands, and huge pasture areas used for grazing sheep. While in the king's hands, it returned by far the largest income (£325) of any of the Templar estates in Lincolnshire. South Witham, the origin of which is uncertain,[209] appears to have been a small house of unknown value and cannot be compared with the other preceptories in the county. Indeed,, when the Hospitallers took it over, they wisely subordinated it to Temple Bruer.[210] For a time, Mere, just outside the city of Lincoln, may have been a preceptory; but if so, it was early placed under the jurisdiction of Eagle and later under Willoughton.[211] Each of these preceptories — together with the lands, churches, and mills associated with them — ultimately came into the possession of the Hospitallers.[212]

In the counties to the north and west of Yorkshire and Lincolnshire, the Templars had no preceptories and only very small holdings.[213] In Northumberland, the Templars held lands at Thornton worth £47; in Westmorland, at Temple Sowerby of unknown value; in Nottinghamshire, at Flaufor, and in addition, small churches at Markham and Sibethorp, and mills at Bekingham, the total returns of which were £52 in 1308; and in Lancashire, small areas not specifically identified.

In the counties near or bordering Wales and in southwest England, the Templars held only small estates which, however, were more numerous than those in the counties just mentioned. In Shropshire, several hundred acres were held in the area of Staunton and Halston;[214] and it is possible that a preceptory existed at Halston.[215] In Worcestershire, the Templars had several minor holdings — e.g., the advowson of Bromsgrove, which they claimed to have held since the time of Richard I; a messuage at Feckenham where they raised sheep and cattle; land at Temple Broughton, part of which had been granted to them by Henry III; and the manor of Temple Laughern, which they had purchased in 1249.[216] In Herefordshire, there were enough holdings to form two preceptories:[217] one at Garewy worth £106, and another at Upleden worth £60. In the southwestern counties, the chief center was at Temple Combe in Somerset,[218] a preceptory in a cattle and sheep raising area which returned £78 in 1308. In Wiltshire, there were a number of holdings, the largest of which were Temple Rockley — probably a preceptory — and Chiryton which together contained over five hundred acres, not including pasture for well over a thousand sheep,[219] but returned only £20 according to the royal survey. In addition, the Templars had small holdings at Connerton in Cornwall, Templeton in Devonshire, and Wileton in Somerset.[220] The chief of these holdings — Upleden, Garewy, Rockley, and Combe — came into the hands of the Hospitallers, and probably the lesser ones did, too.[221]

In the eastern and southeastern counties, Templar holdings were greatest in Essex, Kent, and Sussex. Essex, as seen above, was the site of the first establishments of the Templars in England, and Temple Cressing, the gift of Queen Matilda, was the preceptory in that area.[222] Closely associated with Cressing was Witham — the manor, market, church, and pasture lands — which similarly received royal favor.[223] The two estates together, consisting of well over one thousand acres, returned £77 in 1308. Reyndon, Sutton, Uphall, and Rivenhall were additional Templar centers in this county.[224] In Kent, Temple Ewell, worth £26, served as the preceptory and was closely associated with the Templar manors at Strood, Dertford, and Waltham.[225] In Sussex, though no information was returned in the Inquest, the Templars already held an estate at Shipley[226] and soon were to hold Saddelscomb and minor estates elsewhere.[227] Shipley was definitely a preceptory and possible Saddelscomb was also. The two of them together returned £45 in 1308. In the other eastern and southeastern counties, Templar holdings were few in number and small in size. In Norfolk and Suffolk, the Templars held practically no land in the twelfth century and not very much in the thirteenth.[228] Indeed, their estates here were so small and of such limited value that they appear to have been appended to the Cambridgeshire holdings and to have returned about £15 per year only. Apart from the manor of Widflete, which they rented from 1161 on, the Templars held practically nothing in Surrey except part of the manor of Merrow which returned £17 in 1308.[229] In Berkshire, the Templars had a preceptory at Temple Bistlesham, appraised at £55 per year, and possessed subordinate houses at Bisham, Templeton, Wescott, and Clewer[230] which probably date from the late twelfth or early thirteenth century. In Hampshire, land was held in North, South, and Milford Baddesley, the various holdings making up the preceptory of Baddesley which was in existence by 1240.[231] Generally speaking, all these lands in the eastern and southeastern counties, except Saddelscomb,[232] eventually came into the hands of the Hospitallers.

The holdings of the Templars in the counties in central England, or the Midlands, were second in number and importance only to those in Yorkshire and Lincolnshire. Not all the counties were equally significant, however, as the following paragraphs will show. To facilitate treatment here, the counties will be divided into three groups on the basis of geography and revenue: first, Leicester, Warwick, Gloucester, and Oxford; second, Cambridge, Hertford, and Middlesex; and third, Rutland, Northampton, Huntington, Bedford, and Buckingham.

The first of these groups of counties was the most important both in number of holdings and in revenue. In Oxfordshire, the Templars began their acquisitioins with the grant in 1136 by Matilda of the manor of Cowley[234] which, enlarged by later donations, came to be known as Temple Cowley and early became a preceptory of considerable value. In the 1150's, the manors of Sibford Gower, Merton, and Hensington were obtained.[235] These were followed by the grant of land and a church at Broadwell by 1185, the manors of Littlemore and Warpsgrove in the early years of the thirteenth century, the manors of Horspath and Overhorspath in 1225, and the manor of Sandford-on-Thames in 1239-40.[236] Sandford soon became a preceptory and exercised jurisdiction over Templar holdings in Hampshire and Berkshire as well as in southern Oxfordshire. The wealth of the properties in this county is indicated by the returns of 1308 which credit Temple Cowley with £60, Sandford with £58, Broadwell with £46, and Merton with £44. In Gloucestershire, there were numerous small holdings; but the chief center was at Temple Guiting, the original grants of which — lands, mills, and the advowson of the church — were made in the middle of the twelfth century.[237] Guiting, returning £206 in 1308, was clearly one of the chief Templar preceptories in England. In addition, in the southern part of the county, Bristol served as a financial center not only for its immediate area but also for the counties of Cornwall, Devon, Somerset, and Dorset.[238] Before the dissolution of the order, however, Bristol appears to have been subordinated to Temple Combe in Somerset.[239] In Leicestershire, the holdings which became the preceptory of Rothley started with a small grant of land by a noble in the time of John (probably in 1203) to which Henry III (1231) added the manor of Rothley and the advowson of its church.[240] At the dissolution, this preceptory, worth £195, included lands in thirteen neighboring areas, several mills, large pastures for grazing sheep, and five dependent chapels.[241] Numerous small holdings belonged to the Templars in Warwickshire, chief among which were lands at Sherborne, Warwick, and Fletchamstead.[242] But the major center was the preceptory of Balsall[243] which returned £104 in 1308.

In the second group of counties, Middlesex claims pre-eminence as the county in which the central headquarters of the Templar order in England was located. As has been indicated above, New Temple, London, served as a preceptory for the area as well as the central headquarters of the order. In addition to their chapels and lands in the suburbs of London and their lands and mills along the Thames, the Templars held small estates at Lilleston, Hamstede, Hendon, Crawnford, Hakeneye, and Charring.[244] But none of these holdings, including New Temple, brought in much revenue inasmuch as only £85 was reported in 1308. In Cambridgeshire, which was omitted from the Inquest, the Templars held numerous estates which, for the most part, were subordinated to the three preceptories of the county — Denney (worth £37 in 1308), Duxford (worth £22), and Great Wilberham (worth £59). Some of the individual grants go back to the twelfth century, but most of them seem to have been made in the thirteenth.[245] Templar properties in Hertfordshire, among the oldest holdings of the order in England, appear to have been about the same in number and value as those in Cambridgeshire. Lands, churches, mills, and markets at Hitchin, Preston, Dinsley, Weston, and Baldock date back to 1147-48 when they were given to the Templars by such great lords as Gilbert de Clare, William Marshall, and Bernard de Balliol and were confirmed by King Stephen.[246] These initial grants, and subsequent additions to them, were consolidated under Temple Dinsley which probably had become a preceptory by the end of the reign of Henry II. Another important center in this county, about which very little is known, was Langenok[247] which by 1308 was worth £55 as compared to Temple Dinsley's £60.

In the third group of counties in central England, Templar holdings were small in number and value: the church of Stretton and lands at Melton Mowbray and Stonesby in Rutland;[248] lands at Blakesley, Guilsborough, and Harrington in Northamptonshire;[249] a variety of holdings in Huntingdonshire of which Ogerston-Washingley and Sibeston,[250] worth £25 together, were the most important; the manors of Swanton, Stocton, and Sharnbrook, worth about £17 each, and land, a mill, and a church worth £13, in Bedfordshire;[251] and lands at Radnage—granted by John in 1212 — Marlow, Temple Wycombe, Ham, Loudwater, Calverton, and Bulstrode, worth less than £30 all together, in Buckinghamshire.[252] None of these counties had a preceptory except Buckingham where Bulstrode had become one by 1278. The origin of most of the holdings in this group of counties is difficult, if not impossible, to determine, and the disposition of them after the dissolution of the Templars is not always clear either. But in general, they, like most of the Templar properties, ultimately came into the possession of the Hospitallers.[253]

To be complete, something must be said of the Templar holdings in Ireland, Scotland, and Wales. It is estimated that 13 manors, 21 churches, and miscellaneous parcels of land, returning a total of £411 in 1308, were held in Ireland.[254] In Scotland, where information on the Templars is more controversial than abundant, property returning a total of £25 was held at Blantrodok, Culthur, Templiston, and Berwick-on-Tweed.[225] In Wales, land worth £3 was held at Lammadoch.[256]

Although much more could be written on the holdings of the Templars, enough has been given to suggest that they were extensive and profitable. It would be interesting and pertinent to determine the size and value of the Templar properties, but the lack of essential information and the inconsistency of such data as survives makes the task impossible. One can only say that Templar holdings varied in size from a plot of a few acres to huge estates — like Balsall, Upleden, and Cressing — between five hundred and one thousand acres,[257] and in revenue from petty sums of a few pence to large sums — as at Temple Guiting, Ribston-Wetherby, and Temple Bruer—of over £200 or £300 per year.[258] To this it can be added that the Templars were among the great landholders of the realm though it is doubtful if they held as much land as such other religious groups as the Benedictines, Augustinians, and Cistercians.[259]

Recruitment and Training

Practically nothing is known of the manner in which the Templars obtained their members or of the numbers of men involved. In their Rule, only a few items of information are to be found: the basic requirements for membership,[260] the procedure and vows of initiation,[261] the animals and equipment allowed to individual Templars according to their rank and assignments,[262] and the modification of the dominant western ideas and practices of war by eastern or Turkish influences.[263] All that can be said is that the Templars were a relatively small and elite group, that they were at the start and remained till the end predominantly cavalrymen, and that their valor and *espirit de corps* — as shown time and again in the wars and skirmishes in the Holy Land —

had won for them a reputation which must have provided them with
more candidates for membership than they could normally accept. Yet,
there must also have been times — as, for example, after certain campaigns in which their numbers had been decimated[264] — when they
direly needed new members, perhaps more than they could obtain.

Nor is information on their training available. Obviously, the Templars were initially thoroughly trained in western methods of warfare.
This meant that chief reliance in war was put on the charge of the
heavy-armed cavalry whose knights *(milites),* wearing helmets, hauberks,
and coats of chain mail, equipped with swords, lances, and triangular
shields, and riding large but slow horses, launched all-out attacks upon
the infidel, not so much in a single, mass formation as in successive
squadrons of one hundred to one hundred and fifty men each.[265] The
way for the cavalry charge was usually prepared by the preliminary
activities of the light-armed foot soldiers *(pedites)* who, equipped with
spears, clubs, and bows, were stationed in front of the cavalry, between
it and the enemy forces.[266] So long as the knights could mount their
attack and could maintain their formation, they were likely to drive all
before them. And when it came to hand-to-hand combat following the
charge, the more lightly armed Turks proved inferior to the more heavily
armed Franks. But the Turks, relying chiefly on their light-armed cavalry, especially on mounted archers — bearing shields, lances, swords,
and clubs as well — and riding smaller and faster horses, enjoyed greater
speed and maneuverability than the Crusader forces. Because of their
ability to attack, retreat, reorganize, and attack again so easily, the
Turks were able to do great damage to the Christians and often to upset
the latter's plans and formations. In imitation, the Templars, and other
Christian groups and leaders as well, organized their own light-armed
cavalry troops, which, equipped primarily with bows and arrows, proved
highly effective and became a vital part of Christian armies employing
modified western tactics.[267] These troops, known as Turcopoles, were
recruited from the native population, being often offspring of parents
of different religions, and were used for reconnaissance work as well as
for fighting as regular light-armed cavalry units.

It would be interesting to know what sort of training was given the
Templars in the West, but lack of information permits us only to wonder
whether or not the lessons of the eastern campaigns and the new methods
employed by the Templars were brought back to their recruits and
brothers in Europe.[268] That some sort of training was given is inevitable
in view of the military nature and purpose of the order and the likeli-
hood that many a Templar would be sent East. Though the existence of
training fields or parade grounds cannot be determined with complete

certainty, Fickettscroft in London, across the Thames from New Temple, must have been such a field;[269] and other preceptories may well have had such facilities as well. Without doubt, the Master of the Temple in England was in over-all charge of military training. This task, however, was probably directly under the supervision of the preceptors who in turn relied upon lesser persons — perhaps the heads of the individual houses — to do most of the actual work. Though tournaments might have formed a convenient means of testing their training, there is no indication that the Templars participated in them. The only references which can be found are those in which a Templar is one of a small group of persons sent by Henry III to stop a proposed tournament at Northampton and an actual tournament at York.[270]

When a Templar became sick or too old and infirm to fulfill his duties, he was well taken care of.[271] In England, there were two centers for such persons — one at Eagle, in Lincolnshire,[272] and the other on the Isle of Ely, associated with the preceptory of Denney, in Cambridgeshire.[273]

Though information is limited, enough is known to state that the Templars first came to England about 1128, that they were few in number but great in wealth, that their privileges were very extensive in theory but were limited in actual practice, and that the Templar units and organizations were centralized under the Master at New Temple but were allowed considerable local autonomy.

chapter three

Political and Economic Activities

IN THE PRECEEDING CHAPTER, some consideration was given to the political and economic activities of the Templars, primarily as reflected in their organization, privileges, and land holdings. It is now necessary to examine these activities, and the administrative as well, in some detail, as they pertain to the crown — for which there is considerable information — and to other persons or groups — for which there is little material. The Templars will be found as officials, envoys, and advisers of the crown; they will be found represented in Parliament; and they will be found the recipients of royal gifts and favors excluding the privileges discussed in the preceding chapter. It will also be apparent that they actively engaged in agriculture, trade and commerce, and banking. New Temple, their central headquarters in England, will be seen to be a place of lodging for both lay and clerical persons, of assembly for political and ecclesiastical meetings, of deposit for valuables and money, of monetary exchange and banking activity, of convenience from which royal business of various kinds was carried on, and of burial.

Political Activities

The earliest official position given a Templar by the English kings was that of royal almoner. Roger, a Templar serving as an almoner to John, acted in addition as a royal agent entrusted with the regulation of sea-borne commerce between England and Gascony.[1] Under Henry III, there were at least three different Templars serving as royal almoners. Geoffrey, who held this position from 1234 to 1239, handled a great variety of other tasks for the king as well.[2] As keeper of the king's wardrobe, he held inquiries regarding certain lands and issued licenses and letters of protection as well as writs pertaining to the king's business.[3] That he did a thorough job is suggested by Matthew Paris' statement that his dismissal was an event longed for because of his "arrogance."[4] Another Templar, also named Roger, was dismissed as royal almoner by Henry III in 1253 when the Templars and Hospitallers refused to provide the king with the five thousand marks which had been promised to Richard de Clare if the latter would have his eldest son marry the daughter of the Count of Angoulême.[5] And in 1241, John, a Templar, serving as almoner, was sent by Henry III to stop a proposed tournament at Northhampton.[6] Perhaps Richard, a Templar in King Alexander of Scotland's Council,[7] had been royal almoner in that country. A chance reference to a certain Morinus, a Templar, serving as almoner to Hugh, Bishop of Lincoln,[8] suggests that the Templars may also have been almoners to persons other than kings. As almoners, at least as almoners of the king, they served as individuals and not as Templars as is shown by Henry III's promise to Robert de Sanford, Master of the Temple in England, that the Templar order should not be bound to answer for anything done by Geoffrey as royal almoner.[9]

Frequently the Templars were used as messengers and envoys of the king. John and Henry III repeatedly sent them *"ad partes transmarinas"*[10] as well as to persons and places in England. Sometimes the reason for their dispatch is not given; but when it is, it can be seen that important matters were often entrusted to them. Under Henry II in 1164, two Templars were sent to treat with the Archbishop of York at the Council of Clarendon regarding the possible appointment of the archbishop as papal legate.[11] And it was from a Templar that Henry received the message that Louis VII of France was concerned about the delay in the marriage of Richard and Alice, the son and daughter respectively of the English and French kings.[12] Under Henry III, Templars were often sent, along with other persons, on missions for the king. The Master of the Temple in England, Alan Martel, was sent (1224) to deal with Louis of France on the subject of a truce[13] and, almost immediately thereafter, to look into the possibility of effecting an agreement with Leopold, Duke of Austria, for marriage of King Henry to the duke's daughter.[14] A decade later, Robert de Sanford, then Master in England, was one of the royal representatives in the negotiations leading to the king's marriage to Eleanor, daughter of Count Raymond of Provence, and was a member of the royal party designated to escort her to England.[15] In 1252, Roscelin de Fos, Master of the Temple in England, was in charge of discussing violation of the truce in Gascony; of negotiating an agreement between Simon de Montfort, Henry III's governor of the duchy, and the leaders of the Gascons who were dissatisfied with his administration; and of conserving the truce he succeeded in making.[16] Two years later (1254), the king sent a Templar to Scotland on matters pertaining to the queen of that country.[17] In the same year, when in southern France, Henry directed that certain royal valuables be brought to him by either a Templar or a Hospitaller.[18] Shortly thereafter, a

Templar was one of six royal envoys sent to Italy to deal with Pope Alexander IV on Sicilian affairs.[19] Between 1261 and 1265, on four separate occasions, a Templar was sent, along with one or two other persons, to discuss terms of peace between France and England.[20] During this period, a Templar is also found as a royal envoy to an English noble.[21] Under Edward I and Edward II, the use of Templars as royal messengers and envoys seems to have been discontinued.

There is little information on the use of Templars in England as envoys and messengers by persons other than the king. In 1234, Templars were used as messengers between Richard, son of William Marshall, Earl of Pembroke, and the Irish nobles, in Richard's campaign in Ireland;[22] and in 1235, Emperor Frederick II sent a delegation, including two Templars, to ask for the hand of Isabella, Henry III's sister, in marriage.[23] Quite probably a more thorough search of the sources, though they are concerned primarily with royal affairs, would provide additional examples.

On two occasions, the kings of England found it desirable to entrust disputed areas to the safekeeping of the Templars. In the first instance (1158-61), Henry II of England and Louis VII of France, arguing over possessions of the castles of Néaufles and Gisors in the Vexin, agreed that when Henry's two sons were married to Louis' two daughters — all four were small children — the castles should be handed over to Henry, but that in the meantime, the Templars were to hold them in safekeeping. This they did until Henry, in considerable haste, had his older son, Henry, married to Louis' older daughter, Margaret. For handing the castles over to Henry at this point, the Templars were rebuked by the French king but were rewarded by the English.[24] Later, in 1186, they seem to have had a part in the arrangement by which Queen Margaret of France renounced her claim to the castles.[25] In the second instance, when, en route to the Holy Land, a disagreement between Richard of England and Philip of France arose over which of the two kings should raise his banner over the Sicilian city of Messina, it was decided to entrust the city to the Templars.[26]

On a number of occasions, the Templars are found as advisers to the king. Richard de Hastings, Master of the Temple in England, along with the Bishops of Salisbury and Norwich and the Earls of Leicester and Cornwall, played a prominent part in the Becket controversy (1164).[27] Apparently he and the others sought to effect a reconciliation between the archbishop and the king by urging Thomas to yield to Henry II. Aymeric de St. Maur, Master of the Temple in England, showed himself a faithful adviser to John for over a decade.[28] In the crucial phase of John's dispute with Innocent III, it was two Templars, who had been

sent to the king by Pandulph, the papal legate, who arranged for the
meeting leading to John's submission. These two Templars, doubtlessly
after consultation with Aymeric, advised the king to submit and accompanied him to the Preceptory of Ewell, near Dover, from which
John left to submit to Pandulph and receive his realm back as a fief of
the papacy.[29] Indeed, the gold mark which John offered the church
when absolved from excommunication was borrowed from none other
than Aymeric.[30] This same Templar advised John in the contest with
the barons which led to the issuance of *Magna Carta*. It appears that
Aymeric was one of those lords who, though on the side of John at
Runnymede, advised the beleaguered king to sign the proposed charter
of liberties and rights.[31] Certainly the liberties and rights of the Templars
are to be considered among those confirmed and guaranteed by this
charter[32] and also by the earlier charter of rights and liberties of the
clergy which, interestingly enough, had been signed by John in January
at New Temple.[33] Specific instances in which the Templars served as
advisers to Henry III are not readily found; but in view of the great
favor he showed to the Templars and in view of his frequent visits to
New Temple, it is quite probable that such masters as Alan Martel,
Robert de Sanford, and Roscelin de Fos, who were sent on many a
royal mission,[34] may also have served as royal advisers. Under Edward I
and Edward II, however, there is no evidence to prove nor reason to
suspect that the Masters of the Temple served as royal advisers.

Since the preceding paragraphs do not quite give a complete picture
of the political relations of the Templars with the crown, a few additional
points should be mentioned. Under Stephen, when the Templars, whether
from wisdom or necessity, were playing both sides in the years of civil
strife, one of their number is found in the list of witnesses to the charter
which provided for settlement between Stephen and the Empress Matilda
whereby the latter's son, Henry of Anjou, was to succeed to the English
crown.[35] As part of his penance for the Becket murder, Henry II promised, among other things, to pay the Templars the sum necessary to
maintain two hundred knights for the defense of the Holy Land for a
year.[36] In the hope that Henry could also be convinced to come east at
the head of a large force, an impressive delegation from Jerusalem —
consisting of the Patriarch, the Prior of the Hospitallers, and the Grand
Master of the Templars, who died in Italy en route — was sent to England. But the king, relying upon a convenient opinion of Parliament
(1185), finally rejected the request on the grounds that reasons for his
remaining in England were more compelling than those for his going
to the Holy Land.[37] However, in his will, Henry remembered the Tem-

plars, Hospitallers, and several other religious groups in England, with five thousand silver marks each.[38]

The relations of Richard with the Templars, which are as colorful as they are popular, are more a part of the history of eastern than of English affairs. From the incident at Messina, referred to above, it is clear that a number of Templars, some of whom no doubt left England with the king, accompanied Richard all the way east. While in the Holy Land, Richard found the Templars loyal allies, as was especially proved at Ascalon.[39] When it came time for Richard to return to Europe, even though he had not been able to accomplish all he had wanted to, it was in a boat provided by Robert de Sable, Grand Master of the Templars that he set out for the west (October 9, 1192).[40] Wearing the habit of a Templar, and accompanied by four Templars and a number of attendants, he sailed first to Corfu and then to the northern shore of the Adriatic Sea where he finally landed in the area of Aquileia and Venice. Retaining his Templar disguise and accompanied initially by several priests and two Templars, but later by only one attendant — in order to make capture less likely — the English monarch proceeded inland through territory belonging to his enemy, Leopold, Archduke of Austria. Recognized and captured at a small town near Vienna, he was held prisoner for thirteen months, first by the Archduke and then by Emperor Henry VI, before being brought to trial on a variety of charges at a diet at Worms. At his trial, Richard defended himself with such vigor and eloquence that he was finally put up for ransom — 100,000 silver marks.[41] To this ransom, laity and clergy in England without distinction were compelled to contribute (1193). Privileges and immunities were suspended. The English Templars doubtlessly had to pay their share — as William of Newburgh said, even the Cistercians had to pay.[42]

John, and his son, Henry III, as has been shown above, relied heavily upon the Templars for a variety of services and for advice. Furthermore, both kings were frequent guests at New Temple and at other Templar houses where they carried on royal business.[43] Indeed, the close relationship between the Templars and the crown reached its height in the first half of Henry's reign. Indicative of this royal favor were Henry's choice (1236-37) of New Temple as his burial place — a choice with which his bride concurred — and his bequest of £8 sterling for three chaplains to say mass there daily.[44] Actually, however, upon death, Henry's body, though claimed by the Templars, was not entombed at New Temple but rather in the church of the shrine of Edward the Confessor.[45] Like Henry II, his grandfather, Henry III assumed the cross (1252) but did not actually undertake a crusade although the Templars, Hospitallers, and Teutonic Knights had been instructed to make preparations for the king's passage.[46] While in Paris (1254), it was at the Old Temple there, the Templars' headquarters in France, that Henry chose to stay.[47] Also suggestive of the close ties between Henry and the Templars is the gift of a crystal vase allegedly containing a portion of the blood of Christ which William de Sonnac, Grand Master of the order, sent him in 1247.[48]

The political relations of Edward I and Edward II with the Templars were limited, though both monarchs had frequent financial dealings with them. It should be pointed out, however, that the Templars rendered military service to Edward I in his campaign against Scotland (1298-99) — the Master of the Temple, Brian de Jay, and presumably certain other members of the order, being summoned for this campaign.[49] Indeed, Brian de Jay and another Templar were killed in the crucial battle of Falkirk.[50] Interestingly, too, this same Brian de Jay — apparently while still Preceptor of Scotland and just before his selection as Master in England — had earlier (1296) been called to do fealty to the English king. [51] As this is the only notice of the sort, it raises but does not answer the question of whether or not the Templars regularly rendered fealty to the king. Most likely, the demand for fealty from the Preceptor of Scotland was part of Edward's general policy of seeking to bring all the important lords of that country more directly under his authority, an especially urgent matter inasmuch as Scotland had recently (1295) allied itself with France. In the absence of additional data, then, one cannot assume that fealty was normally demanded of the master and preceptors in England. Apart from their arrest, trial, conviction, and dissolution — which will be dealt with below in Chapter IV — the political relations between the Templars and Edward II are limited to one insignificant event, namely, that they, along with the Hospitallers, should furnish three carts for the king's use, with recompense to be made out of the funds of the king's wardrobe.[52]

The political prominence of the Templars, and of other religious orders and their heads as well, is shown by the regular attendance of the Master of the Temple in England at sessions of Parliament. From 1295 to 1306, he was summoned by name, along with other leading clerics and lay lords, to be present;[53] but unfortunately, exactly what he did at these sessions cannot be determined.

Associated with the political activities of the Templars, but to a lesser degree than with their economic activities, is the administrative role of New Temple. As suggested above, various kings made frequent visits to New Temple — and to other preceptories upon occasion as well — and, during their residence there, carried on royal business as close and patent letters clearly reveal.[54] The subject matter of these letters was as varied as similar royal correspondence written elsewhere: the election of clerical officials, the assignment of church benefices, the holding of assizes, the issuance of letters of safe-conduct and protection, the licensing of merchants and goods, the collection of taxes, the grant of royal gifts and privileges, and the like.

New Temple was repeatedly used as a convenient place for political and ecclesiastical meetings. The council, led by Simon de Montfort, which discussed what should be done regarding Henry III's misrule, met at New Temple in 1260.[55] The parliament which met in November, 1272, upon the death of Henry III, to recognize Edward, abroad on a crusade, as the new king, and to make the necessary arrangements for carrying on the government until his return, was held at New Temple.[56] And in 1299, Parliament was summoned by Edward I to assemble at New Temple.[57] A number of times, when Henry III was king, New Temple was used as the place where those who wished to see him should come.[58] On at least nine occasions between 1256 and 1299, the English clergy, either the prelates alone or the prelates and the lower clergy jointly in convocation, met at New Temple to discuss their various problems and to decide upon a course of action.[59]

Both clerics and laymen found New Temple a convenient place of lodging. Besides the kings who frequently stayed there, prominent clerics like the archbishops of York, Cologne, and Toledo were lodged there.[60] Papal legates seem to have made it a point to stay there — Martin, legate of Innocent IV, for example, resided there for several years (1244-46).[61] And foreign diplomats, such as envoys of the King of Castille, were put up at New Temple.[62] The church even served as a burial place for a number of prominent persons — William Marshall, first Earl of Pembroke; his son, William, second Earl of Pembroke; and his great grandson, Gilbert, fourth Earl of Pembroke.[63] As mentioned above, it had originally been planned that King Henry III and his wife should be buried there.

New Temple was used for other administrative purposes, too. Upon occasion, the great seal of the realm was deposited there for safekeeping,[64] as were royal vestments[65] and valuables—e.g., a large book belonging to the queen[66]— and royal records and charters.[67] Even wine and herring belonging to the king and set aside for charitable or hospitable purposes were found there.[68] And, as will be indicated below, New Temple served both as a place where agreements of all sorts were made and as a place where copies of those agreements were filed.[69]

In view of all of these activities and services engaged in by the Templars, it is not surprising to find them the recipients of favors and gifts. The privileges granted them by kings and popes and the lands given them by kings and laymen have already been discussed. A few additional gifts from the crown can, however, be cited. For almost every year under Henry II, Richard I, and John, the Pipe Rolls authorize annual grants of alms to the Templars ranging from one-half mark to four marks — one or two marks being the rule.[70] Since these grants were authorized for approximately thirty of the counties of England and for such cities as London, Winchester, and Waltham, and since they were made with great consistency, though the sums tend to be smaller under John than under Henry II and Richard I, the total sum involved was considerable. To these gifts of alms are to be added under Henry III and Edward I frequent grants, usually of fifty marks, made to the Master in England rather than to individual houses.[71] Especially under Henry III, annual gifts of wine and venison are repeatedly made to the Templars. These grants, which actually started under Henry II and John,[72] include one, two, or three casks *(dolia)* of wine[73] and five to ten deer from the royal forests[74] and are usually made to the Master and Brothers of the Temple at the time of their annual chapter meeting. Sometimes, however, the grants are made to a particular preceptor[75] and for some other reason.[76] In addition, the Templars are repeatedly authorized to use two to seven oaks per year from the king's forests for construction and repair of mills, windmills, and the like.[77] Individual and non-periodic grants were also made — e.g., the grant of a silver chalice worth five marks for use in religious services,[78] the grant of vestments for the same purpose,[79] the grant of fish for stocking a pool,[80] the grant of one hundred silver marks for an undisclosed purpose,[81] and the payment for construction of a chapel at New Temple.[82] Without doubt extensive grants, apart from land, were also made by persons other than the kings; but surviving forces do not provide much specific evidence on this point.

Economic Activities

The economic activities of the Templars were varied and far-reaching, extending as they did to agriculture, trade and commerce, and financial transactions. Other religious orders and many lay groups were involved in these activities, too. Some religious groups, for example, engaged in agriculture to a greater degree; and some lay groups, in trade and commerce; but few groups, lay or clerical, were involved actively in all three fields simultaneously, and none of them (except possibly the rising Italian bankers) were as deeply involved in financial transactions as the Templars.

Unfortunately, there is no way of determining the total income of the Templars from their economic activities at any one time or in any one area. Their land, churches, and mills listed in the Inquest of 1185 provided an annual income of £857. Not surprisingly, Lincolnshire and Yorkshire, where most of the Templar holdings were located, provided the largest part (£81 and £47 respectively) of the total. But the total figure given in the Inquest omits demesne holdings, which probably were equal to those rented out, as well as services and payments in kind, which were numerous. Furthermore, the Inquest itself did not include all the Templar lands, nor even all the counties in which they had property.[83] The most comprehensive survey that is available is the one made by royal officials in 1308 at the time of the arrest of the Templars and the seizure of their goods. But this survey, too, is incomplete. It purports to give the income received by the king from the Templar properties — lands, mills, and churches — in his keeping. However, the value of crops and animals, the revenue from trade and commerce, the profit from financial transactions, and the income from perquisites of court are not included. Adding up the figures from the reports of the sheriffs and keepers, as given by Perkins,[84] one gets a total income of £4,351 — a considerable sum for the period even though much of the Templar wealth is not included in it. Again, Yorkshire and Lincolnshire, reporting £1,130 and £934 respectively, provided nearly half the total. Oxfordshire, Leicestershire, Warwickshire, Essex, and Gloucestershire follow in that order, with amounts ranging from £268 to £216. Below them, between £167 and £116 are the counties of Hereford, Hertford, Cambridge, Shropshire and Stafford (jointly), and Somerset and Dorset (jointly). The remaining counties varied from the £72 of Sussex to the £2 of Cornwall.

Agriculture

The earliest and most extensive of the economic activities of the Templars was agriculture. Such information as we have on the subject, which is surprisingly little, is gained from legal documents, such as the Inquest, corrody agreements, and miscellaneous references in the public records and in narrative sources. The division of lands and methods of production, as is to be expected, were based primarily on the manorial system and the modifications in it which the Templars retained when control fell to them. This meant, on the one hand, that land was divided into arable, pasture, garden, and waste; and on the other, that it was utilized largely on the basis of the two- or three-field system.[85] That strip farming was widely used, and that at the same time some degree of consolidation was going on, is suggested by the rental units of land varying in size from an acre or two at rates ranging from several pence to several shillings, depending upon the quality of the soil — as is revealed in the Inquest — and by the large units of one hundred or more acres repeatedly referred to in the Hospitaller's Report of 1338. Especially noteworthy were the vast areas of pasture, much of it former waste land, especially in Lincolnshire and Yorkshire, which the Templars reclaimed.

The exact role played by the Templars in agricultural production and management is open to question. The preceptors no doubt exercised a general supervision over agriculture as well as over other matters in their preceptories. The small houses and farms *(casaux),* which the Templars themselves occupied, were managed by the *frères casaliers,*[86] whom we might in some respects compare with the lay brothers of other orders.[87] Perhaps more often than not, the *frères casaliers* personally worked the land along with a few peasants. The larger estates, under the responsibility of the preceptor or certain *frères sergens* designated by him, were usually rented out to lay lords who left the actual work to the usual manorial officials, specialists, and peasants.[88]

Since some consideration was given to specific Templar holdings, rents, and commutation of feudal fees and services into monetary payments in the preceding chapter, the major concern here will be with the crops and livestock raised on the Templar estates. Since the Templars tended to maintain the specialty of the region in which they acquired land, certain areas were devoted to the growing of grains; others, to the pasturage of livestock; and still others, to the utilization of water and water rights.

Grain — wheat, oats, rye, and barley — was raised throughout the areas held by the Templars, but especially in the Midlands and Essex.[89] In only a few instances, in the inventories of Templar movables made by the royal keepers,[90] is a specific indication of the grain raised found. At Hanningfield (Essex), 31 acres were planted to wheat; 7, to rye; and 52, to oats. At Rothley (Leicestershire), the granaries contained 166 quarters of grain; at Copmanthorp, Temple Newsam, and Temple Hirst (Yorkshire), the amounts were 180, 712, and 274 quarters respectively. The question arises of whether or not the Templars produced grain for sale. Rogers, writing in general terms, says that because the market value of grain tended to be low in the Middle Ages, landlords were better off to use their surplus production for fattening livestock than for sale.[91] But Gras, whose work supersedes Rogers' on this subject, disagrees saying that English landlords sold grain on the local market from the twelfth century onward and on the foreign market after the middle of the thirteenth century[92] and specifically shows that the sale of their surplus was encouraged by the fact that the price of wheat rose from 4½ d. to 22½ d. per bushel between 1150 and 1350, a five-fold increase.[93] Furthermore, in the south and east of England surplus grain —

not only wheat but oats and barley as well — was sold as early as the first decade of the thirteenth century as the well-known Pipe Rolls of the See of Winchester for the years 1208 and 1209 clearly show;[94] and by the end of the thirteenth century, both the total amount of grain raised and the percentage of the total production sold had increased.[95] This information, plus the one specific reference to their sale of grain,[96] makes it certain that the Templars, who specialized in the growing of grain and who were constantly in need of cash, did produce grain for sale. The same regions that raised grain seem also to have raised legumes — peas and beans being the only ones listed in the sources — as repeated references to "messuagium cum gardino" or "manerium cum gardino" suggest.[97] And certain areas, especially the county of Kent,[98] where small garden plots were very numerous, seem to have specialized in the raising of fruit as well as legumes.

The grazing of livestock — cattle, sheep, and swine — on their meadows, pastures, and forest lands constituted a major part of the Templars' agricultural program. All of these animals were valuable for their meat, hides, and manure; but cattle were most valuable for dairy products and sheep for wool. Wherever the Templars had reasonable amounts of land they kept their own flocks though certain counties, such as Yorkshire, Lincolnshire, Essex, and Wiltshire which had already become especially famous for grazing, had far more than others. The following list, based on the very small portion of the inventories made at the time of the arrest of the Templars which have been published[99] and upon the Report of the Hospitallers[100] after they had gained control of most of the Templar estates, gives some indication of the numbers of cattle and sheep on Templar lands: Ribston, Copmanthorp, Temple Hirst, and Temple Newsam (Yorkshire), 20, 22, 90, and 97 cattle respectively; Eagle (Lincolnshire), 20; Cressing and Witham (Essex), 32; Lockridge and Rockley (Wiltshire), 16 and 17 respectively; Swanton (Bedfordshire), 35; Feckenham (Worcestershire), 10; and Rothley (Leicestershire), 15. Rockley, Lockridge, and Chiryton (Wiltshire), 900, 300, and 260 sheep respectively; Cressing and Witham (Essex), 600; Eagle (Lincolnshire), 400; Temple Combe and Lopene (Somerset), 200 and 100 respectively; Temple Newsam and Temple Hirst (Yorkshire, 1,036 and 644 respectively; Feckenham (Worcestershire), 60; and Rothley (Leicestershire), 525. The approximate number of sheep at a given Templar preceptory, or in a given county, can be theoretically estimated on the basis of the number of sacks of wool sold at any given time — assuming that it took about two hundred fleeces to make one sack.[101] In 1298, the Master of the Templars complained to the king that his officials had taken forty-nine sacks in Yorkshire without payment or provision for payment.[102]

and in 1308, the king's officials seized thirty-eight sacks in Lincoln-shire.[103] On the basis of this data, wholly inadequate as it is, it can be estimated that the Templars had at least 9,800 sheep in Yorkshire and 7,600 sheep in Lincolnshire. Without doubt these figures are decidedly low. If more information were available, it might also be possible to find out whether or not the Templars, like so many owners of great estates, pastured the flocks of strangers in return for a share of the animals or a payment in money.

For swine, horses, and oxen, which the Templars must have had in considerable numbers, practically no information is available. The Inquest occasionally refers to *pannagium* (the privilege of feeding pigs);[104] and the Templars, like many others, held forest lands. In the reports of the keepers of Templar lands, some mention of swine is made — e.g., there were 30 at Temple Newsam, 22 at Temple Hirst, 40 at Swanton, and 45 at Rothley.[105] Of horses, there is even less mention although obviously the Templars needed many, especially for military and training purposes. In one reference, it is stated that 30 palfreys and 3 sumpter horses, valued at £ 78, were taken into the king's hands by the royal keepers.[106]

Associated with agriculture were the Templar mills which proved highly profitable. Exactly how many there were cannot be determined though the Inquest of 1185 lists eighty-one. Most of these were grain mills to which the Templar tenants, and many others in the area, brought their crops to be ground. The Templars themselves seem to have run many of them; and the others were rented out at annual rates usually ranging from five shillings to five marks,[107] depending upon the size and value of the mill. The Castle Mills at York, however, were especially valuable and were rented at fifteen and one-half marks annually.[108] Some of the mills, one at Barton in Gloucestershire and one at Temple Newsam in Yorkshire, appear to have been used for fulling purposes[109]— the earliest such known in English history.[110] Whether or not the Templars and their tenants participated directly in the production of cloth is uncertain, but it seems likely that they did — at least the probability is sufficient to warrant further investigation.[111]

The millponds and the rivers on which Templar mills were located also provided fish, as did the bays along the coast and the sea. Probably fishponds of one sort or another existed on all the larger Templar estates.

In general, it can be said that the Templars were orthodox and efficient in the production of agricultural goods and in the management of their properties. Perhaps earlier and to a greater extent than other lords, they sought to convert their agricultural produce and their income from rents into cash;[112] but just how successful they were in this and exactly how much money they obtained cannot be determined.

Trade and Commerce

Wool, wine, dairy products, grain, fish, hides, salt, timber, and metals were among the standard items of medieval trade. In varying degrees, all the great English estates of the twelfth and thirteenth centuries produced for purposes of sale and exchange as well as consumption.[113] The old generalization that medieval economy, including that of the religious orders, was in essence self-sufficient is now universally recognized as a gross oversimplification. The Templar estates certainly were not self-sufficient; not only basic commodities such as wine, fish, and timber, but also luxury items such as fine cloth, special horses, leather, and metal ware were needed. For the Templars, as for most others, most of these goods were to be obtained through exchange and purchase at local or regional markets and fairs or by trade with foreign merchants. In payment for these goods, the Templars could offer wool, grain, and cash to the foreign merchants, and grain, fish, and livestock to the local merchants.

Wool, the chief commodity the Templars could offer for sale and exchange, was sold by grade—good, medium, and lock—either to agents of the king or to foreign merchants, Flemish or Italian. In 1298, royal agents of the king contracted to buy 16 sacks, 27½ stone of wool from the Templars in Lincolnshire for £134 15s. 7½d.; 6 sacks, 18½ stone of good wool and 3 sacks, 22 stone of medium wool at Temple Bruer; 2 sacks, 25 stone of good wool and 1 sack, 12½ stone of medium at Willoughton; and 1 sack, 16½ stone of good wool and 17 stone of medium at Eagle.[114] At the same time, they purchased 3½ sacks of wool for 22 marks 10 shillings from the Templars at Wilberham in Cambridgeshire and 5½ sacks for 44 marks from the Templars at Temple Guiting in Gloucestershire.[115] In addition, the royal agents took without payment or provision for payment 49 sacks of wool in Yorkshire and 24½ sacks in Lincolnshire.[116] The price the crown promised to pay for the wool purchased in Lincolnshire and Cambridgeshire was £10 per sack for good wool and six marks (£4) for medium wool.[117] These prices compare favorably with those the Cistercians were receiving at the same time and would appear to be in line with the standard rate paid for English wool in the late thirteenth century.[118] No specific prices were quoted for inferior (lock) wool, probably because the variation in quality was so great.

Foreign merchants also purchased Templar wool, probably at such major fairs as the one at Boston.[119] As royal licenses indicate, the Templars were active in shipping their wool abroad, especially to Flanders, through the ports of Boston and Southhampton, usually free of customs duties,[120] and without limitation except in time of war between England and Flanders.[121] The value of this exemption is immediately apparent when one remembers the export duties put on wool by Edward I — 7s. 6d. per sack in 1275, 5 marks in 1294, and 3 marks in 1297.[122] Unfortunately no figures are given on the amount of wool shipped abroad, and no contracts survive to indicate the terms of sale. It would be interesting to know whether or not the Templars, like the Cistercians and some other religious groups, found it necessary, in their need for cash, to commit their clips to foreign merchants for years in advance.

The finest wool in England was produced in such areas as Lincolnshire, Shropshire, and Herefordshire; high quality wool was raised in much of Yorkshire, the Lindesey region of Lincolnshire, and the Cotswold Hills of Gloucestershire; and the Midlands tended to provide medium grade wool. In each of these areas, but especially in the undeveloped northern counties, the Templars held sizable lands; and in all of them except Shropshire, they pastured large flocks of sheep and maintained major preceptories. However, the Cistercians certainly, and perhaps the Premonstratensians and the Gilbertines as well, were more famous and important in this respect than the Templars.[123]

Wine was the second major item in the foreign trade of the Templars, an import as wool had been an export. So far as can be determined, the exchange was to a large degree limited to the Templar houses in Poitou and Gascony.[124] The ships which plied the seas between the English ports of Dover, Portsmouth, and Boston and the Angevin ports of La Rochelle and Bordeaux were often owned by the Templars[125] — one of them, fittingly was named "La Templère."[126] In general, provided their ships and cargoes did not fall into the hands of the king's enemies,[127] did not carry goods belonging to other persons,[128] and did not go to other than English ports,[129] the Templars were granted freedom from customs duties both for exports and imports.[130] On one occasion, in 1242, when he found the Templars violating these terms by taking other persons' wines to places other than England, Henry III temporarily cancelled the Templars' commercial exemptions.[131] It might be added, too, that John and Henry III, and perhaps some of the other monarchs as well, found it convenient to purchase wine for the royal household from that imported by the English Templars.[132]

In addition to wine, the Templars were permitted to import and export free of tolls and customs other goods *("alias res et merchandisas")*.[133] What these goods were, is at no time specified. Perhaps they included grain, fish, and dairy products; and possibly, in view of the Templars' many commercial associations, such things as spices, silk cloth, and armor.

Two Templars, by name Roger and Thomas, were employed at different times by Henry III in his naval service as officials entrusted with the regulation of commerce both of seaports and on the high seas. In this capacity, probably more administrative than commercial they aided the bailiffs of the port cities in the inspection of vessels and cargoes and even stopped ships and seized goods at sea.[134] They also were commissioned to procure win for the king.[135] And for a time, Thomas was put in charge of one of the king's larger ships sailing between England and southern France on royal business.[136]

Markets and fairs were a regular medium for the exchange of goods in the Middle Ages and were a convenient source of profit to the owner. It is not surprising, therefore, to find that the Templars obtained from the kings, who claimed exclusive jurisdiction over the issuance of such franchises, the grant of markets and fairs on certain of their properties.[137] The first such grant to the Templars, made by Stephen, was a weekly market (on Sunday, later changed to Tuesday) at Witham (Essex). This was followed by John's grant in 1199 of a weekly market (on Wednesday) at Baldock (Hertfordshire) and an annual fair of four days — later changed to three (September 20-23) at the same place. It was Henry III, however, who made the largest number of such grants to the Templars. He authorized them to establish a weekly market (on Wednesday) at Newburgh (Yorkshire), and both weekly markets (usually on Sunday) and annual fairs, usually of three day's duration, at Wetherby (Yorkshire, July 24-26), Walnesford (Essex, August 28-30), Balsall (Warwickshire, April 22-24 and September 20-22), and Kirkeby (Lincolnshire, July 24-26). Some years after his original grant, Henry III cancelled the market and fair at Walnesford but substituted a weekly market (on Thursday) and an annual fair (June 23-25) at Werriby, in the same county, instead. Edward I also made several grants of markets and fairs and subsequently changed one of them. He granted a weekly market (on Monday) and an annual fair at Rothley (Leicestershire, June 10-12) and at Southcave (Yorkshire, June 2-5) and then substituted a weekly market (on Wednesday) and an annual fair (June 10-12) at Gaddesby (Leicestershire) for the one at Rothley. Under Edward I, also, a weekly market (on Thursday) and an annual fair (July 24-26) at Bruer (Lincolnshire), originally granted by Henry III but hitherto not made use of, was authorized. Though the profit from these markets and fairs is unknown and though none of them were among the most celebrated and wealthy ones, they must, nonetheless, have proved both profitable and convenient to the Templars.

Financial Activities

When we think of English finances in the late Middle Ages, the Templars, the Italians, and the Jews come quickly to mind. The Jews were active both before and after the Templars, but they seem to have been little more than pawnbrokers and money-lenders of limited means; and the Italian merchants and bankers did not become important until the late thirteenth century, especially as they took over the collection of papal revenues and as they enlarged their own resources. But during most of the twelfth and thirteenth centuries in England, neither the Italians nor the Jews could be ranked in financial power or influence with the Templars.

In a period of rapid economic development, it was the Templars, with their center at New Temple, London, to whom the Angevin kings, papal legates, great and small lay and ecclesiastical lords, merchants, and others in England turned for guidance and aid. There were several reasons for this: the traditional sanctity of centers of religion and the strength of their buildings, the confidence and security associated with the Templars as outstanding men of religion and arms, the abundance of their riches, the international scale of their operations, the conveniences and permanence of their houses, and the independence of the order from most lay and ecclesiastical authorities. To kings and feudal lords who were almost constantly on the move and who had few, if any, persons to whom they could turn for financial aid or places where they could safely store their wealth, the use of the Templars and their facilities must have seemed the answer to their problems.

The financial activities[138] of the Templars were numerous and varied, simple and complex, successful and unsuccessful. Knowledge of them, despite the general absence of their account books and of other pertinent data and the need to rely upon brief and often incomplete entries in the public records and upon occasional references in the chronicles, is sufficient to present a general picture showing that the Templars engaged in the exchange of money, the acceptance of valuables and cash for deposit and disbursement, the lending of money, the international transfer and transportation of funds, the issuance and use of credit instruments, and the trusteeship of future interests. From these many activities, it is apparent that in an age before the appearance of banks proper the Templars engaged in most of the activities normally associated with banking. And, in addition, they served as financial officials of the kings and fiscal agents of the popes.

Evidence for the exchange of money by the Templars is indirect. References are made to the import and export of specie; to the receipt and disbursement of money in terms of English pounds and of pounds

Tournois; and to dealings with French, Flemish, and Italian merchants. Obviously these transactions could only have been performed by the exchange and evaluation of money, both domestic and foreign.

The deposit and disbursement of cash and valuables made New Temple both a treasury and a bank. Hundreds of entries in the public records dating from the last years of Henry II to the early years of Edward II, but mostly from the reign of Henry III, indicate the large scale of these operations. However, since these references are in a large part incidental and unsystematic, there is no necessary relationship between what was paid in and what was paid out; and, though funds may have been deposited for a certain purpose, they were not always so used. Consequently, the true scope and method of these transactions cannot be determined.

The term treasury *(thesaurium)* was often used in the Middle Ages to mean a storehouse where valuables of various kinds were placed for safekeeping.[139] New Temple served as a treasury in this sense for the kings, for members of the royal family, and for important men in the realm. Except for one reference to John depositing the royal jewels in New Temple (1204-1205),[140] all the surviving data pertaining to the royal family date from the reign of Henry III. In 1232, Henry placed royal jewels worth three thousand marks (£ 2,000) there for safekeeping.[141] Some of them were withdrawn in 1242.[142] Later (1254), the remaining jewels were ordered transferred to the queen at Portsmouth[143] and were finally (1261) sent to Queen Margaret of France who, after taking careful inventory, had them deposited temporarily with the Templars at Paris.[144] In 1264, however, the royal jewels were returned to London for safekeeping at New Temple.[145] The treasure of Hubert de Burgh, former justiciar, and his wife, Margaret, was stored at New Temple.[146] Chests of valuables belonging to Simon the Norman (1242),[147] for a time keeper of the royal seal, to an unnamed merchant of Ghent (1259),[148] and to the Bishop of Rochester (1278)[149] were also kept there. The above examples are known either because they involved the crown or because something out of the ordinary occurred. There must have been many other instances of which no record has survived.

Taxes, both royal and papal, after being collected and stored locally, were frequently transported in strong carts under guard to New Temple for deposit and safekeeping.[150] So, for example, tenths,[151] fifteenths,[152] twentieths,[153] thirtieths,[154] fortieths,[155] carrucage,[156] the tallage of the Jews[157] and of cities such as London and Lincoln,[158] subsidies for the Holy Land,[159] issues of eyre,[160] revenue from Ireland,[161] and clerical contributions to the crown[162] — as well as income derived by the king from ecclesiastical benefices[163] — were deposited or ordered to be deposited there by John, Henry III, and Edward I. Sometimes, however, the treasury at Westminster or in the Tower of London was cited as an alternate place of deposit.[164] Papal procurations,[165] subsidies for the Holy Land,[166] and Peter's pence[167] were frequently stored at New Temple though they were sometimes entrusted to the Hospitallers, Cistercians, and Italian merchants as well.[168] There is no way of knowing just how much money might have been on deposit at any one time; but the fact that taxes (e.g., £2,900 and £1,388, the thirtieth of only the two centers of Nottingham and Bristol[169] in 1238) and the extensive deposit of funds by many persons were entrusted to the Templars make it obvious that very large sums of money were involved. Indeed, in 1307 just before their downfall, the amount of money in New Temple was so large that Edward II was able to seize the enormous sum of £50,000 at one time.[170]

The question of the safety of the deposits at New Temple inevitably arises. Though the money and other valuables were normally secure, a number of exceptions can be cited. After the fall from power of Hubert de Burgh, Henry III, having learned of his former justiciar's great wealth in the custody of the Templars, and being in need of money as usual, summoned the Master of the Temple and demanded that Hubert's treasure be handed over (1232). This the Master said he could not do without the permission of the depositor. Though Henry seems to have been ready to use torture to get Hubert's approval and to use force to get the treasure from the Temple, neither was necessary as the prisoner consented to the king's demand.[171] Ten years later (1242), the treasure of Simon the Norman, recently dismissed as keeper of the royal seal, was ordered removed from New Temple.[172] This seizure appears to have been made over the strong protest of the Templars as Henry's guarantee that they should not be questioned about the matters suggests. In 1254, Richard of Cornwall, then serving as regent for his brother, King Henry, who was in Gascony and in immediate need of money, invaded the treasuries both at New Temple and at Westminster and may have carried off certain valuables.[173] The Poitevins, forced to withdraw from England because of their unpopularity (1258), left behind at New Temple a large sum of money which was confiscated and expended "at the option of the king and barons for the benefit of the kingdom."[174] About the same time, the fortune of William de Valence, which Paris says was of "astonishing magnitude," was seized by King Henry, William's half-brother.[176] In 1263, when his misrule had caused the barons led by Simon de Montfort, Earl of Leicester, to seize control of the government and when Henry and the queen had taken refuge in the Tower of London, the young Prince Edward and Robert

Walerand, the king's seneschal, went to New Temple to obtain badly needed funds. Demanding to see the queen's jewels, Edward and Walerand were admitted to the Temple treasury where they broke open a number of chests and carried off a large sum of money belonging to others — variously reported as £1,000 or £10,000.[176] Some years later, in 1277, after a band of robbers had broken into the Templar treasury,[177] and at a time when many of the barons and knights of the realm were departing for the campaign in Wales, it was suggested by a group of prelates meeting at New Temple and by the king that the papal tenth then being collected should be entrusted to Italian firms like the Ricciardi, instead of being deposited at New Temple.[178] At one point (1295), Edward I temporarily appropriated funds the Templars were about to send to Cyprus but, on the earnest demand of the pope, restored them.[179] And finally, in 1307, Edward II had £50,000 in silver, plus gold and jewels, which had been deposited in their treasury by Bishop Langton, his father's treasurer, seized and handed over to his favorite, Piers Gaveston.[180]

These examples certainly prove that the Temple and its treasure were neither inviolable nor impregnable. Yet most of the cases of violation involved the king, against whom the Templars dared not take too positive a stand lest they be deprived of valuable privileges and immunities or be restricted in their possessions and activities. What happened to the Templars could and did happen to others. For example, the goods of the Jews were repeatedly seized, and the loans of Italian bankers were sometimes repudiated. Yet, the Templars' record of one hundred and twenty years of active financial operations was one in which losses and confiscations were rare and security the rule. It is doubtful if depositors could have found more trustworthy persons or a safer place for their wealth.

Money was regularly, and on a large scale, deposited at New Temple, sometimes for safekeeping, but more often for use. If for safekeeping only, it was usually stored in strong boxes under double lock and key (with one key for the depositer and another for the Treasurer of the Temple) or the instructions for deposit directed that the money "be kept under seal,"[181] or some such phrase. Normally this sort of deposit was held until the depositor showed up in person to reclaim possession. The principle and practice here is identical with the storage of valuables, such as jewels, mentioned above. On the whole, most deposits would either be (1) general — in which case the funds were disposed of according to specific directions of the depositors as they were received — or (2) conditional — in which case the disposition was indicated at the time of deposit and the funds were not to be used for any other purpose.[182] The Templars were careful in the handling of these general accounts and normally released funds only upon written instructions bearing the signature or seal of the depositor as well as the date, the name of the payee, and the sum involved.[183] This authorization fulfilled the chief function of our check and has been referred to as a primitive form of check though there was no transfer or endorsement possible.[184] That the Templars insisted upon this procedure is well illustrated when King Henry III was informed that Hubert de Burgh's money could not be handed over to him without the depositor's authorization.[185] As a further safeguard, the Templars often demanded that the person obtaining the money sign a statement of receipt.[186] In the case of the conditional accounts, care was taken to see that the terms were fully met, or if a change of terms was to be made, that the change was agreed upon by all parties concerned.[187]

Deposits might also be classified as regular or irregular. If the former, the money was not to be touched except by order of the depositor; if the latter (e.g., the open account of the King of France and possibly of the King of England), the management of the funds seems to have been left to the discretion of the Templars with the possible consequence that a sum of money supposedly deposited for a given purpose (e.g., a special levy for a proposed crusade) might actually be used for some other purpose (e.g., payment of a royal debt to Italian merchant-bankers.)[188]

Under certain conditions, it would seem that funds could be transferred without the actual movement of specie from one account to another — not only between accounts of a given house but also between accounts of different Templar houses. This seems clearly to have been the case in many of the transactions of the London and Paris Temples which will be discussed below. The details of the procedure are lacking; but from what is known of the Templars and of other financial groups in this period, or a little later, the transfer may well have been effected either on the basis of written statements or on the basis of oral agreements made by the parties concerned in the presence of the appropriate Templar official.[189]

To the question of whether or not the Templars paid interest on money deposited with them, no positive answer can be given. There seems to be no evidence that they did although it was not unusual for bankers to do so under the form of a gift or bonus.[190]

The kings, royal officials, members of the royal family, lay and ecclesiastical lords, religious organizations or units, merchants, widows, and the like — practically all classes of persons and corporations — had accounts with the Templars at one time or another. Public authorities carried the largest and most active accounts and, at least upon occasion, even overdrew their balances in their general or current accounts. When this happened, the Templar treasurer might permit the overdraft in view of funds in the client's conditional accounts or might make short-term loans available to cover the shortage.[191]

Henry II in 1182 and again in 1188 deposited money with the Templars for use on his projected crusade to the Holy Land.[192] John entrusted 20,000 marks[193] on one occasion, 10,000 marks on another, 7,000 marks on still another, and other sums totalling at least £5,000 to the Templars.[194] From time to time he ordered the Templars to pay out certain sums — e.g., 1,000 marks to Emperor Otto IV, his nephew (1212); 8,500 marks again to Otto (1213); 9,000 marks to the Earl of Salisbury and Falkes de Breauté a Norman adventurer in the king's service, for official purposes; 6,000 marks to Pandulph, the papal legate; and 3,000 marks to be sent to the Bishop of Rochester.[195] For Edward I and Edward II, there are very few references — probably because they turned increasingly to the Italian bankers in financial matters, especially for loans. Yet, the Templars still appear as custodians of royal revenue and as bankers to the crown. So, for example, Edward I used £2,000 from the tallage of the Jews on deposit at New Temple to cover expenses for his visit to Paris (1274) on his way home from the Holy Land. On two different occasions (1276) he withdrew 1,000 marks each; and he repeatedly ordered the Treasurer of New Temple to pay out various sums from tenths and the like entrusted to the Templars for expenses of the royal household, for repair and construction work at the Tower of London, and so forth.[196]

The numerous and sizable deposits and disbursements of Henry III suggest the close relationship which existed between him and the Templars. Indeed, as will be indicated below, Henry came to use New Temple as a royal treasury and the treasurers of New Temple as royal treasurers. Since a complete listing of Henry's financial dealings with the Templars would take many pages, only representative examples will be cited here. Sometimes individual sums, apart from the revenue from the tax levies referred to above, were deposited without indicating their purpose — so for example, £1,000 in 1225, 1226, and 1246;[197] £700 in 1224;[198] £510 in 1221;[199] £200 in 1223;[200] 5,000 marks in 1247;[201] 2,000 marks in 1224 and 1247;[202] 1,400 marks in 1224;[203] and 1,000 marks in 1226 and 1240.[204] Sometimes funds were deposited for a definite purpose — so, for example, 10,000 marks in 1237 for payment of the remainder of the dowry of his sister, Isabella, wife of Emperor Frederick II;[205] 1,000 marks for papal tribute in 1222, 1239, 1246, 1247 and 1250;[206] 3,300 marks for expediting the king's business at the Roman Curia in

1225;[207] 300 marks, £1,000 and £200 for Simon de Montfort in 1245, 1250, and 1251;[208] 1,500 marks for the Count of La Marche in 1224;[209] 2,000 marks for the Holy Roman Emperor in 1235;[210] the same amount for his mother-in-law, the Countess of Provence, in 1224;[211] £1,000, 10,000 marks, 6,000 marks and 2,000 marks for Richard, Earl of Cornwall, in 1225, 1237, 1238, and 1245;[212] 500 marks for Ferrand, Count of Flanders, in 1229-30;[213] the same amount for the king's affairs in Gascony in 1221, 1222, and 1224;[214] and 400 marks for use in Wales in 1231.[215] These sums were to be held until proper certification by the king or his officials directed their release.

As the following examples attest, other persons had sizable accounts at New Temple, too. At the time the barons forced him to leave England (1258), William de Valence, the king's half-brother, had a large but unstipulated sum subsequently increased by deposit there during his absence of the revenues from his estates.[216] The Earl of Pembroke had on deposit an undisclosed sum for the use of Simon de Montfort (1245).[217] Hubert de Burgh, a powerful noble and former high official of the realm, had £150 in cash in the Templar treasury in 1232.[218] Falkes de Breauté on one occasion (1226) deposited 40,000 marks there — most of it apparently belonging to the king.[219] Various Poitevins in their hasty flight from the country left behind their deposits in New Temple (1258).[220] That merchants and magnates of the realm had funds there is proved by the fact that some of the money seized by Prince Edward in 1263 belonged to them.[221] Also, on the basis of royal Scottish records from Edinburgh (1282), certain English magnates had deposited money at New Temple apparently to be used to win the support of the Scottish king in their contest with Henry III.[222] Moreover prominent clerics like Walter de Merton and John Bradfield, Bishops of Rochester (prior to 1278), and Walter Langton, Bishop of Lichfield and Coventry (1307), had funds there.[223] So did the Bishop of Exeter who in 1227 collected the 4,000 marks which W. Bruer, his uncle, had bequeathed to him and had deposited in New Temple.[224] This is obviously an incomplete list as it is composed only of those persons whose funds were recorded in the rolls because they came into the hands of the king.

Associated with the deposit and disbursement of funds was the use of New Temple as a place for the payment of debts of all kinds. Sometimes, the money involved seems to have been paid through the Templar bank; but at other times, the Temple seems to have been used merely because of its convenient location. To determine which category any particular case falls within is frequently impossible. Kings and prominent persons paid debts at New Temple. For example, Henry III promised to pay Prince Louis of France 6,000 marks there for his withdrawal from England (1218);[225] Peter, Duke of Brittany, 6,572 marks (1234);[226] Richard of Cornwall, King of Germany, 250 marks (1226);[227] his uncle, Thomas of Savoy, 500 marks (1253);[228] and his wine merchant, £500 (1270).[229] Prince Edward was to pay £200 to an unknown creditor there for two years (1256-57);[230] another £200 annually for five years to his uncle, Archbishop Boniface (1256-62);[231] a total of £1,000 owed to his mother over a period of years starting in 1269;[232] and £10,000 Tournois, starting the same year, to King Louis IX of France for funds lent to him for his crusade.[233] Other payments made at New Temple included those of the Count of Salisbury, who paid money owed to the city of Bordeaux (1226);[234] the Count of Warren, who had agreed to pay an undesignated creditor £20 annually for an unstated period (1227);[235] Richard de Clare, Earl of Gloucester, who paid 1,000 marks as surety for Prince Edward (1253);[236] a certain John of Balun, who paid 140 marks to Guy de Lusignan, Henry III's half-brother (1257);[237] Henry, the nephew of King Henry, who repaid a loan of 200 marks (1259);[238] various persons who paid sums of varying amounts owed to William de Valence, another of Henry III's half-brothers (1259-70);[239] William de Valence himself, who paid 3,500 marks to Richard de Clare in three installments for custody of certain lands and tenements (1270);[240] and John and Hugh le Despenser, prominent lay lords, who paid Eleanor, consort of Prince Edward, £220 in 1271 and William of Camp Bello 1,600 marks in 1282.[241]

Clerics also found New Temple a convenient place for the payment of debts. A certain Arnold de Bosco paid the Bishop of Norwich £120 there in 1259;[242] the Abbot of St. Albans paid a debt of 115 marks there (1252);[243] and Hugh of Gloucester paid the Abbot of La Couture ten marks per year there, starting in 1206.[244] The Prior of the Cluniacs at Bermondesey owed Adam of Stretton 700 marks to be paid off at New Temple in seven annual installments, starting in 1271;[245] and Ralph of Grendon owed the Bishop of Bath and Wells £200 to be paid there (1290).[246] Additional cases involving clerics could be cited.[247]

Merchants frequently used New Temple as a convenient place for the payment of debts owed to them and often specifically designated New Temple in their contracts as the place of payment.[248] Henry III repaid loans to Florentine and Sienese merchants there[249] — as did such members of the royal family as Queen Eleanor and Prince Edward;[250] such clerics as Fulk, Archbishop of Dublin, the Abbot of St. Albans, and Anthony Bek, Bishop of Durham;[251] and numerous private citizens whose names are otherwise unknown.[252] This use of New Temple — and the chief fairs of England, which were also so used — as a place for the repayment of debts owed to foreign merchants must have served as a precedent for the Statutes of Acton Burnell (1283, 1285) by which Edward I and his council decreed that merchants could register their loans before the mayors of London, Bristol, and York and that official action would be taken to promote repayment at the agreed upon time and place.

Because of its convenient location, ordinary debts between private citizens were often paid at New Temple. Numerous examples of this could be cited;[253] but for the purpose of illustration, it is only necessary to indicate that the men and sums involved ranged from the £900 which Simon of Pateshull, a financial official of the king, owed to John Gifford (1268)[254] to the twelve and one-half marks which John, son of Alan, paid to Thomas of Aldeham (1267).[255]

Some of these debts were repaid in a single payment; and some, on an installment basis. Information is available on this payment of private debts at New Temple because both debtors and creditors found it to their mutual advantage to appear before the officials of the Chancery to have their oral agreements recorded.[256] Consequently, the contracts became a part of the public records, with copies frequently being made and sent to New Temple.[257] Then, when the debt was paid, a new entry was inserted by the clerks of the Chancery to that effect or the words "Cancelled because the debt was paid" were inscribed after the original entry.[258]

Lending money was another of the financial activities of the Templars. The loans, probably made out of funds deposited with them[259] as well as out of their own revenues, seem to have been granted usually in rather small sums and for short terms, often ranging from one month to one year. The loan was often granted on the basis of a promise to pay on a given date although collateral or guarantees of a stronger sort — for example, jewels or control of revenue from certain properties — were sometimes demanded. Though complete details of the contracts entered into are lacking,[260] penalties, as will be seen, were exacted for failure to pay on the due date. On the basis of surviving records, the English kings are found to have been by far the chief and most frequent of the Templars' clients.

The earliest financial services the Templars rendered John involved more than a mere loan. On the king's instructions, they arranged for as well as paid the ransom of William Brewer (1204), Petrus de Arcanaca and Gaufridus de Moher (1205), and Gerard d'Athies (1206), subjects of John captured on the continent.[261] These services were followed by a loan of 1,500 marks in 1206 for repayment of a debt owed to Philip Augustus of France.[262] There is no indication of whether or not these loans were repaid. John again borrowed from the Templars — 1,100 marks from the English Templars[263] and 1,000 marks from the Templars of Poitou[264] in 1215 and another 1,000 marks from the Templars of Aquitaine[265] in 1216. These sums were used to bring troops from the continent to England and to pay them for their services in John's struggle with his barons.[266] Always direly in need of money and consequently without funds to repay, John proved a poor risk. Aymeric de St. Maur, then Master in England and one of John's advisers, apparently did not press very hard for repayment; but the Templars on the continent were more determined. Finally, in view of their persistent demands for repayment, John ordered a part of his revenue from his fiefs in Gascony handed over to the Master of the Temple at Poitiers;[267] and his revenues from the city of Bordeaux, to the Templars at Aquitaine.[268] At the time of his death, these loans still had not been completely repaid as is shown by the arrangements to continue payment made by William Marshall and Hubert de Burgh,[269] who were heading the government of England during the minority of John's son and heir, Henry III.

The chief royal client of the Templars was Henry III. In 1221, he borrowed the 500 marks needed for making peace with France, promising to repay at the rate of £120 per year out of the income from the royal manor of Godmanchester.[270] Three years later (1224), another 300 marks were borrowed; and this time, "full seisin" of the manor was assigned to the Templars until the total debt should be discharged.[271] In 1225, Henry is listed as owing the Templars 330 marks.[272] Whether this was a new loan or the loan of the preceding year with an increase in sum due to non-payment is unclear. In 1234, reference is made to two loans obtained from Robert de Sanford, then Master in England — the first, a royal order for repayment of an earlier loan of £200; and the second, a new loan of 300 marks to be repaid within the year.[273] The next year, what amounted to still another loan, this time totalling £1,000 — to be repaid out of income from royal lands at the rate of £200 per year for five years — was arranged for payment by the Templars of money Henry owed to Hugh de Lusignan, Count of La Marche.[274] Five years later, in 1239, in order to raise 1,000 marks for the use of Thomas, Count of Flanders, Henry again went to Robert de Sanford and borrowed the necessary amount.[275] In 1244, 500 marks were paid to Hugh of Stocton, Treasurer of New Temple, for a loan which the Templars of Paris had made the previous year to a certain Roger, Henry's representative abroad.[276] In 1247, the king, on behalf of Guy de Lusignan, obtained a loan from the Templars of Jerusalem in the amount of £1,000;[277] and in the same year, he requested the Templars at Paris to lend Gaucher de Chastilon £400 to be repaid at the rate of £100 per year.[278] The first payment seems to have been delayed, however, a year beyond its due date.[279] Then, not until 1260, over a decade later, is there specific evidence that Henry again borrowed from the Templars. At this time, he obtained £2,800 Tournois from the Templars at Paris to be repaid within the year.[280] This was soon followed (1262) by another loan, this time for £700, from the French Templars.[281] And in 1268, he paid the Templars of Paris 2,000 marks on a loan of £28,189 Tournois which his son, Edward, had obtained in the Holy Land and in France.[282] Though the loans indicated here may not have been the only ones he obtained from them, they are sufficiently large and numerous to show how often and how heavily Henry III relied upon the Templars for financial aid.

Edward I also borrowed on occasion from the Templars. In 1274, he paid the balance of the huge loan (£24,974 Tournois) he had received in the Holy Land; the next year, £200 or £300 Tournois for the sum borrowed from the Templars in Paris for the conduct of certain royal business in France; and four years later 3,355 marks for other money he had borrowed in the east.[283] In 1299, evidently pressed for cash by the Frescobaldi, merchants of Florence, he resorted to the device of transferring his debt of 2,000 marks to them to the Templars whom he promised to repay at an early date.[284] In general, however, Edward I, unlike his father, did not find it necessary to borrow repeatedly from the Templars — not because he did not need money, but more likely, because he preferred to do business with the Italian merchants who had become important as money lenders some time after the middle of the thirteenth century.[285] For Edward II, there is no evidence of loans obtained from the Templars.

Loans were also made to people other than kings though there is little surviving evidence of this. That Hubert de Burgh, at the time of his imprisonment (1233), was in debt to the Templars is known by the fact that King Henry permitted the Master of the Temple to speak to Hubert about the debt — no amount is indicated — but about nothing else.[286] On one occasion (1279), on orders of the king, the Templars lent the Bishop of Bath and Wells £69 17s. 7d. and £49 5s. 2½d. out of royal funds on deposit at New Temple.[287] In several instances, the Templars are shown as creditors of Italian banking houses. Thus, in 1304, merchants of the Mozzi company of Florence owed the English Templars 2,000 marks; and in 1305, merchants of the companies of the Galerani of Siena and the Frescobaldi of Florence owed them 879 marks, a sum which was paid shortly thereafter at New Temple.[288] Other cases involve only small loans: 30 marks owed them by John de Erde of Kent (1306);[289] £10 owed them by Bartholomew of Badlesmore (1306);[290] and 300 marks repaid them by Stephen de Burgherssh, a knight (1307).[291]

The question now arises of whether or not the Templars profited from their lending transactions. Since canon law and the prevailing Christian attitude were opposed to usury,[292] one might well conclude that the Templars certainly were not apt to have practiced openly what their religion forbade. Furthermore, inasmuch as surviving documents invariably provide for the repayment of the same sum as borrowed, one might also assume that loans were made without the expectation of profit. However, that the Templars should have foregone all remuneration is neither reasonable nor likely in view of what we know of commercial activity in the Middle Ages.

It might be truthfully argued that the Templars received good-will, gifts, privileges, and protection in return for their loans; but they received these things without lending money, too. However, the specific exemption from import and export duties on wine and wool and the grant of gifts in land and cash, both of which have been mentioned above, may have been a more direct reward. So, too, protection, especially by the crown, was very valuable as the following incident of 1304 suggests.[293] Certain merchants of the Mozzi company of Florence, in return for a loan of 1,300 marks from the English Templars, issued letters promising the sum would be paid by members of their society in Paris. Before the sum was paid, it was reported to the king that other merchants of the same company, still in London, who owed the Templars 700 marks for wool, seemed to be preparing to leave without paying. Thereupon Edward ordered his sheriffs to seize all members of the company in England and, after ascertaining by oath of other merchants what goods the Mozzi had in the area, to seize and hold these goods until further order. Though the outcome of the case is not known, the implication certainly is that the crown seriously intended to protect and aid the Templars.

A few explanatory remarks are necessary before responding to the specific question "Did the Templars exact usury?" The whole complicated issue of usury was evolutional in definition and interpretation and becomes rather technical, involving considerations of both act and intent.[294] Gathering together statements from the early Latin Church Fathers and from such early councils as that of Nicaea, and supporting prohibitions of Charlemagne found in his Capitularies, Gratian[295] treated the issue briefly, directing attention initially to a prohibition of usury to all clerics, but later applying the prohibition to laymen as well. For Gratian and most canonists of the late Middle Ages, usury consisted primarily of demanding back more than was given — i.e., receiving something in excess of the principal, whether open or hidden. Technically speaking, the canonists and theologians tended to hold that usury pertained only to a loan *(mutuum)* and not to other contracts unless a loan was implicit in them.[296] What their discussion of principles and cases adds up to is this: a person certain of making a profit commits usury; one not certain of making a profit does not. As Hostiensis explained it, it is wrong for a lender of money to make a profit on a loan because ownership and risk have been transferred to the borrower and for the lender to do so would be to pay him for what is not his.[297] Rather, where a loan is made, it should be granted out of a feeling of Christian charity and not out of the motive of gain. This amounts to a refusal to recognize that the creditor is inherently running a risk in lending out his money and may be justified in demanding recompense. Moreover, even the lender who does not demand a sum in addition to the principal from his debtor but only hopes for gain — e.g., an unsolicited gift from his debtor — becomes guilty of usury.[298]

Yet, there were instances in which canon lawyers sanctioned the receipt of something in excess of the principal. Two such instances are pertinent to the present discussion. The first was that of the "free gift" *(gratis dans, donum)* made by the debtor to the creditor on a wholly voluntary and unsolicited basis.[299] So long as the creditor neither expected nor hoped for such a gift, he was held free to accept it. The second was the penalty exacted by the creditor from the debtor for his failure to repay his loan on time *(poena nec in fraudem),* provided no fraudulent intent was involved and provided that the penalty was designed to serve only as an incentive for prompt repayment.[300] The idea involved here is clearly based on the assumption that non-payment has caused the creditor to suffer an unjustifiable loss and is similar to the Roman law concept of *"interesse"* (or damages) which became due to the injured party when the other party to a contract defaulted. Roman law *interesse, id quod interest* involved determination of (1) the difference between the creditor's present situation and what it would have been if the loan had not been made — i.e., actual damages *(damnum emergens)* — and (2) compensation for the gain which was lost to the creditor by the debtor's failure to repay — i.e., lost profit *(lucrum cessans).*[301] *Interesse* as it pertained to actual damages suffered was acceptable to most medieval canonists. Indeed, from the 1220's on, due to the treatment of the subject by the Roman legist Azzo in his glosses on the Code of Justinian, the single word *interesse* came to be used by the canonists to refer not to something paid in addition to the principal of a loan but to the difference to be made up to the injured party (the creditor) by the defaulting party (the debtor) who had failed to meet his obligations.[302] But *interesse* as it pertained to profits lost was not widely accepted by medieval canonists before the fourteenth century.[303] Hence the term *"interesse"* is not to be equated with our term "damages." Similarly, usury refers technically only to unauthorized receipts in excess of the principal of a loan and not to all receipts in excess of the principal.

Many a medievalist specializing in economic history has held that the bankers of the Middle Ages did not lend money without charging interest. They have pointed out that it was easy to conceal their profits within rates of exchange wherein a loan might be made in one currency but made repayable in another at a value in excess of the original grant, that interest could be hidden by levying it at the time the loan was made or by adding it to the total due in such fashion that the debtor repaid a sum larger than the amount he actually received, and that penalities for late payment might be agreed upon with the informal understanding that repayment would not be made on the due date so that the debtor would be open to assessments for damages as determined by the creditor.[304] Only Piquet, however, makes an explicit statement that the Templars found ways to get around the Church's prohibition[305] though he can hardly prove this in a documentary manner.

Illustrative of the theory of damages or compensation for losses in operation is the example preserved in a document incorporated by Matthew Paris into his history.[306] In this particular document, the merchants of Cahors demand as compensation for losses the payment every two months of one mark for every ten marks borrowed if the loan was not repaid on time – 60% interest per year. But because the canonists held that the setting of specific rates determined purely by the time of delay created a presumption of usury, it became common, as notarial records show,[307] to stipulate penalties as being double the sum lent if the terms of the contracts were not met. But for the Templars, there are no surviving contracts with precise and detailed terms showing that they did, and if so by what means, get around the restrictions laid down by the Church. It is reasonable to assume, however, that Templar contracts and methods were not markedly different from those of secular business men. It appears that John's original loan (1215) of 1,000 marks from the Templars of Poitou had grown by 1218 to 1,157 marks.[308] Exactly what was meant when Henry III assigned the English Templars "full seisin" of the manor of Godmanchester until "full satisfaction" had been obtained[309] is uncertain, but a sum in excess of the original loan may well have been involved. On the surface, the Templars appear to be involved in a mortgage, prohibited to the clerics by Pope Alexander III (1163) – i.e., they appear to be granting a loan, or the extension of a loan, on the security of a piece of property placed in their hands to retain until the debt had been paid, with the fruits of the property accruing to them and not being used to reduce the principal of the debt.[310] But that this is necessarily the correct interpretation is open to question. In January of 1260, having borrowed £2,800 Tournois from the Templars at Paris and having promised payment "within the month of Easter next," Henry III agreed that if the debt was not paid by then, he would "make good all losses, interest, and expenses" occasioned by the default, accepting the word of the Templars as to the amount of the loss.[311] The terms of this loan are not markedly different from those Henry agreed to in a contract with certain Florentine merchants by which he promised under penalty of 200 marks, in addition to losses, interest, and expenses to repay by a certain date at New Temple the 780 marks borrowed. Incorporated in this same loan was an earlier unpaid loan of £100 and a payment of 80 marks "of the king's gift for their grace in lending."[312] It is conceivable, though there seems to be no specific evidence, that the Templars were accustomed to receive such "gifts" for their grace in lending. The most explicit evidence that the Templars received something in excess of the principal for their loans is to be found in the acquittance issued by William Beaulieu, Grand Master of the order (1274), to Edward I for repayment of a loan (£24,974 Tournois) made to him in the Holy Land and for receipt of an additional £5,333 6s. 8d. Tournois "tam super principali quam super custibus, dampnis, et interesse"[313]— the extra payment being due to the king's failure to fulfill the terms of the original contract.

The material cited here, although it is not as precise and detailed as one might wish, is nonetheless pertinent and convincing evidence that the Templars were compensated for their lending and that they did receive sums in excess of the principal of their loans. But the evidence does not prove that the Templars were guilty of practicing usury in the sense of the term as defined and discussed by the canonists. It only shows that the Templars received what today would be called interest and damages. Furthermore, had there been any grounds at all for a belief that the Templars engaged in usurious activities, such a charge would surely have been included in the indictment drawn up against them at the time of their arrest and trial.

The international transfer and transportation of funds was another of the useful activities engaged in by the Templars. Carrying money over long distances was at best a precarious operation in the Middle Ages, and especially before the widespread use of gold coins, was a laborious task, as details in the public records show. Until credit instruments came into existence, only persons who were reliable and capable of defending themselves could be used. During the era of the Crusades, there was probably no group safer or more reliable than the Templars. The direct and specific instances in which the English Templars actually transferred and transported funds at a distance are not too numerous though the implication of many passages is that they did do so. Quite possibly the English Templars, rather than carry funds for the Holy Land directly to the east, normally brought them to the Temple at Paris, the headquarters of the order in western Europe, whence they were taken east. Yet, in 1241, the king ordered that money which had been raised in England for the Holy Land should be delivered to a Templar and a Hospitaller "to be taken at first passage" to Richard, Earl of Cornwall, in the Holy Land.[314] Whether this involved the transportation of the cash or the use of letters of credit is uncertain.

Most information from England, however, is limited to the carrying of money for the king between England and France. In 1228, Aymeric, Master in England, was ordered by Henry III to have an unstated sum taken to the Paris Temple for ultimate payment to citizens of St. Emilio for certain claims they had against the crown.[315] The £200 which Henry agreed to pay annually for five years (starting in 1235) to the Count of La Marche at the Paris Temple for the Isle of Oleron was to be carried there "at the peril of the king."[316] In 1238, three or four Templar knights were ordered by the king to accompany two royal clerks, no doubt to guarantee the safe conduct of the money, delivering 6,000 marks to Paris for the use of Richard of Cornwall.[317] In 1254, a Templar, Alan of Kent, was ordered to take £1,500 in February and £1,460 in March "safely except for the peril of sea, fire, and thieves" to Alphonse, Count of Toulouse, at Paris in payment of damages committed by Henry's troops during his recent campaign in Gascony and an additional 4,671 marks in August and 4,000 marks in October to Gascony for the king's use there.[318] In the same year, Henry III, while still in southern France, sought to borrow money for a pilgrimage to Pontigny and directed that it be sent to him by a Templar, a Hospitaller, or other sure messenger.[319] And in the next year (1255), three Templars took money owed by the king to three citizens of Toulouse and returned with the jewels the king had deposited as collateral.[320] There are other examples where the English Templars may have transported specie from one place to another,[321] but the matter is not certain. Likewise, though it is most probable that they did so, there is no specific evidence in English sources of the Templars transporting papal funds to Rome, except via the Temple at Paris.[322] All that can be said is that in the years before the appearance of credit instruments and in the early stages of their development, it is most likely that the Templars carried funds, their own and those belonging to others, with a considerable degree of regularity and with great reliability. To obviate the need for the actual physical transfer of specie, credit devices were needed.

The widespread use of credit in the late Middle Ages, beginning in the Italian city-states as early as the eleventh century and spreading rapidly in the period of the Crusades and thereafter, is now a familiar subject,[323] though the precise distinctions between the different forms of credit instruments used and the technical points in their actual operation are not wholly known or agreed upon.[324] Similarly, there is no questioning that the Templars employed credit instruments, but there is considerable doubt regarding the type and working of the ones they used. This uncertainty is due to the fact that we do not have the Templars' contracts and correspondence which would give precise details but must rely primarily upon brief instructions and requests, mostly royal, directed to the Templars.

For the Templars in England, only two examples involving specific and unquestionable use of credit instruments have been found. The first, dated 1255, is a reference to a letter of credit for twenty-five marks issued to three English Templars going abroad on a mission for the crown.[325] What is involved here is simply an authorization for them to use this letter to meet their expenses and a guarantee to any person honoring the letter that the sum stated will be paid. The second, dated 1304, is a reference to a letter obligatory (or possibly an *instrumentum ex causa cambii*) worth seven hundred marks issued in favor of the English Templars by the Mozzi of Florence upon purchase of wool worth that amount.[326] To receive actual payment of the sum, the Templars had to present the letter at the offices of the company in Paris. Since there are many examples in the public records of the use of letters of credit by the crown, it would seem likely that the Templars used them quite regularly despite the small number of specific references found.

There are many transactions — e.g., long distance payments or transfers between Templar houses, especially between the London and Paris Temples — which seem to assume the use of credit even though the references contain no statement to this effect and no indication of the procedure to be employed. The typical transaction is one in which money would be deposited at New Temple and the appropriate Templar house on the continent would be expected to discharge that sum to the designated party abroad. Before discussing the instruments and procedures of credit which might have been used, a number of examples of the transactions involved must be given.

The settlement (1186) between Henry II and his son's widow, Margaret, to be discussed below, involved sums handled by the Templars of England and France. In 1213, John allotted 2,000 marks at New Temple for the use of the Earl of Salisbury, then in Flanders, to be obtained from the Paris Temple.[327] In 1218, it was provided that the 2,150 marks which Henry III still owed Louis of France for his departure from England should be paid by the Templars of Paris after deposit of the sum at New Temple.[328] The same arrangement was made three years later for 500 marks which Henry owed Philip Augustus.[329] Similarly, in the same year, another 500 marks were deposited at New Temple for Henry's affairs in Germany.[330] In 1221 and 1224, two payments of 500 marks each were made, apparently at London, to be credited to the Templars of La Rochelle who were to pay out the thousand marks for the execution of the king's affairs there.[331] In 1226, money owed by the Count of Salisbury to the city of Bordeaux was deposited at New Temple for payment by the Templars at Bordeaux.[332] An especially good example is the payment by Henry to his step-father, Hugh de Lusignan, Count of La Marche. In 1224, 1,500 marks were brought to New Temple for payment to the Count by the Master of the Temple *"citra montes"*;[333] and in 1235, it was arranged that Henry should deposit £200 yearly for five years in London and the Temple at Paris should pay the count that sum for the same period.[334] In the same year (1235), there are two references – one of 2,000 marks and the other of 10,000 marks – to payments in England for funds to be made available to the emperor by the Templars on the continent.[335] The 3,000 marks to be paid by the Temple at Bordeaux (1242) for the truce expenses[336] was most likely a credit transaction. In 1266, Henry deposited at New Temple 250 marks for the use of Richard of Cornwall, King of the Germans, who was to obtain the money from the Templars on the continent.[337] Perhaps the best example of all is the arrangement whereby the £70,000 Tournois owed Louis IX of France by Prince Edward of England were to be repaid in installments of 5,000 marks twice a year by deposits at New Temple and disbursements by the Templars of Paris.[338] There are other examples, but these are enough to suggest the sort of credit transactions involved and to show the need to work out some system for the balance of deposits and disbursements between the various Templar houses.

Credit and exchange operations in the late Middle Ages took a variety of forms:[339] letters of credit and contracts of exchange as well as simple letters designed to meet specific current situations. A common type of letter of credit was a formal document issued by a king (or some other prominent person whose financial position was known and respected) authorizing the bearer(s) to incur indebtedness of a given amount which would be paid off later by the king upon presentation of the letter by the person (or his representative) who had honored it before the proper official at the royal court. That the Templars were acquainted with this device, which so conveniently obviated the need for carrying large amounts of specie, has already been shown. However, surviving materials do not permit one to say whether or not the Templars issued such letters in their own name.

A variety of contracts of exchange[340] were employed in this period. The simplest was the *cambium minutum* which involved on-the-spot exchange of coins and was usually limited to petty exchange between money-changer and client. In their capacity as bankers, the Templars engaged in this activity, probably not so much in England as on the continent. More complicated was the *instrumentum ex causa cambii,* the prototype of the bill of exchange, which involved the extension of credit in the form of a loan, the transfer of funds, and the exchange of currency. Commonly used in the thirteenth and early fourteenth centuries to cover a multiplicity of transactions, and normally involving only two parties (the creditor and the debtor), the *instrumentum* recorded the loan of money in one currency (e.g., English pounds) and called for its repayment in another currency (e.g., pounds Tournois) at a definite time and in another place. Clauses of indemnity for expenses and damages in the case of delayed repayment and the posting of collateral were familiar provisions in these contracts. Hundreds of contracts of this kind made by Italian merchants survive because the two parties concerned agreed to terms in the presence of a notary who wrote them down and entered them in the records of such cities as Genoa. Many of the loans made by the Templars, such as some of those extended to Henry III and Edward I discussed above, may well have fallen into this category since all the necessary elements of the *instrumentum* were present. This type of contract may also have been employed in the transfer of funds from England to the continent or from the continent to England without the actual shipment of specie since the funds involved could easily have been expressed in terms of credit and exchange. An additional incentive for the use of the *instrumentum* was the fact that it was looked upon by canon lawyers as an operation of exchange and not as a loan *("cambium non est mutuum")* and as such did not come under the restrictions pertaining to usury.

The *cambium per litteras,* or true bill of exchange, also involved a loan, a transfer, and an exchange of currency, but it was more complicated than the *instrumentum,* involving four parties (two at the place of issue and two at the place of payment), two payments, and two bills of exchange — one of change and one of rechange. This type of contract made possible for the first time, according to Usher,[341] systematically doing business between parties not present in the same place, and like the *instrumentum* had the advantage of not falling in a category of transaction subject to prosecution for usury. The English Templars had nothing to do with this type of contract since its details were not worked out by the Italian merchants who created it until the last half of the thirteenth century, and since they did not introduce its use into England before the middle of the fifteenth century, long after the Templar order ceased to exist. Furthermore, the bill of exchange was not usually handled by banks of deposit and transfer but rather by merchants who found it useful in their purchase and exchange of goods.

Most likely what the Templars ordinarily used in lending and transfer operations were separate letters for each individual transaction, working out and improving upon details and techniques with time and experience.[342] So, for example, the English Templars may have sent a letter to the Paris Temple requesting that house to pay out a certain sum, at a given time or at stated intervals, to a specified party, for a particular purpose. Then, quite likely, the Paris Temple sent back a letter of confirmation and execution. Over an extended period, the requests, deposits, and disbursements between houses may have been reasonably well balanced so that the facilities and commitments would not get too far out of line. However, if they should, the transfer of specie or of credit could easily and speedily be effected.

Like modern bankers, the Templars also accepted responsibilities of trusteeship. By this is meant that they became involved with the administration of what might be called future interests — e.g., dowries, revenues, pensions, and wills. As has been indicated above, the castles of Gisors and Néaufles were held in trust by the Templars (1158-61) until the marriage of Henry and Margaret, the son and daughter of Henry II and Louis VII respectively.[343] In 1259, the Templars stood guarantee for Louis IX of France in his promise to pay Henry III, in accordance with the treaty just made between the two monarchs, the cost of maintaining five hundred knights for two years.[344] The dowry of Berengaria, the wife of the late King Richard, as agreed upon between her and John — £1,000 per year — was to be paid at New Temple and entrusted to the Templars.[345] In 1214, John sent £2,500 to the Templars of La Rochelle, to be paid in five annual installments to Alice, Countess of Angoulême, as her dowry.[346] Similarly, the dowries of Isabella, sister of Alexander III of Scotland (1228),[347] of Eleanor, King Henry's sister and wife of the Emperor, Frederick II (1239),[348] and of Alice, daughter of William de Valence and fiancée of Gilbert, son of Richard de Clare (1255),[349] were handled through the Templars. The income from properties of absentee owners — e.g., those of William de Valence[350] and Guy de

Lusignan[351]— were frequently entrusted to the Templars for deposit in New Temple. Pensions were also paid through the Templars. In 1186, after the death of her husband, it was agreed that Margaret of France should receive an annual pension of £2,750 — the sum being paid through the French Templars — at the expense of the English crown in return for withdrawal of her claim on certain lands.[352] John, in order to strengthen his own position on the continent, sent £30,000 to the Templars of La Rochelle for the payment of £6,000 annually to Ralph, Count of Eu, for his neutrality.[353] Other pensions paid for the king by the Templars included those of John's uncles, Thomas and Amadeus of Savoy; Peter Saracen, Vicomte de Thouars; Hugh, Bishop of Ostia; a certain Hubert Huese; and Ferrand, Count of Flanders.[354] A pension of £400 per year, in the absence of her husband, William, was authorized to be paid by the Templars to Joan de Valence (1258).[355] And a pension of £20 yearly for life was to be paid to Bayamund de Vicia by arrangement made by William, Abbot of Malmesbury, with the Templars.[356] After the deaths of the Earl of Salisbury (1227), of W. Bruer (1227), and of the Bishop of Ely (1257), the execution of their wills, insofar as certain debts and other financial matters were concerned, was entrusted to the Templars.[357] Though additional examples could be cited, those given here are sufficient to indicate the type and scope of trusts engaged in by the Templars.

Since their record books have not survived, practically nothing is known of the system of accounting used by the English Templars. However, it must have been essentially the same as that used in France where some information is available because of the survival of a part of the Journal of the Paris Temple covering the period from March 9, 1294 to July 4, 1296.[358] An examination of the cash book, the most comprehensive and informative of the surviving documents, shows that the Templars divided their receipts into two major classes: those pertaining to their own business and goods and those pertaining to the transactions of their clients. In the first category, are the returns or surpluses turned in from time to time by the preceptors or commanders of the various houses for crediting to the Treasurer or Master of the Paris Temple representing the order in France and the disposition to be made of those amounts. In the second, are the receipts and expenditures of individual clients, most important of whom was the king. From the cash book, entries were made into the appropriate accounts or books, perhaps as many as twelve different ones. So, for example, there are the *liber regis* in which records of the king are entered, the *magnus liber* in which entries pertaining to other clients and to the Templars themselves are kept, the *liber ad debemus* in which deposits for payment on a given future date are listed, and the *liber ad debetur* in which information concerning various clients of the Templars and the debtors of those clients is recorded. Beween the various accounts, however, there is so much overlapping of subject matter that it is often difficult to understand why a certain item of information is found in one book instead of another. The same is true for the keeping of records on the income and expenditures of their own order, for which the Templars at Paris kept at least five separate accounts: the *liber in magnis fratrum,* the *liber pilosus,* the *parvus liber novus,* the *parvus liber vetus,* and the *liber in parvis ad vad-*[*imonia*]. Though the Templars kept a great many separate accounts, they could easily extract from them a credit and debit statement, and did in fact do so three times a year for their major clients. At Candlemas (February 2d), Ascension (in April or May), and All Saints (November 1st), the king received such a statement in two parts: a General Account or summary of totals of receipts and expenditures and a series of Appendices in which was given a detailed breakdown of receipts showing types, sources, and amounts credited to his account and of expenditures showing individual sums listed by major categories with a final statement of the credit or debit balance clearly indicated.

The great weakness of the Templars' system of accounting was their failure to keep a general account which would have provided themselves with an analysis of their financial position as a whole at any given time.[359] Though the material for a balance sheet was available, such a record was never compiled. Consequently ignorance of their precise overall financial condition must have caused many a business decision to be made on the basis of incomplete and inadequate data, if not on the basis of chance.

Despite the lack of as much explicit information as might be desired, the foregoing discussion of the Templars as a financial group has shown that their organization was well worked out, their activities were varied, their methods were basically sound and successful, and the scope of their operations was broad. Although most of these things were not wholly apparent till the thirteenth century, they presuppose an evolutionary development extending well back into the preceding century.[360] This financial activity is especially interesting inasmuch as the Templars were not professional traders or bankers but rather seem to have been drawn into banking because of their wealth and international connections. On a comparative basis, the Templars are to be seen as financial leaders, especially in banking and credit activities, and with few peers or significant rivals during much of the period. It is doubtful if most writers, excluding Delisle and Piquet, have given the Templars as much credit as they deserve for the breadth and depth of their financial activities and for the influence they had on the development of medieval finance and credit operations. This is true despite the fact that England was an economic backwater and that the Italian merchants were performing in various areas on the continent the services the Templars were performing in England.

𝔉inancial and 𝔄dministrative 𝔘se of the 𝔗emplars and of 𝔑ew 𝔗emple

So far, a considerable amount of material has been introduced to show the activities of the Templars as bankers. Now it remains, in order to complete the general picture, to show that the Templars were used as financial officials and agents by the kings of England and by various popes and that New Temple was used as a center for the administration of some of the financial activities of the kings.

As royal officials, the Templars served as collectors, receivers, and keepers of the king's revenue, and as auditors for the crown. Tenths, fifteenths, and other such levies, both lay and ecclesiastical, were frequently collected by a local committee composed of one Templar, one Hospitaller, and one or two other persons. The use of Templars as royal collectors first appeared in 1184;[361] and the policy of using a Templar and a Hospitaller jointly was laid down at the time of the first Saladin tithe (1188).[362] Interestingly enough, the bad precedent which was then set by Gilbert of Ogerstan,[363] a Templar who was found guilty of embezzlement of some of the funds — for which he was severely punshed by the Master of the order — seems not to have limited the practice as the collections of subsequent years show.[364] If the example from Bristol is a guide, the same local committees which collected the funds were responsible for seeing to it that they were safely conducted to New Temple for deposit.[365] Another duty assigned the Templars by the king was the auditing of accounts. So, for example, the Master of the Temple in Ireland, along with the Archbishop of Dublin and two royal officials, audited the accounts of the Justiciar of Ireland in 1242, 1250, and 1281;[366] in 1253 and 1279, along with the Prior of the Hospitallers in Ireland, and two royal officials, he audited the accounts of the Treasurer of the Exchequer of Dublin;[367] and in 1252, he audited the account of Simon de Montfort for the administration of Cusac castle.[368] Except for one occasion (1285), when the account of the Templars for the twentieth then deposited at New Temple was audited by order of Edward I by a merchant of Lucca,[369] there is no indication that the Templar accounts were themselves checked. Royal confidence in the financial knowledge and experience of the Templars is further suggested by

Edward I's appointment of Richard de Herdewyk and Richard de Fetham, preceptor and treasurer of New Temple, to a committee of three — Richard de Boclaunde, sacristan of St. Paul's Cathedral, London, being the other member — to determine adjustments necessary for the conversion from the old money to the new (1294).[370]

Since the Templars were so involved in the collection and receipt of royal revenue, it is not surprising to find them serving — at least from 1238 to 1242, and most likely for a longer time than that — as keepers of the king's revenues, along with such other persons as certain Hospitallers and the royal constables at the Tower of London.[371] Indeed, at one time, as indicated above, Geoffrey the Templar served as keeper of the wardrobe — the only Templar ever to hold that position.[372] Nor is it surprising to find certain of the treasurers of New Temple serving as royal treasurers.

Use of Templars as messengers and officials through whom royal funds were paid or transported has already been dealt with — Roger,[373] Thomas,[374] and Geoffrey[375] being the best known examples. Likewise, the use of Templars as agents for the collection and receipt of papal revenues has already been covered.

Important, but not wholly clear, was the relationship of the New Temple Treasury to the Exchequer and the Wardrobe which by the end of the reign of Henry II were the two major financial offices of the English government. The former had come to enjoy a certain degree of independence from the king and had its own treasury at Westminster, subsequently moved to London; and the latter, wholly under the control of the king, served as his private treasury, normally accompanying him wherever he went. By the time of Henry III, the Wardrobe was gaining in power and importance though income still seems to have been deposited without much distinction in either the Wardrobe or the Exchequer.[376] In view of this trend, Henry III found it desirable to establish treasuries, in the sense of storehouses or places of deposit, for the Wardrobe at the Tower of London and at New Temple so that regular and permanent places for the deposit and safekeeping of royal income would be provided.[377] The practical wisdom of this move is suggested by the fact that New Temple served as a royal treasury for approximately a century. Whether or not New Temple ever became a treasury in the sense of a center for the determination and administration of royal financial policy is unclear. If certain references are to be taken literally, it would seem that it did for a brief period. At least, the Wardrobe, whose officials helped determine and administer royal financial policies, seems to have been temporarily established at New Temple (1225). For, in that year, royal orders directed the deposit of funds *"in garderoba domini regis apud Novum Templum Londonie.*"[378] Usually, however, royal orders merely called for the deposit of income at New Temple and for the disbursement of funds *"de thesauro nostro [qui est] in domo Novi Templi Londonie.*[379] The reasons for the choice of New Temple as a royal treasury would seem to have been these: its permanence and convenient location, the physical strength of the Templars and their buildings, the known financial competence of the Templars, the piety of King Henry III and his strong sympathy for the Templars, and especially the need for such a financial center in the years before royal administrative institutions had evolved sufficiently to assume full control of all royal functions and responsibilities.

The question arises of who was in charge of royal funds deposited at New Temple. That normally the treasurer of New Temple was is shown by the great number of royal orders addressed to him directing him to accept deposits of various sorts, to pay out certain sums of money to a named official or private person, or to permit a particular official or individual to have what is necessary to accomplish the specific tasks designated in official letters.[380] A number of times, however, other persons seem to have been in charge — for example, the Bishops of Bath and Salisbury in 1225;[381] Peter Chaceporc, Keeper of the Wardrobe, in 1247;[382] the treasurer of the Hospitallers in 1270-71;[383] and Joseph de Chauncey, the king's treasurer, in 1276.[384] These instances, however, seem to be the exceptions rather than the rule. The important thing to note is that the treasury at New Temple remained directly under the control of the king and was not under the control of the officials of the Wardrobe or of the Exchequer in the sense that deposits and disbursements were made on the basis of royal orders rather than on the basis of orders of Wardrobe or Exchequer officials. This qualification has to be added, however: when the Exchequer deposited certain of its funds at New Temple, as it occasionally did, those funds remained under the control of the Exchequer as is indicated by certain orders sent from the officials of the Exchequer to New Temple directing payment of the indicated sums "out of our treasury which is in the New Temple in your custody."[385]

The closeness of the Templars to the crown and the reliance of the kings upon the services of the Templars are especially manifest in the use of two of the treasurers of New Temple as royal treasurers and keepers of royal funds at the Tower of London. Hugh of Stockton, treasurer of New Temple from approximately 1229 to 1242, and Robert of Sicklinghall, treasurer of New Temple from approximately 1245 to 1260, were repeatedly used during their terms as royal treasurers by Henry III.[386] Under Edward I, however, the Templars, though they still were of service to the crown and though they continued to accept on deposit the revenues of the kingdom, declined in importance, probably because Edward was building his own administrative staff and was turning to Italian bankers who may have been more willing to lend large amounts of money than the Knights.

Conclusion

The survey of political, administrative, and economic activities of the Templars given in this chapter reveals the interrelationship of these activities and the variety of Templar undertakings. Most of their activities, except for those that were wholly within the sphere of their own affairs, were closely associated with those of the crown. In all three fields, they served the kings of England, with very few exceptions, with distinction. Honesty and efficiency must have characterized their actions or else their services would not have been so sought after or so relied upon.

In political affairs, the Templars were mainly used as representatives of the king in missions abroad and as advisers to the king. In these capacities, however, they were merely a few of the king's many envoys and councillors. Accordingly, though they were powerful and influential, they were no more so than many other groups, clerical or lay.[387] In administrative affairs, the Templars played a more prominent role. In their capacity as financial agents of the crown and in the use which the king made of their treasury and offices at New Temple, they became for a time a direct part of the king's administration, thus contributing significantly to the development of the royal administration. In economic affairs, the Templars played their most important role. Wealthy from their own lands and goods which they managed efficiently, constantly active in trade and commerce which they profited from, and deeply concerned with matters of finance in which they engaged effectively and creatively, the Templars became expert accountants, outstanding administrators, and active promoters of credit and credit instruments. In a very real sense, during the late twelfth and all of the thirteenth centuries, they were the greatest bankers in England, easily overshadowing the Jews but being eventually themselves overshadowed by the Italian merchants. It is not surprising, then, to find that for almost a century much of the financial business of the English crown passed through the hands of the Templar order whose men and facilities were freely used by all the kings from Henry II through Edward II. But the height of their influence was reached under Henry III whose favors to them and whose use and reliance upon them were great.

Though details cannot be gone into here, it is safe to say that the Templars were active in the political, administrative, and economic affairs of other countries, too. In no state was this more apparent than in France where the kings seem to have relied upon the Templars to an even greater degree than did the English kings.[388] In the field of finances, this reliance was most noticeable and most significant. Throughout the thirteenth century, under Philip II, Louis IX, Philip III, and Philip IV, the treasury of the Templars at Paris was intimately associated with the crown as existing documents show. M. Delisle even contends that for all practical purposes the Templar treasury was also the royal treasury and that the Templar treasurers were royal treasurers as well.[389] More cautious, M. Piquet says only that the royal treasury was at the Temple.[390] This situation continued till Philip the Fair, at the end of the thirteenth century, established a sort of private treasury at the Louvre which he used in conjunction with the Temple treasury.[391] And it was under the same king that the French Templars, perhaps too powerful and too influential, fell from favor to disgrace. But it might be asked for France as for England whether a private organization of a religious and military nature like the Temple could continue to manage effectively the complicated financial affairs of the crown and whether the Templars could, had they chosen, compete with the activities and ambitions of the Italian banking houses.[392]

It is necessary now to turn to a consideration of the forces and events which led to the arrest, trial, and dissolution of the Templars, first in France, and then in England and the other countries of western Europe.

chapter four

Trial and Dissolution

The Fall of the Templars in France

THE CONDEMNATION of the Knights Templars, which the distinguished historian Henry C. Lea has called "the great crime of
the Middle Ages,"[1] constitutes one of the most interesting and dramatic
chapters in the history of medieval Europe and serves as an especially
good example of "man's inhumanity to man." The trial and dissolution
of the order, reflecting the age-old rivalry between church and state,
involved considerations of economic and political advantage to a greater
degree than elements of religion and morality. In the recurring struggle
between church and state in France, where currently the ambitious and
ruthless king, Philip IV (the Fair), was vying for control with the
weak and vacillating pope, Clement V, the Templars, caught between
the two parties, were destined to be sacrificed. Indeed, for some time
the Knights Templars had been a source of uneasiness to the rulers
of both the church and the state. This uneasiness increased with the loss
of the Holy Land and with the settlement of the Templars, with their
great wealth and power, on a more permanent basis in the states of
Europe. In no country was this tension more obvious than in France;
but the attack on the Templars, though it started in France, was not to
be limited to that country. It was to extend to all areas where Templars
were found.

In citing reasons for the fate which befell the Templars, one must
distinguish between alleged and real reasons. The practice of heresy,
idolatry, immorality, and all sorts of indignities and irregularities was
given as their motive by many who wanted to see the Templars
destroyed.[2] A more fundamental reason for the attack, however, was
the hostility and rivalry which the Templars had aroused because of
their extensive privileges and immunities, their apparent power and
influence, their arrogance, and their occasional perfidy. The Knights
Hospitallers, the Teutonic Knights, the various monastic orders, and
the secular clergy were all envious and perhaps even fearful of the Templars. The bitter rivalry between the military orders had repeatedly been

brought out into the open, and the attitude of many of the secular clergy was well expressed by those bishops who had regularly protested the exemption of the Templars from their jurisdiction and had been understandably concerned over the growth of Templar wealth and power. Secular rulers, too, had good reason to be disturbed at the growth in their realms of Templar wealth and power over which they had no control. Moreover, now that the Templars were no longer actually fighting the infidel, their continued existence seemed less compelling. But the crucial and the immediate reason for the attack on the Templars was financial — Philip the Fair's pressing need for money.[3] Philip had already dealt with this problem in a variety of ways, but without lasting success. He had, for example, taxed the clergy, confiscated goods of his vassals, robbed the Lombards, seized the wealth of the Jews, imposed new levies on trade and property, and devalued the currency over fifty per cent in a decade. The Templars, who had both land and money, seemed a desirable victim to Philip.

The details of Philip's plans and the execution of them, significant and enlightening as they are, cannot be carefully gone into here.[4] Suffice it to say that Philip's campaign, though filled with risk and moments of seeming failure, succeeded in the long run. However, the steps in this campaign against the Templars in France must be mentioned briefly as a contrast to what happened in England. Seizing upon rumors unfavorable to the Templars which had been circulated almost periodically over the last four or five decades, Philip's lawyers, led by William de Nogaret, drew up a long list of charges against the order, a copy of which was forwarded to Pope Clement V who, however, took no immediate action and referred to the charges as beyond belief.[5] Pressed with the threat of initiating proceedings to condemn Boniface VIII, his predecessor, and with the demand to make Philip's brother, Charles of Valois, Holy Roman Emperor, Clement soon consented to an investigation of the Templars.[6] Philip, having gained his point, and being determined both to prevent the pope from conducting the inquiry and to prevent the Templars from organizing a defense, had secret instructions for the arrest of the Templars prepared and delivered (September, 1307) to his seneschals and to certain other royal officials.[7] These letters, not to be unsealed, on pain of death, until October 12th, directed the royal officials, effective October 13th, to imprison the Templars, to seize their goods, to make an inventory of their possessions, and to hold everything at the discretion of the king. All this proceeded as planned — a remarkable demonstration of the effective organization and force Philip had created. At this point, a propaganda campaign against the Templars was undertaken. The clergy and people of France were informed of the charges against the order and were told, untruthfully, that Clement had consented to the king's action and that Philip had acted only after being requested by William of Paris, chief inquisitor in France — who was also private confessor to the king — to help stamp out the heretics and idolators.[8] The French clergy, both secular and regular, largely dominated by the crown, fell into line and openly denounced the alleged evils of the Templars. And the French nobility, perhaps partly in hope of political and economic concessions, but more probably in fear of Philip, in view of the king's earlier successes, did not protest. The Templars, being now officially informed of the charges against them, were examined — at times by Philip's political agents, at times by representatives of the Inquisition, and at times by both[9] — and were promised leniency if they confessed but death if they did not. To facilitate the process, torture was used openly and effectively.[10] Under these conditions, a number of "free and spontaneous" confessions were obtained although many of them were later repudiated as having been obtained under duress. Armed with these depositions of heresy, immorality, and indecency, Philip intended to force Clement to make further concessions. But Clement, when he learned what Philip had done, denounced the action in the strongest possible terms, declaring the seizure of the Templars an unjustifiable interference in the rights of the papacy and expressing the opinion that there was no truth to the charges. Furthermore, as an indication of papal anger and determination, William, Inquisitor of Paris, was deposed.[11] For the moment, then, it looked as though Clement meant to stand his ground. Just what would have been his next step is uncertain, but it is likely he meant to have the Templars examined under more favorable conditions. Philip, however, filled with rage at Clement's hostile action and having no intention of conceding to the pope, determined to bring to bear enough pressure to compel Clement to renounce his recent statements and to permit Philip to proceed with his campaign against the Templars. Vigorously pressing anew his plans for the condemnation of Boniface, pointedly insisting that the secular arm had come to the aid of the ecclesiastical at the latter's request, dramatically stressing the evidence of heresy and wrongdoing, and shrewdly acquiring the specific support and approval of the archbishops of France, Philip forced the pope to give in. In a new bull — *Pastoralis praeeminentiae*[12] — issued November 22, 1307, Clement submitted, not only saying that since his bull of a month earlier new and convincing evidence of the guilt of the Templars had been laid before him but also going on to praise Philip for his zeal as a faithful son of the church and devoted defender of the holy faith.

Philip had obviously won — the Templars were to be examined.

However, since the matter had not yet been agreed upon, Philip, in his determination to gain papal acquiescence to a trial procedure not inimical to his own interests, resorted to the tactic of summoning a carefully selected Estates-General — which met in May, 1308 — whose duty it was to support him and to arouse the people. By mid-July, Philip had obtained from Clement a satisfactory compromise solution: the trials of the Templars were to be conducted in each diocese by the bishop and six lesser clerics, with the services of inquisitors available at the discretion of the local bishop. It was also agreed that the goods of the Templars were to be entrusted to curators, half of whom were to be named by the bishops and half by the king. These concessions were balanced by Clement's announcement that the goods of the order were to be reserved solely for the use of the Holy Land and that the results of the inquiry were to be submitted to a church council which would meet at Vienne and would decide the fate of the Templars.[13]

Accordingly, episcopal commissions of inquiry were set up in each of the dioceses of France, and papal commissions of investigation were established at such key centers as Paris where an especially important investigation was held. There William Imbert, Inquisitor of France, and his colleagues, together with representatives of the king who were always present, examined Jacques de Molay and other Templars (November, 1309 to March, 1310).[14] When Molay, claiming he could be tried before the pope alone, refused to assume the defense of the order, the task fell to two Templar priests, who did most of the work, and two knights.[15] All this was preliminary to the trial proper which began in April, 1310. The first group of witnesses at the formal trial was composed, except for a few Templars or former Templars, of secular clerics and laymen who testified to the guilt of the order.[16] The second group to testify consisted of the imprisoned Templars who, one after another, denied the charges alleged against them and their order and publicly repudiated their earlier confessions of guilt as the product of torture.[17] Philip became understandably concerned as his case against the Templars seemed to be collapsing. From a reluctant pope, he hastily gained approval of the appointment of a certain Philip de Martigny, Bishop of Cambrai and brother of one of the king's most trusted ministers, to the vacant archpishopric of Sens which had jurisdication over the diocese of Paris. The new archbishop, within a month of his appointment, summoned a provincial council to met at Paris (May, 1310) to deal with the Templar matter. Promising leniency for those who confessed and life imprisonment or death for those who made no confession or retracted confessions already made, the council, working rapidly and diligently, interrogated the Templars and handed fifty-four of them over to the secular arm as

relapsed heretics.[18] Meanwhile, the papal commission, though it continued to sit at Paris and to hear the Templars, was limited in its
activities by the action of the provincial council; and individual Templars, mindful of what had happened to their brothers after denying the
charges against the order and renouncing their individual confessions
before the provincial council, were hesitant to testify before it. Finally,
in June of 1311, the papal commission at Paris adjourned and trans-
mitted its records without comment for the use and guidance of the
Council of Vienne.

The Council of Vienne,[19] which finally assembled in October of
1311, was presided over by Pope Clement, who, as seen above, had,
as early as November of 1307, committed himself to the guilt of the
Templars and who had openly supported the use of torture against
them. When the council members, despite papal orders, seemed hesitant
to condemn the Templars without a hearing, a select committee — which
also proved reluctant — was appointed to consider the matter. Though
Clement had held earlier that the Templars should be permitted to defend themselves, he nonetheless had no Templars brought before the
council. Indeed, when, in November, six renegade Templars, shortly
increased by two, did show up requesting permission to defend their
order and claiming to represent between fifteen hundred and two
thousand of their brothers who had taken refuge in the mountains of the
Lyonnais, they were imprisoned without being heard. The months
dragged on without progress or decision, with Philip the Fair anxiously
awaiting the outcome and appearing with a small army first at Lyons
and then at Vienne. Finally, Clement issued a bull — *Vox in excelso*,[20]
dated March 22, 1312 — to the effect that, though the evidence did not
justify the definitive condemnation of the Templars, yet, the order had
been so scandalized that no honorable man could hereafter enter it and
that its possessions could not be maintained unimpaired. In view of this,
he said, it was expedient for the Holy See to abolish the order provision-
ally. The council approved this bull in April of 1312; and in short order
(May 2, 1312), also ratified another bull — *Ad providam*[21]— which
abolished the Templar order irrevocably and declared excommunicated
any person presuming to enter the order or to wear its habit. Hence, the
Order of the Knights of the Temple was abolished without being convicted, even without being heard.

It still remained to dispose of the persons and the property of the
Templars. According to Clement's recent bull — *Ad providam* — the
property was assumed by the Holy See and was declared transferred to
the Knights Hospitallers, with exceptions in the Iberian peninsula. All

those who failed to hand over the property within a month after summons were to be pronounced excommunicated. The disposition of the persons of the Templars, except for the chief officers who were reserved for papal decision, was to be determined by provincial councils which were to summon all Templars — knights, sergeants, and chaplains — to appear within one year before their bishops for examination and sentence under pain of excommunication for non-appearance. The unrepentant and relapsed were to be dealt with locally, with the severest penalties being authorized; and the penitent were to be placed in former houses of the order or in monasteries where they were to be decently maintained out of the proceeds of the order. This policy was general and was to be applied throughout Europe. How well this directive was carried out in France, and elsewhere, is not wholly certain; but enough is known to say that some of the Templars died in their dungeons, some were burned as relapsed heretics, some wandered about Europe as homeless vagabonds, and some worked as manual laborers.[22] Meanwhile, the fate of the leaders of the order was decided by a commission of cardinals appointed by Clement. On March 9, 1314, in Paris, Jacques de Molay, the Grand Master, and three other high officers, heard their fate: perpetual imprisonment. But de Molay and Geoffrey de Charney, Master of Normandy, arising before the assembled throng, proclaimed the innocence of the order and denounced the charges and confessions as fictitious and false. Thereupon, these two men were handed over to the provost of Paris, a royal official, and on order of an infuriated king and council, were, on the same day, burned as heretics without having been held for the formal decision of the church.[23]

What happened to Templar property in France cannot be dealt with in detail here. Apparently the treasure of the order fell into Philip's hands and was never accounted for;[24] and the landed estates, despite a pretense of being surrendered to the pope, were retained by Philip till his death. (Interestingly — and prophetically for some — Philip and Clement both died within a year of the execution of de Molay.) The revenues from the estates and the debts owed the Templars were also collected by Philip. By the final settlement in France (1317),[25] the French king was to retain all claim to the income of landed estates which the crown had held for ten years and was to retain most of the movable goods which had belonged to the Templars; but the remaining Templar lands and goods were to go to the Hospitallers who were to assume the expenses of the imprisoned Templars. Meanwhile, rulers, great lords, religious houses, and former donors seized or claimed Templar lands and goods wherever and whenever the occasion permitted. Only after extended and costly legal suits did the Hospitallers gain sound title to part of the former Templar possessions in France.

The Trial of the Templars in England

As in France, the Templars in England were effectively prosecuted. But the dissimilarities of the campaign against them in England were of greater significance than the similarities. Instead of the ruthless prosecution which was carried on by the French king, his officials, and many of the French clergy, the trial of the Templars in England was characterized by relative leniency and proceeded largely in accordance with the principles and procedures of English law which were more advantageous to the accused than those practiced in France. The English Templars were also aided by a popular attitude which was not nearly so hostile as that in France and by a king who seemed less than convinced of their guilt and who was less determined in his policies and actions than the French monarch.

Uncertainty regarding the status and future of the Templars in England first arose in October of 1307 when Philip the Fair, King of France, dispatched Bernard Peletin, a trusted messenger, to King Edward II, his future son-in-law, with a secret communication enumerating the alleged wickedness and crimes of the Knights Templars and urging Edward to take action against them as he, Philip, had already done in France.[26] Edward's reaction was not what Philip had hoped for. Instead of immediately proceeding against the Templars in his realm, Edward defended them. In his letter in reply (October 30, 1307), Edward dismissed Philip's charges as "incredible" to himself, his priests, earls, barons, and others of his council.[27] Furthermore, writing on behalf of the order to the kings of Portugal, Castille, Aragon, and Sicily (December 4, 1307), Edward pointed out the great reputation of the Templars for devotion and probity, recalled their distinctive services to the faith, urged his fellow monarchs to turn deaf ears to the slanderers who were moved more by greed and envy than by zeal for righteousness, and called on them to permit no injury to the Templars or their property unless the alleged wrongs were lawfully established.[28] Edward also sent a letter to Pope Clement (December 10, 1307) in which, expressing amazement and horrer, he declared that the great esteem in which the master and brothers of the Temple were held by him and by all his kingdom prevented him from believing the charges.[29] Further, suggesting that the charges might well be the work of evil-disposed persons who were turning the good deeds of the order to works of perversity for their own advantage, he urged the pope by some fair inquiry to clear the order of the charges being brought against it. But Edward's letter to the pope was to be of no avail; for, as previously noted, Clement had already committed himself to the guilt of the order.[30] Though Edward had not yet received a copy of Clement's recent bull — *Pastoralis praeeminentiae* — he soon learned that in this papal dispatch Clement, after speaking of the crimes of the Templars and of the action taken against the order in France, asserted that the Grand Master — as well as many of the brothers — had publicly and spontaneously confessed certain of the charges and that he himself had examined a knight of the order of high birth and authority who had fully and freely confessed. Because of these things, Edward was instructed with caution and secrecy to arrest all of the Templars in his kingdom on one day and to take their property into safe custody.[31]

Adhering to his initial conviction but briefly, Edward in short order turned against the Templars.[32] To determine motives for human actions is always difficult. In this case, there seems no reason to assume that Edward actually became convinced of their guilt. On the one hand, his original statements and the subsequent failure of the examinations of the Templars in England to produce positive proof would make such an assumption doubtful; on the other hand, his hesitation, as a monarch and as a Christian, to challenge the formal policy and decision of a pope seems a probable reason for his change of attitude. His realization of the problems involved in pursuing a policy opposed by the papacy and his knowledge of what had happened to certain earlier kings who had done so must have influenced him. The possibility of gains for the crown must also have been considered. At any rate, his subsequent action, as will be indicated below, shows that some of the wealth and property of the Templars went to the crown.[33] In addition, his impending marriage to Isabelle, daughter of Philip the Fair, may well have caused him to think twice about following a policy not in agreement with that of the strong-willed French monarch.

By December 20, 1307, sealed instructions of arrest and confiscation, to be effective January 8, 1308, had been drawn up and sent by sworn clerks to the sheriffs of England, the justices of Wales and Chester, the Keeper of Scotland, and the Justiciar of Ireland.[34] Only after each official involved had taken an oath to keep the contents secret were the writs opened and their contents disclosed. In accordance with the royal directive, between January 8th and 11th, approximately one hundred and fifty Templars in England were arrested; and their property was taken into the king's hands. Though some Templars escaped,[35] it is not known how many. The prisoners, apparently treated considerately, were taken to a central castle in each county to be held pending further order, being, according to royal command, guarded "in a fitting place" and not confined "in a hard and vile prison."[36] It was also provided that each Templar was to receive for his support a liberal allowance, to be taken out of the income from the land of the order, of four pence per day.[37] William de la More, Master of the Temple in England, was taken to Canterbury Castle where he was given clothes and equipment, was authorized a daily stipend of two shillings, and was permitted the company and services of any two Templars he desired.[38] Shortly, on May 27, 1308, at the intervention of the Bishop of Durham,[39] one of the greatest lords in England, he was released on his honor and was not again imprisoned until six months later (November 28th), due probably to papal insistence.[40]

The charges brought against the Templars in England were essentially identical with those brought against them on the continent, the eighty-seven articles listed by Clement[41] serving as the basis for the examinations. The charges fell into five major classes. Heresy, including idolatry, was the major charge. The Templars were accused of denying Christ, God, Mary, and the saints (article 1); rejecting the crucifixion (article 5); worshiping a statue (articles 37, 46-57) or a cat (articles 14-15); disbelieving in the sacrament of Holy Communion (articles 16-19); failing to have their priests consecrate the host in the celebration of mass (articles 20-23); and permitting the Grand Master or the local masters to grant absolution from sin (articles 24-26). Disrespect and profanation, as represented by spitting and stamping on the cross at reception (articles 9-11), were alleged. Improper action, as represented by confessing only to their own priests (article 74), and greed, as represented by a concerted effort to increase the wealth of the order by every possible means (articles 77-78), were charged. Indecency, as represented by kissing (articles 30-33) and homosexual practices (articles 40-45), was stressed. And secrecy, as represented by the holding of secret initiations (articles 69-73) and chapters (articles 36-39), was alleged.

The basic procedure to be followed in examining the English Templars was set down by Clement in his bull of August, 1308,[42] in which the archbishops and bishops of England, in conjunction with the papal inquisitors, were directed to secure evidence on the charges listed. After the individual brothers had been examined, provincial councils were to be summoned to determine the guilt or innocence of the order and the disposition of its individual members. However, because of delay, the trial itself did not begin for well over a year.

It was not until September 13, 1309, twenty months after the arrest of the Templars in England, that the papal inquisitors finally arrived.[43] On the next day, new royal writs were sent to the sheriffs to arrest all the Templars in their counties — meaning, apparently, those Templars who for some reason were still at large — and to send them without delay, together with those already in custody, from the county prisons to the Tower of London or to York and Lincoln castles.[44] On the same day, writs were sent to the constables of these three strongholds to receive the prisoners, to keep them safely, and to produce them on request for examination.[45] The boards of inquiry — composed of the Archbishops of Canterbury and York; the Abbot of Lagny (in France) and the French notary, Sicard de Vaur, papal inquisitors; and the Bishops of Durham, Orleans, Lincoln, Chester, and London[46]— were now almost ready to begin work. But first, on September 22, 1309, before the actual examination of the Templars had begun, the Archbishop of Canterbury, acting in accordance with papal orders, had had published and read in all the churches of the country a papal bull in which Clement declared his conviction that the Templars were guilty and announced the excommunication of all persons, regardless of rank, station, or profession, who should aid or counsel the Templars and the imposition of the interdict on all cities, castles, and places which might harbor any of the accused.[47]

What is known of the trial of the Templars in England pertains chiefly to the examination at London. Most of the prisoners were concentrated there,[48] and the examination of them falls conveniently into five phases. During the first phase — between October 21 and November 17, 1309[49]— forty-three Templars were questioned on a number of matters, but primarily on the procedure used by their order for confession and absolution. In this initial phase in which no torture was applied, most of the Templars denied the alleged charges and failed to make any specific confessions of wrongdoing though their testimony suggested a degree of unclearness in the matter of confession and absolution.[50] When a number of outside witnesses also failed to provide any significant or incriminating evidence, it became rather apparent that the desired confessions would not be obtained without the use of torture. Accordingly, at a meeting of the southern provincial council at Lambeth at the end of November, where the papal bull calling for a general council to meet at Vienne was read, the inquisitors requested permission to proceed "*secundum constitutiones ecclesiaticas.*"[51] On December 11 (1309), the appeal of the bishops was called directly to the attention of Edward who, four days later, conceded by issuing orders to the custodians of the Templars to allow and assist the prelates and inquisitors to do as they wished with the bodies of the prisoners "according to ecclesiastical law."[52] Nonetheless, there was still considerable hesitation on the part of the royal officials to proceed in this fashion — at least Edward's order had to be repeated.[53]

In the second phase of the examination at London — from the end of January into March of 1310 — two stages can be observed. Initially, thirty-four Templars were questioned, again apparently without torture being used and with no confessions obtained.[54] Shortly (February 8th), new royal writs were issued ordering the jailors to obey the prelates and inquisitors so as to help them deal with the Templars "according to ecclesiastical law" and appointing William de Dien to oversee the employment of torture.[55] Then, a month later, solitary confinement was authorized and the orders to use torture were repeated.[56] Even so, no headway was made inasmuch as those Templars who were again examined failed to confess.[57]

In June (1310), the inquisitors drew up a statement addressed to the Archbishop of Canterbury[58] in which they attributed their lack of success to their inability to find persons to carry out the torture which had been authorized and recommended the following ways by which the Templar affair could more quickly be brought to a successful conclusion: removing the prisoners from the care of the king's officials; putting the men on a bread and water diet; making public the confessions from France so as to arouse public indignation to the point that torture could be applied *"sine scandalo populi"*; and transferring the Templars to Ponthieu, an English possession on the continent, where torture could be more fully and freely applied. After some time had passed without any action on these recommendations being taken by Edward, Clement wrote the king (August 6th) to the effect that he had heard reports that the crown had prohibited the application of torture as contrary to the laws of England and that the work of the inquisitors had thereby been impeded.[59] At the same time, the pope wrote to the English bishops condemning them for negligence and urging them to aid the inquisitors.[60] In response to these papal criticisms, Edward, on August 26th — and again, in slightly modified form, on October 23d — ordered the Templars in the Tower to be delivered to the sheriffs of London whenever requested by the inquisitors for the application of ecclesiastical law.[61] Meanwhile, the southern provincial council which had again met at Canterbury (September 22, 1310) ordered that the Templars should be examined further and should be tortured provided no mutilation, permanent dismemberment, or effusion of blood resulted.[62] It would seem that the bishops were concerned on the one hand lest no confessions be obtained; and on the other, lest popular opinion be aroused against the use of torture.

Edward, occupied with his campaign in Scotland, cooperated so that the third phase of the examination at London — October through December, 1310 — was conducted more in accord with papal wishes. From Scotland, he directed the Constable of the Tower to deliver the Templars in his keeping to the sheriffs of London when the prelates and inquisitors desired, to permit the inquisitors to do as they pleased with the bodies of the prisoners, and to receive the Templars back when their examination was over.[63] The Templars handed over to the sheriffs were now confined in prisons attached to the city gates where it seems the sterner treatment was meted out.[64] Edward, in instructing the Mayor, aldermen, and commonalty of London to obey his orders, stated that he was allowing the proceedings against the Templars *"ob reverentia Sedis Apostolicae."*[65] Similar letters were sent (November 22d) to the Constable of Lincoln ordering him to hand over the Templars in his custody to the bailiffs of Lincoln for imprisonment in the city gates there.[66] Finally, on December 12th, Edward ordered the Templars hitherto detained at Lincoln to be transferred to London where all the Templars in the southern province were being collected in anticipation of the meeting of the southern provincial council which would determine the guilt or innocence of the order in England.[67] During this period, the Templars were re-examined,[68] and torture was probably employed; but still, there is no indication that any confessions were obtained. Clement, again making known his dissatisfaction with the course of affairs in England and indicating his lack of confidence in the efficacy of ecclesiastical law as applied in England, suggested (December 23d) – but to no avail – that Edward follow the recommendation of the inquisitors that the whole matter be transferred to Ponthieu where their work could be carried on without hindrance.[69]

Meanwhile, during the spring and summer of 1310, the Templars at York were examined.[70] Though the papal bull of accusation had been heard there with astonishment by all concerned,[71] the royal officials made the prisoners available to the designated ecclesiastics who proceeded to interrogate them as directed by Clement. The use of torture, as authorized by papal and royal letters, caused extended debate at the meeting of the northern provincial council which seemed quite uncertain as to whether it was to be applied by lay or clerical officials.[72] In fact, torture does not appear to have been used against the Templars at York at all, and perhaps as a consequence not a single confession of guilt was obtained.

The fourth phase of the trial at London – beginning in March and lasting throughout April (1311) – provided no more convincing or incriminating evidence against the Templars than the earlier phases. When re-examination of the Templars, after several months of more rigorous treatment, produced admissions of irregularities on only the most trivial of points, the inquisitors turned to outside witnesses – approximately sixty in number, only six of whom were not ecclesiastics –

most of whose testimony was second or third hand and of little credibility.[73] For example, one priest testified that another priest had told him that a certain Templar had confessed to every single crime now charged against the order. However, both the priest and the Templar concerned, being dead, were unavailable for confirmation or denial. A certain knight affirmed that his grandfather, who had died after becoming a Templar, was believed to have been murdered by his brothers for refusing to take part in heretical practices. And a Franciscan testified that he had been told by a woman, who had been told by a man, who had been told by someone else, that a servant of the latter's acquaintance had been put to death when caught watching the Templars worship an idol. On April 22, 1311, after the present phase of the examination had been completed and the testimony of outside witnesses had been heard, the Bishops of London and Chichester and the papal inquisitors finally offered the Templars eight days to prepare and to present any defense they might desire.[74] The invitation was rejected with the comment that the aid of anyone who could give them competent advice was denied them — the reference being without doubt to the bull of Clement which the Archbishop of Canterbury had had read throughout England back in September, 1308. Instead, at the end of the eight days, William de la More, Master of the Temple in England, joined by other Templars, replied that the Templars believed all the doctrines of the church, denied all heresy and iniquity alleged against them, and called for all except their enemies to come forward to speak of the good conduct and activities of the order.[75]

The subsequent treatment of the Templars is somewhat unclear. Arrests of renegade Templars were pressed anew;[76] stricter confinement was practiced; and the use of torture was again authorized by the king.[77] It must be stressed, however, that there is no evidence to suggest that any Templar in England died from torture as so many had in France. During the fifth and last phase of the examination at London — late June and early July (1311) — three confessions were gained. Stephen de Stappelbrugge, a renegade Templar who had only recently been captured (June 10th), under imprisonment and probably under torture, confessed (June 23d) the truth of many of the charges. Especially, he said there were two initiations: one was good and proper; the other was *"contra fidem"* and involved denying Christ and spitting on the cross.[78] Thomas Tocci de Thoroldsby, another renegade Templar who had just been arrested, confessed initially that the Templars were urged not to confess to priests outside the order. On June 29th, after a lapse of four days during which it is quite probable that torture was used against him, he further admitted that the Templars renounced Christ, spat beside the cross, favored the Moslems over the Christians in the Holy Land, and permitted their lay officials to exercise priestly functions.[79] And on July 1 (1311), John de Stoke, a chaplain of the order and recently treasurer at New Temple, London, after having initially denied all the charges against the order, admitted that the Templars denied Christ and were told that Christ was an imposter. To the other charges and questions, however, he pleaded ignorance.[80] Whether or not torture was applied to him cannot be ascertained. With the testimony of these men, the public examination of the Templars in England was concluded. Although very little specific or convincing evidence had been gained either from the Templars themselves or from the non-Templar witnesses, it was evidently the best and most that could be obtained under existing conditions and was deemed sufficient for present purposes by those in positions of authority.

Hence, the "trial" of the Templars in England had been completed; and the decision of guilt or innocence would normally follow. But, as seen above, the final decision had already been made; and it now remained only for the general council at Vienne, and the local provincial councils in England, to announce the disposition of the Templars and their goods in accordance with papal mandates.

Disposition of Templar Property in England

The question of what should be done with the lands of the Templars in England proved to be a major problem. A considerable amount of confusion and conflict arose both with respect to the establishment of a policy and the practical implementation of it.[81] For present purposes, the problem can be most effectively treated by discussing briefly the three periods through which it passed.

The first period (1308-12) was one of indecision by both pope and king. At one time, Clement argued that their lands should be held in safekeeping for the Templars until a definite decision was reached on their guilt or innocence;[82] at other times, he maintained that the lands should be held for use in the recovery of the Holy Land.[83] Edward initially seems to have expected that he would acquire a goodly portion of the Templar lands for the crown; later, however, he was willing to satisfy himself with the use of the income from the Templar lands and possessions of only a few of the Templar estates.

In January, 1308, at the time of their arrest of the Templars, the king's sheriffs, in accordance with royal mandate, had seized the property of the Templars as well as their persons.[84] As the months passed and the trial of the Templars did not begin, Edward seems to have begun to dispose of the property at will. As early as October 4, 1308,

Clement, concerned over a report that the king had transferred or sold certain Templar properties, wrote to Edward ordering that possession or control of the property should be entrusted to certain prelates and certain other fit and proper persons.[85] In his reply, Edward asserted that he had thus far done nothing improper with the possessions of the order, that he had no intention of doing anything he had no right to do, and that he would deal with the goods in a manner acceptable to God.[86] Clement subsequently (February 25, 1309) advised Edward to transfer the goods to the papal commissioners designated to handle them — the archbishops of Canterbury and York and the bishops of Lincoln and Durham — and urged him to aid the commissioners regain lost goods, but there is no evidence that Edward paid any attention to this order.[87]

Edward soon proceeded to the task of the appraisal and supervision of the Templar wealth. As early as February 10, 1308, he ordered his sheriffs, under whose control the goods had been placed, to learn by inquisition of local juries the extent and value of the Templar possessions.[88] A year later, on March 4, 1309, the treasurer and barons of the exchequer were ordered to have another survey made so as to learn the annual value of the property "in demesnes, services, rent, villenages, and all other issues"[89] and were further directed to commit the properties of the Templars "to faithful men who will answer to the king for the value appraised."[90] This meant — as was gradually done during the rest of the year — that the sheriffs were to be relieved of their control over Templar property and that special keepers were to be appointed instead. Furthermore, by 1310, though the title as such was not officially used, there had emerged a general keeper of all Templar lands — Roger de Wingfield, clerk of the king's wardrobe[91] — whose task it was to supervise the local keepers and to see that accounts were made directly to the king's central officials.[92]

In the meantime, it would appear that certain persons followed the king's lead in taking over various Templar estates — or perhaps they had even anticipated his action. In order to check these seizures, Edward appointed special agents to inquire into the value of the property carried off and ordered the sheriffs to summon juries to get at the truth.[93] Perhaps the fact the public records provide scanty information on this subject means the trend was checked, at least for the time being.

It is possible to trace in considerable detail what Edward did with the Templar properties held in his name. First, he had the revenue of the Templars — including the debts owed to them[94] — paid into the royal treasury or wardrobe for use as he might direct.[95] For example, there are royal orders to the officials of the exchequer to pay out given sums for services rendered,[96] for specified debts,[97] and for bounties due the

Scotch refugees of his recent campaign.[98] What is more, even the grain,[99] timber,[100] and livestock[101] of the Templars were used or sold as the king desired. Second, the king granted Templar lands and revenues to various persons. For example, he dispensed churches, vicarages, prebends, and the like;[102] he gave lands as dowries, as royal favors, and in return for services rendered to him;[103] and he assigned the use of revenue from Templar possessions.[104] Third, without equivocation, Edward paid the Templars the regular allowance authorized for their subsistence both when imprisoned and when confined to monasteries.[105] Fourth, the king recognized lawful claims against the Templars. For example, Templar corrodies and pensions were recognized after their validity had been determined;[106] expenses for necessary repairs of Templar property were allowed;[107] rent owed by the Templars for lands they held of others was paid;[108] and debts to or debts contracted on behalf of the Templars were honored.[109] Moreover, individuals who could produce proper authority for holding former Templar lands were permitted to retain them.[110] Fifth, the king, and other lords as well, under certain circumstances were assigned Templar lands as escheats and were permitted to exact feudal reliefs of their tenants.[111]

Some indication of the amount of money the king received from the Templar property can be given. The careful work done on this problem by Perkins[112] suggests that for the period 1308 to 1313 the king received a net income from Templar goods of £9,256 — £8,840 being derived from England; £390 from Ireland; £25, from Scotland — or an average of £1,542 per year.[113] Using such figures as are available on the total annual income of the crown for these years, based on wardrobe receipts, Perkins estimates that the Templar income constituted approximately four per cent of the total normal annual income.[114] These figures suggest that the Templar possessions provided the king with a considerable amount of money but that this sum was by no means of decisive importance. It must be noted, however, that these figures do not include the movable goods—for which we do not even have probable estimates—possessed by the Templars and used or disposed of by the king.

Not much information is available on either the amount or the value of the Templar movables — i.e., cash, grain, livestock, clothing, household equipment, agricultural implements, armor, weapons, ecclesiastical robes and objects, books, and the like. Not only is complete data missing, but only parts of the inventories which do exist in manuscript form have so far been utilized.[115] The impression one gets, however, is that the Templar movables were far less than the king and his officials had anticipated. For example, instead of great treasures of gold, silver, and jewels at New Temple, London, the royal officers found only ecclesiastical movables worth £121 and other movables worth £68.[116] At some key manorial centers, such as Faxfleet and Foulbridge in Yorkshire, the movables were of greater value, being worth £290 and £254 respectively.[117] Even more surprising is the fact that the total cash seized from all the preceptories in England amounted to only £36.[118] Two possibilities suggest themselves: either some Templars may have escaped with or secretly disposed of the valuables of the order or the Templars did not possess extensive movable property. It is true that a few Templars did escape, but a rigorous search by the king's officials and the inquisitors produced only nine.[119] The one known instance of a Templar bribing his keeper to permit him to escape involved the rather small sum of forty florins.[120] Two cases,[121] the only such known, were concerned with a definite effort on the part of the king to acquire Templar movables allegedly in the hands of private citizens. In the one, a certain man and his wife were ordered by the king to account for twenty-three shillings— a small sum — supposedly left with them by a Templar. In the other, the outcome of which is also unknown, the king demanded that a chest of money, said to contain the rather large sum of one hundred marks sterling and two hundred gold florins, which the Templars had supposedly left in Warwickshire, be produced. Then, there is also the royal order instructing the new sheriff of Gloucester to secure those Templar possessions, including movables, which his predecessor had not yet obtained.[122] It would be unwarranted, on the basis of this information, to argue that any appreciable number of English Templars escaped or that much Templar wealth was successfully sequestered. It is more reasonable to argue that the Templars' movable goods were actually quite limited. Very likely, the Templars in England lived relatively simple and unostentatious lives and sent the greater part of their portable wealth to the Templar headquarters in the Holy Land or in Cyprus.

The second period (1313-24) was concerned with a struggle to see whether or not the Knights Hospitallers were actually going to come into possession of the Templar properties. The position of Clement, as taken at the Council of Vienne, was that with the condemnation of the Templars their goods should be transferred to the Hospitallers. Accordingly, on May 16, 1312, Edward was directed by a papal bull to deliver the property of the Templars in England to the Hospitallers forthwith.[123] This, however, the king was reluctant to do[124] and instead, for over a year, did nothing except to order (August 1st) the Prior of the Hospitallers to cease his efforts to gain control of the Templar possessions until parliament again met.[125] Ultimately, but under protest, Edward did yield, pointing out that he was doing so only from fear of dangers to himself and his realm if he refused,[126] referring probably to his fear of ecclesiastical censures. But at the same time, he insisted that his own rights and those of his subjects should not be prejudiced by any restitution of such lands and goods as might be effected and that he and his subjects should be allowed to sue for their rights in the proper courts. It was not until November 28, 1313, a year and a half after Clement's order, that Edward specifically instructed his keepers to hand over the lands to the Hospitallers.[127] Having transferred the lands concerned, Edward, on February 8, 1314, ordered the Prior of the Hospitallers henceforth to pay out of the revenue of former Templar property in his possession the regular allowance of four pence per day for each Templar placed in a monastery to do penance, except for Himbert Blanke, the ranking Templar in England, who was to receive two shillings per day.[128] Always watching out for his own interests, Edward, before he had ordered the transfer of the Templar lands, had made sure that his keepers, or others involved, had first been instructed to hand over to the king's representatives all the movables (especially the livestock) of value.[129]

With the removal of direct royal control, there appears to have been a scramble for the Templars' lands involving both the lesser and the great lords. Certainly the Hospitallers got some of the property without much difficulty;[130] but lacking most of the records of the Templars, they were hard put to defend their claims and to protect what they did obtain.[131] Even as late as August 1324 and August 1325, the Hospitallers complained of not having received the Templar charters.[132] Matters were further complicated when the great lords—including such men as Thomas of Lancaster, Robert de Holand, John de Mowbray, Guy de Beauchamp, and Aymer de Valence[133]— seized and claimed certain lands as heirs of the original donors or as lords by escheat. These actions on the part of the secular lords were not only tolerated by the king[134] but were practiced by him as well.[135] Meanwhile, Clement attempted without much success to aid the Hospitallers by ordering the king, the nobles, and the clergy to assist the order in gaining possession of their legitimate properties.[136] Edward assumed a rather indifferent attitude, pointing out that he himself had given up the Templar lands and could proceed against his lords only according to the law and custom of his realm.[137] Nor did the clergy as a whole seem very anxious to help despite the papal bulls and the strong efforts of Archbishop Reynolds.[138] Thus the matter dragged on for several years until May 23, 1322, when John XXII, a more determined pope than Clement, ordered the bishops to unite in parliament in order to expel the lay occupants of the Templar estates and to use ecclesiastical censures to enforce the restitution of the lands.[139] After some delay and much discussion, Parliament, on March 26, 1324, finally decreed that no lord had any title or right to Templar lands or appurtenances by escheat or otherwise;[140] however, as a concession to the lay lords involved, the statute recognized the right of individuals to prosecute their claims in the proper courts. In executing this statute, King Edward, on May 16th following, ordered his sheriffs to seize Templar properties in his name so that they could be delivered to the Hospitallers,[141] but with the proviso that all movables on the estates were to be returned to their owners and that the Hospitallers were to pay for the crops already sown.[142] By July 1, 1324, the royal keepers in the different counties had been instructed that they must permit the sheriffs to hand over the land;[143] and some time later, the sheriffs and others concerned were told to deliver Templar charters and records to the Hospitallers as well.[144] Thus, the decision to grant the Templar lands to the Hospitallers had definitely been made, but it still remained to enforce and implement the decision.

The third and last period (1325-38) was concerned with the concerted efforts of the Hospitallers to get actual possession of the lands (and records) guaranteed to them by pope, king, and parliament. In some instances, certain lands were handed over without any apparent difficulty;[145] in other instances, litigation, which had already been resorted to, was continued or pressed anew even though it proved time-consuming and costly.[146] In 1328, Philip de Thame, Prior of the Hospitallers in England, wrote to the Grand Prior of his order that for the current year he had received only £458 from the Templar lands.[147] Ten years later, this income had increased to £1,441 per year[148] — a sum still less than the average income of £1,542 for the years 1308-13 when the Templar property was in the hands of the king.[149] When the king, the great lords, and royal officials still proved reluctant to give up certain Templar lands under their control, the Hospitallers, in their effort to gain actual possession of the larger part of the Templar lands and to win the necessary support of influential persons, began to employ a new and more successful method — a method which might be called bribery. After granting certain former Templar lands and/or revenues, without restrictions and in perpetuity, to the king,[150] to influential lords and officials like Hugh le Despenser and Hugh the Younger,[151] and to lesser, but nonetheless important, people at the royal court,[152] they found it easier to acquire the bulk of the lands they had so long and unsuccessfully sought. They now found that royal orders (1332-33) directing the sheriffs to again take former Templar lands into the king's hands on behalf of the Hospitallers resulted in the prompt delivery of them.[153] Furthermore, in 1335, Edward III, a more determined ruler than his father, explicitly confirmed the parliamentary statute of 1324,[154] thereby giving the Hospitallers both moral and legal support. Within a couple of years — by

1338 specifically — the Hospitallers had obtained at least nominal possession of most of the Templar estates not ceded to the king or such important persons as the Despensers.[155] Though some difficulties remained and some court cases still arose,[156] they were few in number and tended to turn out satisfactorily. By and large, these lands which the Hospitallers had gained were to remain in their possession until the dissolution of religious houses by Henry VIII in the sixteenth century.

In summary, then, it can be said regarding the Templar property in England that, though the king was unable to take over any great part of the lands, he was able to dispose of the movable goods and to use the revenue from the lands for some years. Ultimately, however, the great bulk of the property of the Templars did pass to their rival religious-military order, the Knights Hospitallers.

Elsewhere in Europe, the Templar lands were disposed of in various ways. In Portugal, Aragon, and Castille, where the Hospitallers received none of the lands, they were handed over to other military orders, many of them newly established.[157] In France, Italy, and Germany, the Hospitallers had experiences somewhat similar to those they had in England,[158] finally acquiring part of the former Templar property only after long delay and considerable effort. Especially to be noted is the fact that the Hospitallers in France, as indicated at the end of the first section of this chapter, fared far worse than the Hospitallers in England in their attempts to gain possession of former Templar properties.

Disposition of the English Templars as Individuals

The problem of deciding what should be done with the Templars as individuals proved far less troublesome and time-consuming than the problem of deciding what should be done with their property. At the end of their interrogation in the summer of 1311, the Templars were informed by their inquisitors that if they would publicly admit their inability to clear themselves of the accusations levied against them and would agree to submit to the provincial councils, they would be received back into the church.[159] By the middle of July (1311), after abjuring their alleged errors, most of the prisoners at London were formally received back into the church. The southern provincial council meeting at Canterbury then ruled that the men be assigned singly or in small groups to various monasteries to do penance and directed that payments of money, at the rate of four pence per day for each Templar — to be taken out of the income from the order's properties — be made for their maintenance in these monasteries.[160] Similar arrangements for the abjuration of errors, assignment to monasteries, and payment of expenses were made by the northern provincial council (July 29, 1311) for the prisoners at York.[161] Within a reasonable time, the English Templars were placed in a great number of different monasteries throughout the country where they apparently spent the remainder of their lives and conducted themselves in a humble and proper manner.

Only two Templars still remained imprisoned — Master William de la More and Himbert Blanke, Preceptor of Auvergne — both of whom had refused to abjure errors they said they had never committed.[162] More, broken in health, died in the Tower of London (December 20, 1312) before his case could be referred to the pope and council at Vienne;[163] and references to Blanke, who had been ordered retained in prison pending further instructions,[164] disappear from the records.

In Scotland, where two Templars had been arrested and examined, both denied all the charges except that the master had some power in the matter of absolution.[165] Forty-one outside witnesses, all ecclesiastics, were heard, apparently without providing any significant evidence against the prisoners or their order.[166] In Ireland, where fifteen Templars were arrested, no noteworthy results were obtained despite the fact the prisoners were examined up to three times.[167] As in Scotland, the testimony of outside witnesses, thirty-seven ecclesiastical and four lay, provided no significant evidence of heresy or wrongdoing.[168]

Regarding the trial of the Templars in England, it can be said that the proceedings, procedure, and results were less severe than in France and that the English Templars were treated fairly well during their years of incarceration and examination. Though torture was sanctioned, it was applied sparingly, without enthusiasm, and with little success. The few confessions gained, whether resulting from torture or not, proved contradictory and unreliable in content. On the matter of orthodoxy or unorthodoxy, the only point that can be conceded is that the Templars' practice of confession and absolution, though unclear to the Templars themselves, differed somewhat from the system becoming increasingly common in the west. Even the testimony of outside witnesses — of which there were 157, all but 33 of whom were ecclesiastics[169] — was neither very credible nor very damaging. In general, the Templars in England, as will be shown in the next section of this chapter, had been fairly popular and apparently remained so inasmuch as there is no adequate evidence to show that any noteworthy hostility toward the order developed even during the trial. Though the Templars may well have been guilty of misdeeds of one sort or another, the case presented against them as individuals and as an order must be labeled "not proved."[170] Indeed, much of the evidence cited against them would today be dismissed as unreliable and irrelevant by any legally trained or fair-minded person. The greatest disadvantage, and the most damaging factor against the

Templars, was their penchant for secrecy which made possible so many of the charges raised against them and so many of the tales told about them. It was with telling wisdom, insight, and pathos that Himbert Blanke, Preceptor of Auvergne, when asked by the inquisitors at London why secrecy was maintained if nothing but good was done under its cover, answered "through folly."[171]

To make the record more complete, passing reference to the fate of the Templars elsewhere must be indicated.[172] Though Clement persisted in his insistence on the guilt and condemnation of the order throughout Europe, he was not always successful in getting his desires executed. In Aragon, where the Templars defended themselves with arms, it was two years before they were finally arrested and tried. As in England, the use of torture was, to a degree, resisted by the king and *cortes*. The final decision, as reached by the provincial council of Tarragona (November 4, 1312), was an unqualified acquittal of the order and a recommendation that the Templars should reside in the dioceses where their property lay.[173] In Castille and Portugal, the Templars were arrested with dispatch and secrecy and after a trial, the details of which have been lost, were pronounced innocent by a provincial council at Salamanca. In addition, in Portugal, a new order, which some people claim represents a continuation of the Templar order, was established by the king and approved by the pope.[174] In Italy, in the areas most directly under the control of the pope and of Charles of Anjou, King of Naples and cousin of Philip the Fair, the Templars were arrested, tortured, tried, and convicted; but in other areas, very considerable difficulties were encountered in the attempt to arrest, torture, try, and convict them. In Cyprus, where the outcome of the trial is unknown, no significant evidence against the order was gained despite the use of torture. And finally, in Germany, where the number of Templars was not great and where such Templars as were captured refused to give evidence against the order, two separate trials were held, with the Templars in each instance being in essence found not guilty.

The final decision regarding the fate of the Templar order, as seen above, was actually made by Pope Clement V though it was supposed to have been left to the Council of Vienne. But, when the members of the council hesitated to do as the pope wanted, Clement took it upon himself to abolish the order and to assign its property to the Knights Hospitallers. Similarly, the final decision regarding the fate of the individual Templars, as also seen above, was actually made by the pope though it was supposed to have been left to local provincial councils. But, as few of these councils ever met, it was Pope Clement V and John XXII who ordered all former Templars sent to monasteries.[175]

Popular Attitude Toward the Templars in England

In discussing the downfall of the Templars in England, considerable attention must be given to the matter of their popularity or unpopularity even though evidence on this point is difficult to find and more difficult to evaluate. Yet, such information as is available, much of it of an indirect and of a very minute sort, does provide at least a qualified answer to the question raised. Most of the material to be discussed below will tend to be unfavorable in varying degrees for two reasons: the nature of the available data and the need to determine whether or not this unpopularity was an important factor in bringing about or in hastening the fall of the order. For the sake of simplicity, clarity, and brevity, the criticisms of the Templars will be dealt with in a topical manner.

The secrecy of the order aroused a considerable amount of curiosity, suspicion, and distrust from which the Templars certainly did not profit. It permitted fantastic tales to be circulated about them and gave some of the witnesses at the trial an opportunity to make rash and unsupported statements against them.[176] It may well be, as Perkins says, that their secrecy was the chief cause of their unpopularity[177] — but even if it was not, it was at least a major cause.

The pride of the Templars, which was proverbial, aroused great antagonism and assuredly did not help them in their hour of trouble. The best known reference to this pride is the pointed statement attributed to King Richard I. Though there exist various versions, differing only in minor detail, the gist of the story is this: Richard, on a military campaign in France, was rebuked by a French priest, Fulk de Neuilly by name, for having three daughters who cost him dearly; and he was advised by the priest that it would be to his advantage to rid himself of those daughters because only thus could he expect to find favor with God. When Richard denied having three daughters, Fulk informed him that the daughters he meant were Pride, Luxury, and Avarice. With quick wit and insight — so the story goes — he replied that he would forthwith marry off these daughters. Pride he would marry to the Templars [or Hospitallers] "who are as proud as Lucifer himself;" Luxury, to the Black Monks [or the prelates of the church]; and Avarice, to the White Monks.[178] There are other indications of Templar pride, too. Pope Innocent III, in 1208, sternly denouncing their short-comings, wrote the Templars that their unbridled pride had led them to abuse their enormous privileges.[179] Frederick II, Holy Roman Emperor, writing to Richard of Cornwall (1244), complained that the pride of the Templars was responsible for the defeat of the Christians by the Kharizmians.[180] King Henry III (1252), replying to a complaint of the Hospitallers regarding some injury committed against them, stated that the prelates, and especially the Templars and Hospitallers, had such great revenues that they had become swollen with pride.[181] William of Tyre maintained that in his own day (i.e., in the last half of the twelfth century) the Templars, having abandoned their former humility, had by their actions become obnoxious to everyone.[182] Matthew Paris and Roger of Wendover said essentially the same thing, though in different words.[183] Similarly, Walter Mapes, an out-spoken critic of religious groups alluded disapprovingly to the pride of the Templars.[184] To these references can be added the suggestion of H. C. Lea that the many men of the lower class who were admitted to the order as sergeants, or serving brothers, may have assumed the airs of the knightly class, to which they did not really belong, and may have conducted themselves in a more haughty manner than they should, thereby arousing further hostility.[185]

Insolence, closely akin to pride, was not unknown to the Templars and was manifested in a variety of ways and forms. Royal domain and jurisdiction were infringed upon and violated by the Templars as a bull of Honorius III (1222), in reference to the situation in the French possessions of the English king indicates. In this bull, the Templars are called upon, among other things, to cease doing the following: usurping royal domain by erecting their crosses on houses not belonging to them, preventing customary dues from being paid the crown, disregarding the customs of the king's manors, and involving the king's officials in troublesome law suits.[186] A bull of Innocent III (1208) complained that the Templars, upon receipt of a gift or contribution, were so bold as to bury in their church yards even persons under excommunication.[187] The continuous rivalry between the Templars and the Hospitallers – a rivalry frequently involving outright warfare – led Walter Mapes to attribute the misfortunes of the Christians in the East to the corruption of the military orders[188] and caused Matthew Paris (1259) to assert that the Templars' call for members in Europe to be sent to the Holy Land was designed "to take fearful vengeance upon the Hospitallers by force of arms."[189] Paris, in the same passage, further added that he feared that the peace and stability of Christendom would be destroyed "through their extreme fury." In 1253, the Templars (and Hospitallers) dared to refuse to give Henry III, much to his anger, the money promised to Richard de Clare.[190] And Clement IV (1265), reproaching the Templars for their ingratitude, warned them that only the papacy could sustain them against the hostility of the bishops and princes.[191] How right Clement was, the Templars were later to learn.

The Templars were upon occasion accused of treachery – sometimes with reason and sometimes without. In 1170, Thomas Becket, Archbishop of Canterbury, was warned by a friend not to trust or to take the advice of two Templars in the particular matter before him because of their deceit.[192] Writing in reference to the situation in 1244, Matthew Paris remarked that people were uncertain whether or not to believe reports sent to Europe by the Templars (or Hospitallers) because Christians "always suppose them to conceal some fraud and . . . [to] . . . have some wolfish treacheries under a sheep's clothing."[193] Indeed, he went on to say, had there not been fraud and treachery, the many brave western knights would have successfully routed the infidel in their recent encounters.[194] The same author, in a speech attributed to the Sultan (1246), at a time when the envoys of the Templars and Hospitallers were seeking to procure the release of Christian captives, recorded that the Sultan called the Templars (and Hospitallers) "wretched" *(miseri)* because they sought to betray the emperor, Frederick II; because they rejected the efforts of Richard of Cornwall, brother of the English king, to bring peace between the two orders; and because they broke the peace made by the same Richard.[195] In a speech of the Count of Artois (1250), reported also by Paris, the Count, when advised by the Templars to let the soldiers rest and then to proceed only with caution in the attack on Mansourah — good advice as events turned out — made a bitter attack saying:

> See the ancient treachery of the Templars! the long-known sedition of the Hospitallers. . . . This is what we were told long ago; and truly has the augury been fulfilled; the whole country of the East would long ago have been gained, had not we seculars been impeded by the deceit of the Templars, Hospitallers, and others calling themselves religious men. See, the chance of capturing the sultan is open to us, and the ruin of all paganism is imminent, as well as the lasting exaltation of the Christian faith, all of which this Templar, who is here present, endeavors to impede by his fictitious and fallacious arguments. For the Templars and Hospitallers, and their associates, fear that, if the country is reduced to submission to the Christian power, their domination, who fatten on its rich revenues, will expire. Hence it is that they poison, in divers ways, the Christians who come hither girt for the cause of the cross, and, confederating with the Saracens, put them to death by various means. Is not Frederick, who has had experience of their treachery, a most certain witness in this matter?[196]

And again, according to Matthew Paris, Richard of Cornwall (1241) would not commit Ascalon to the Templars, nor would he entrust to them money left behind for the completion of a castle, because of their quarrels with and attacks on other Christians.[197]

As the record occasionally indicates and as reason suggests, certain of the economic exemptions of the Templars aroused resentment and hostility. Being exempted from royal tolls, and sometimes from local tolls as well,[198] the Templars must have been hated and opposed upon occasion by those merchants whom they could undersell at the different markets and fairs, if they so chose. The Templars' exemption, in varying degrees, from certain types of taxes also provided grounds for resentment.[199] For example, the king had granted the Templars (and Hospitallers) exemption from tallage for one man per city, a privilege which with time had been extended, apparently without specific authorization, to additional persons. The dissatisfaction of the townsmen at this extension can be seen, at least in the city of Bristol, in a quarrel, continuing in an off-and-on manner from the reign of John into the reign of Edward I, which arose between the two groups because the townsmen wanted the Templars to pay their "fair share" of the tallage due the king.[200] The fact the Templars were generally exempted from a variety of fees, fines, aids, services, and the like, associated with the land[201] must also have aroused a considerable amount of envy and hatred even though not expressed in such manner as to leave a record of the details either in judicial proceedings or in popular literature.

Various of the judicial privileges accorded the Templars, especially those tending to increase the order's power and independence, aroused antagonism in men of importance, both lay and clerical. The keystone of Templar judicial privileges was the one stating that members of the order could be impleaded only before the king or his chief justice.[202] By using this privilege to their own advantage, the Templars were able to postpone trials and to exhaust their opponents both in time and money as a case which arose in Ireland well illustrates. There the Abbot of St. Mary's monastery in Dunbrody, after having begun (1278) a suit against the Master of the Temple in Ireland over the ownership of seven carucates of land, found himself faced with one delay after another, arising apparently from the Master's claim that he could be impleaded only before the king or his chief justice. Finally, in 1291, after over twelve years of arguing in the courts and after the Abbot had petitioned Parliament for redress, pleading poverty from the extended legal proceedings, a settlement was reached according to which the Master of the Temple was to give the Abbot one hundred marks in return for the latter's acknowledgment of Templar ownership of the land.[203] Hundredors of various counties repeatedly made complaints against the Templar judicial privileges and their misuse. Specifically, they complained that the Templars hindered justice by forbidding their tenants to appear before any but Templar courts,[204] prevented the arrest of persons guilty of crime by receiving them on their property,[205] oppressed people under their jurisdiction by imposing excessive fines or by summoning them to London,[206] and unjustly and without warrant assumed rights of court.[207] Even the crown came face to face with Templar usurpation of rights of court from time to time. For example, Henry II, on one occasion, deemed it necessary to fine a royal servant for going before a Templar court and not before a royal court;[208] and Edward I was especially active in an attempt to check private jurisdiction, including that of the Templars, exercised at the expense of the crown.[209]

The wealth of the Templars did not add to their popularity. Though the extent of this wealth, at least in England, was grossly exaggerated,[210] it was, nonetheless, great enough and sufficiently believed in to have some adverse effect. Both William of Tyre[211] and Matthew Paris[212] put great stress on this wealth, as also did Walter Mapes.[213] It was common knowledge — and it was certainly true, as seen in the two preceding chapters — that the Templars possessed numerous estates, both large and small; that they received a considerable revenue from rent, fees, and services associated with their lands; that they had a goodly income from grain, wool, and the like; that they acquired large sums of money or other valuables yearly as gifts and tithes; and that they profited handsomely from their banking activities. Though it is reasonable to assume that their wealth aroused envy and hatred, yet direct and positive evidence to this effect is hard to find. Rather, it was avarice or greed, which is so closely related to wealth, that evoked open and bitter antagonism and criticism.

Though the charges were often of a general and undocumented nature, the Templars were repeatedly accused of unbounded avarice. Jacques de Vitry wrote, "You profess to have no individual property, but in common you wish to have everything."[214] William of Tyre, in one passage, accused the Templars of delivering Naziredden, a captured Moslem leader, to his enemies for 60,000 pieces of gold though he was on the point of becoming a Christian.[215] Matthew Paris charged that the Templars prolonged the war with the Saracens merely to have a pretext for raising more money.[216] And the well known incident of the Templar purchase of Cyprus (1191) from Richard I for 25,000 silver marks and the sale of it the next year to Guy de Lusignan for the same price after the order had flagrantly misruled the island and exacted excessive taxes[217] was cited as proof of their greed. In addition, the Templars were accused of practicing usury as a means of further satisfying their avarice. So, for example, during their trial, a certain John de Lyndeseye, Rector of the Church of Ratbon in Scotland, swore that he knew the Templars were usurers;[218] and a certain William de Brasl, a witness in Ireland, gave similar testimony.[219]

The best and most concrete illustration of Templar avarice, of which only a few of the many instances need be mentioned here, was their great hunger for land. It is not always easy, however, to distinguish between a voluntary grant to the Templars — of which there must have been thousands — and Templar seizure or covetousness. The repetition of the charges that the Templars illegally seized certain lands and made improper claims to other lands — even seizure of royal lands without warrant are referred to[220]—suggests that the Templars did not always cease their practice despite the complaints and accusations. Nor did Edward I's Statute of Mortmain (1279), designed to limit or prohibit further alienation of land to clerical groups, prevent the Templars from continuing to acquire land, sometimes by special royal authorization of grants in mortmain[221] and sometimes through grants by corrodaries and pensionaries.[222] A Hospitaller charter of 1354 from Hawkerstown, Scotland, referring to an incident of the thirteenth century, well illustrates this hunger for land.[223] On the death of a certain man, who had allegedly conveyed the patrimony of his wife to the Templars for his own lifetime in return for maintenance by them, the Templars claimed the land as theirs. When the deceased man's wife challenged the claim and took the matter to court, where the decision was rendered in her favor, she was twice forcibly removed by the Templars. Finally, when her son later sought to regain the land, the Templars were said to have had him murdered. If this story is true — and Edwards in his article accepts it as true[224]— or if people then accepted it, or other similar stories, as true, then there is good reason to assume that definite hostility to the Templars arose on the grounds of avarice. The statement of a certain Adam of Wedale, a Scottish monk, at the trial of the Templars in Scotland, provides further information on Templar land hunger in the part which reads:

> This order is defamed in manifold ways by unjust acquisitions, for it seeks to appropriate the goods and property of its neighbors justly and unjustly with equal indifference, and does not cultivate hospitality except towards the rich and powerful, for fear of dispersing its possessions in alms.[225]

Also at the Templars' trial, John de Lyberton, a priest, testified that he had heard another priest, Walter de Alberton, who had been in the service of the order for seven years, say that the Templars were avaricious to acquire property for their order.[226] The same idea is brought out by Walter Mapes, who, speaking in general about the greed of the Templars (and Hospitallers), accused them of viciously exploiting the poor and humble by convincing them to hand over their lands to the military orders.[227] It is not surprising, then, to find the Templars' greed for land as one of the charges listed against the order by Pope Clement.[228]

Associated with this land hunger was a steady increase in the number of Templar tenants, an increase which was due not only to the aggressiveness of the Templars themselves but also to the desire of individual persons wanting to profit from the attractive privileges and exemptions which might be theirs as Templar tenants. As in the case of the excessive alienation of land by mortmain, so in this instance, the practice had become so widespread and of so serious a nature that kings like Henry III and Edward I found it necessary to issue special royal orders limiting the number of persons who might qualify as Templar tenants.[229]

The extensive religious privileges and the large degree of independence granted to the Templars by the popes, which have been discussed in Chapter I above, served to arouse the rivalry and enmity of other clerics and religious groups, both secular and regular. One need only recall that the Templars were exempted from the jurisdiction of the local clergy — being in effect subordinate to the pope alone — were immune to ordinary excommunication, were excused from paying most clerical taxes and other levies, and were given the right to collect regular and special contributions throughout Christendom. The bitterness and envy these and other privileges elicited from the clergy are clearly reflected in the testimony, only a small portion of which has been cited earlier in this chapter, of hostile ecclesiastics at the Templars' trial.

Lastly, there were many minor complaints and criticisms raised against the Templars. For example, they were charged with obstructing water courses or roads, of raising walls, and of enclosing common lands to their own advantage,[230] but it would be difficult to determine whether or not such annoyances as these appreciably contributed to the unpopularity of the Templars.

Having thus far presented the adverse criticism, one must now briefly discuss the evidence favorable to the Templars. That this evidence is limited and often indirect is not unexpected inasmuch as historical records are frequently less complete and informative about the good that is done than about the bad. This is especially true in the case of the Templars because they had no contemporary apologists or known writers of their own, because their opponents — led by Clement V — did a remarkable job of silencing those who might have worked or spoken on their behalf, and because even their organizational records have largely disappeared.

The fame, valor, success, and good repute of the Templars as soldiers and leaders on the field of battle — which were briefly referred to in Chapter I above — are too familiar to need recital or documentation here. It should perhaps be pointed out, however, that many of the writers who severely criticized the Templars upon occasion were generous in their praise of them at other times, as can be observed in the works of Jacques de Vitry, William of Tyre, Walter Mapes, and Matthew Paris.[231] A favorable attitude toward the Templars is certainly attested by the numerous and repeated grants of property, privileges, exemptions, and the like, which were freely made to the order by private citizens, clerical persons, public officials, great lords, and kings over the long period of its existence. Furthermore, the difficult time the papal inquisitors faced in their concerted efforts to find witnesses against the Templars suggests that public hostility was anything but widespread. What is more, as has already been noted, the evidence given by the 157 witnesses against the English Templars, of whom 124 were clerics and only 33 were laymen,[232] was either not very damaging or was of doubtful quality and reliability. A careful search through a goodly amount of the popular literature of the period reveals little, if any, material pertinent or helpful to a solution of the problem of popularity or unpopularity.[233] In an indirect and negative sense, this would seem to mean that though the Templars were not popular heroes they were also not the subject of popular ridicule or hatred. Generally speaking, it seems safe to say that the actions of the kings — about which we have the most information — and other Englishmen indicate not only royal favor and good opinion of the Templars but public approval and esteem as well. To be specific, Edward I (May 13, 1304), writing to Jacques de Molay, Grand Master of the Templars, praised William de la More, Master of the Temple in England, for his "great and laudable services" to the crown and called upon the Grand Master to treat William well and to send him back to England with all speed.[234] Later, in 1307, as seen above, Edward II, who had just succeeded to the throne, initially rejected the charges levied against the Templars by the French king and wrote letters on their behalf to the pope and to certain of his fellow monarchs. It was this same Edward who permitted William de la More, and apparently other Templars as well, to be set free on parole after their initial arrest and imprisonment.[235] All this suggests the Templars were not deemed the evil men the charges asserted them to be but rather were held in high esteem by both the king and his subjects right up to the very moment of their downfall.

To many a reader of Sir Walter Scott's *Ivanhoe*, the Templars were men of unusual arrogance, ambition, hypocrisy, worldliness, and luxury. This characterization, however, is based more on fiction than on fact. In Brian de Bois-Guilbert, a not too typical Templar, is to be seen an exaggeration of those human strengths and weaknesses which are dearer to the heart of a novelist than of a historian. If anything, the picture of Beaumanoir, the aged and proud Grand Master, is closer to the truth than that of Brian, the preceptor and candidate for the Master's chair.

The information which has just been cited and the fact that the Templar order was composed of human beings suggest that the Templars were neither all good nor all bad. Without question, there were adequate grounds for friction and animosity between the Templars and other groups in society because of their extensive privileges, which they did upon occasion abuse or take improper advantage of, and because of their many aggressive and selfish acts. These things most certainly did them no good. However, the privileges which they enjoyed and the questionable actions which they engaged in — political, economic, or religious — were far from unique inasmuch as many other religious groups and many lay lords had received similar ones and had done, or sought to do, the same things. Indeed, the complaints levied against the Templars can be, and were, levied equally well against others.[236] Hence, in most cases the Templars as such were not being exclusively singled out for criticism or reprimand. So, for example, when kings or popes proceeded against the Templars, it was often as one of a number of persons or groups. Furthermore, every instance of censure or criticism can be balanced many times over by instances of praise and commendation.

In England, there is no adequate evidence to suggest any sudden or marked increase in grievances against the Templars or any sudden or marked change in the popular attitude toward the Templars in the years just before the trial. Nor is there any indication, even during the trial, of an effective or of a noticeable campaign against the Templars among the laity. Rather, there is evidence of some popular support. The leniency of the king, his sheriffs, and the keepers of the Templars toward the arrested and accused prisoners suggests a considerable degree of sympathy rather than hostility. As the trial revealed, the most bitter and open critics of the Templars were the clerics, many of whom considered the Templars their chief rivals and all of whom had been as a unit committed by Pope Clement to the guilt and destruction of the order.[237] But even so, the leniency and consideration shown by such important clerics as the Archbishop of York suggest that the Templars' judges were not wholly convinced of the guilt of the order. Indeed, when the exaggeration and bias of their critics, especially the clerical, is compensated for, the Templars appear no worse than many other groups which, though sharing many of the same actual and alleged grievances, did not share the same fate. Finally, the hesitation, secrecy, and delay in the trial of the Templars and the propagandistic efforts undertaken during the period of imprisonment and trial, limited as they were in England, suggest that uncertainty about popular opinion necessitated great caution and care by the public officials and clerics involved. Hence, it would be unwarranted to say that the opinion of the British laity —

and for that matter, of the royal officials or the entire clergy in England as well — was in any significant manner unfavorable to the Templars or that their attitude had much actual effect in determining the ultimate fate of the Templars.

chapter five

Conclusion

Summary and Evaluation

The origin and purpose of the Templars were essentially military. To a considerable degree, as its long record of leadership and achievement both during and between the Crusades attests, the order remained military from its humble beginnings in 1118 to its dramatic dissolution between the years 1307 and 1312. Indeed, not realizing that the fall of Acre had ended the Crusades as a major project, the Templars were still anxious to continue the struggle against the infidel; and Jacques de Molay, the last Grand Master, when summoned to appear before Pope Clement V at Poitiers, presented him with a plan for a new campaign.[1] Yet, during the two centuries of their existence, the Templars had also become very much involved in political and economic activities — as can well be seen in the history of the order in England. These other activities, though less glamorous and exciting, were certainly equally as important as their military exploits.

The Templars first appeared in England toward the end of the reign of Henry I, but it was not until the years of civil strife following his death that they made much headway. Then, from the accession of Henry II to the reign of Edward I, they grew rapidly in power, wealth, and influence. Though initially possessing lands in southeast and south-central England, the Templars came to have their largest, most numerous, and richest holdings in the northern counties of Lincoln and York, which were then, so to speak, frontier regions. There, together with other religious groups, they joined in clearing waste areas and converting them into fields and pastures for the profitable production of grain and the grazing of cattle and sheep. The concentration of Templar estates in the north is probably due to the fact that so many areas in the rest of England had already been taken by other religious orders — for example, the Benedictines, Cluniacs, Augustinians, and Cistercians — who had established themselves in England earlier than the Templars and whose holdings were so extensive that they often made those of the Templars seem small by comparison.[2] The scattered lands of the Templars were grouped together for purposes of administration and supervision into preceptories, approximately forty in number, over one-third of which were in the two counties just mentioned. The headquarters of the order, however, were at New Temple in London where the Master of the Temple in England usually resided.

Besides agriculture, which was practiced throughout England and was their major economic concern, the Templars engaged in trade and commerce and in financial operations. Wool, and to a lesser degree, grain, sent to Flanders and France, were the chief exports; and wine from southern France was the chief import. More important than trade and commerce, but less important than agriculture, were the numerous financial activities of the Templars. The exchange of money, the acceptance of cash and valuables for deposit, the transfer of funds, the issuance and use of credit and credit instruments, the execution of trusts, and the grant of loans were systematically and widely engaged in. Indeed, until superseded by the Italian merchants in the last half of the thirteenth century, the Templars were the foremost bankers of western Europe. In England, their chief clients were the kings: Henry II, Richard I, John, Henry III, and Edward I. They had other clients, too, but not much is known about them.

The close relationship of the Templars to the English crown is also to be seen in the grant of privileges to them and in their use as officials and advisers to the kings in matters political and administrative as well as economic. To their religious privileges of exemption from ecclesiastical taxation of all kinds and independence from all ecclesiastical authority save that of the pope, must be added their political privileges — granted to them and repeatedly confirmed by all the kings from Stephan to Edward I — of exemption from secular taxation and ordinary feudal burdens and of jurisdiction over their own lands and persons and over those of their vassals and tenants as well. These privileges made the Templars independent of local ecclesiastical and lay authorities and responsible essentially only to the pope and the king. The kings found the Templars reliable and effective as envoys and advisers and as collectors and keepers of royal revenues; they found them a desirable group to whom to turn in time of financial need; and they found New Temple a convenient and secure treasury for royal funds.

The zenith of Templar power and influence in England came under Henry III, a weak, vacillating, improvident, and pious ruler. Under him, their privileges were more fully maintained than under the other kings; and their influence as royal advisers and their use as royal officials reached their greatest extent. To him they lent more money than to any other monarch; and under him, New Temple and its treasurers were for a time a part of the royal administration. Yet, during the last two decades of Henry's reign and after the mastership of Roscelin de Fos (d. 1253), the power and influence of the Templars in English affairs began to decline. This decline is especially noticeable under Edward I who, instead of turning to the Templars for aid and advice, turned increasingly to the Italian merchants for money and to his own officials for political and administrative service.

The power, influence, and independence of the Templars in England has been greatly exaggerated. Their limited numbers — fewer than one hundred and fifty at the time of their dissolution — their repeated appeals to the king and the pope for maintenance of their privileges, and their reliance upon the crown for support, made it impossible for them to exercise any large degree of independence. They may have been more powerful and influential than their size, actions, and resources warranted; but they were at no time a real threat to the church or state. They did arouse antagonism and hatred among their rivals, the secular and regular clergy and some lay lords; but among the population as a whole, there is no adequate evidence to suggest any widespread or continued unpopularity.

The arrest and trial of the Templars were conducted under questionable conditions. Indeed, many of the charges against them were incredible and obviously suspect; and those who acted as their jailers and judges were not always convinced of their guilt. In England, this doubt on the part of the king, certain of their interrogators, and many members of the church councils which considered their fate is especially apparent. The major charge against them was heresy; but as one historian has said, this was not one of their sins — they were warriors not theologians.[3] They were used and misused by Philip IV of France and by Pope Clement V whose decisions and actions were based not on a careful and impartial examination of the charges and evidence but upon a verdict of guilty which had been determined in advance. In England, where torture was used only sparingly and where none of their members was killed, the Templars fared better than in France though they were nonetheless officially considered guilty. Their lands were initially handed over to the king who succeeded in retaining some of them; but most of them ultimately, after a long struggle, were transferred to the Knights Hospitallers. Their portable wealth, which was never fully accounted for, presumably fell into the hands of the king. And the Templars themselves were assigned to do penance in many different monasteries, only a few being sent to any one house.

The Templars, except for their military character and aristocratic stamp, had much in common with other religious groups and like them

formed a bridge between the ideal and the real and serve as an object
lesson for the moralist. Beginning as a poor and humble group seeking
to serve and defend God and their fellow Christians, they remained
wholly loyal to their ideals only briefly. With success came honor, pres-
tige, wealth, privilege, and power. Their original humility and poverty
were readily forgotten or ignored, and matters other than defense of
God and their fellow Christians received increasing attention. In England, these other activities — political, administrative, and economic —
seem to have become their primary concern. This is not to say that the
English Templars did not devote themselves to the defense of the Holy
Land. They did concern themselves with the Holy Land as their collections of money and recruitment of members suggest. It is only to say
that on the basis of surviving evidence the Templars seem to have been
less concerned with their crusading activities than with their non-military
activities. Quite possibly, many of their contemporaries had a similar
impression.

When all is said and done, the Templars contributed much to western civilization as their participation and leadership in the Crusades and
their services — political, administrative, and financial — to the kings of
England, and to the rulers of other states, indicate. Though they were far
from perfect and certainly deserved censure as well as praise, their fate
was undeserved. It seems safe to say that they were the victims of forces
and circumstances more powerful than themselves. They were also, in
part, the victims of that remarkably effective and formidable institution
known as the Inquisition. In short, for certain leaders, political and
religious, and for certain purposes, likewise political and religious, the
Templars were expendable.

The Question of the Continued Existence of the Templars

To the inevitable question of whether or not the Templars continued to exist as an organization, no final answer can be given. There
are three modern theories on this subject: the first, that the Templar
order was disbanded and did not survive in any sense; the second, that
the Templars survived in Portugal as members of a new organization,
the Order of Jesus Christ, created by King Dionysius; and the third,
that the Templars continued to exist via the Order of Freemasonry.

This is not the place for a detailed discussion of this problem, nor
even for an indication of the many difficulties involved. For present purposes, it is only necessary to state that there is much to be said for the
first and second views, and little for the third. In a sense the papal bull
of dissolution did indeed put an end to the Order of the Knights of the

Temple. But at the same time, there are documents to suggest that in Portugal the Templars did not suffer the fate of their brethren elsewhere and that their lands and possessions were transferred to the new order which was approved in 1319 by Pope John XXII.[4] Apparently former Templars joined this order, but whether or not it was with papal approval is unclear. The association of Freemasonry with the Knights Templars, however, is a different matter. It is claimed that Jacques de Molay, before his death, appointed John Mark Lamernius his successor as Grand Master, and that from that date to the present, the office has never been vacant.[5] Just what happened to the Templars under Lamernius and his successors between the death of de Molay in the early fourteenth century and the uncontroverted existence of Freemasons in the seventeenth century would seem to be a mystery. The few documents which have been presented as proof of the continued existence of the Templars via Freemasonry are, to put it mildly, of doubtful authenticity. A letter by an unnamed writer, quoted in Addison, illustrates the uncritical use of questionable material. This writer refers to a dubious work of a Frenchman writing in the middle of the nineteenth century as proving that the earliest freemason's lodge was probably founded by some recreant and seceding British Templars and that all lodges in the world are offshoots of that early one.[6] Until more convincing evidence is presented, this sort of material can hardly pass for serious history. Much more realistic in their approach to the historical problem of the early origins of Freemasonry are Knoop and Jones who, in their sober and carefully presented study of Freemasonry from its beginnings to 1730, do not even mention the claim that Freemasonry was descended from the Knights Templars of the Middle Ages.[7]

Appendices

Appendix A

A List of the Masters of the Temple in England

Name	Date	Name	Date
Hugh of Argentein	*ca.* 1140	Amadeus de Morestello	1259-60
Otto (Osto)	*ca.* 1150	Ambesard	1264
Richard de Hastings	1155-64	Himbert Peraut	1271
Geoffrey Fitz-Stephen	1180-85	Guy de Foresta	1273-74, 1291-94
William Newham	?	Robert de Turvill	1276-90
Aymeric de St. Maur	1200-18	Jacques de Molay	1295
Alan Martel	1218-28	Brian de Jay	1296-98
Robert de Sanford	1229-48	William de la More	1298-1312
Roscelin de Fos	1251-53		

A complete list of the Masters of the Temple in England cannot be drawn up because of lack of evidence. Nor can complete accuracy in the dates of their mastership be attained. The list here includes those men for whom there is definite evidence in the source materials of the period and several men — Hugh of Argentein, Otto, and William Newham — for whom Miss Lees (pp. xliii, xlviii, lix) gives reasonable proof. For other lists, see Addison, *op. cit.,* pp. 457-58 and Williamson, *op. cit.,* p. 671. Cf. also references in the Register of Bishop Sutton, *op. cit.,* pp. 22, 46, 58, 75-77, 89, 91, 105, 110, 137, 147, 173-74, 177, 188-89, and 203.

Appendix B

A List of the Preceptories of the Templars in England

Berkshire
Temple Bistlesham
Buckinghamshire
Bulstrode
Cambridgeshire
Denney
Duxford
Great Wilberham
Essex
Temple Cressing
Gloucestershire
Temple Guiting
Hampshire
Baddesley
Hertfordshire
Garewy
Upleden [or Bosbury]
Herefordshire
Temple Dinsley
Kent
Temple Ewell
Leicestershire
Rothley
Lincolnshire
Aslackby
Eagle
(Mere)
South Witham

Temple Bruer
Willoughton
Middlesex and London
New Temple, London
Oxfordshire
Sandford
Temple Cowley
Shropshire
(Halston)
Somerset
Temple Combe
Sussex
(Saddelscomb)
Shipley
Warwickshire
Balsall
Wiltshire
(Temple Rockley)
Yorkshire
Copmanthorp
Faxfleet
Foulbridge
Penhill
Ribston and Wetherby
Temple Cowton
Temple Hirst
Temple Newsam
Westerdale
Whitley

This list is drawn up on the basis of information presented in Chapter Two. The centers within parentheses are those for which the evidence is not conclusive.

Appendix C

A List of the Templar Treasurers at New Temple, London

Name	Date	Name	Date
Simon of the Temple	1214-24	Warin	1273-76
Hugh of Stocton	1229-42	William	1288
Robert of Sicklinghall	1239-60	Richard of Feltham	1294
Ralph of Brimsgrave	1259-60	John of Stoke	1308

This list is taken from the article by Miss Sandys ("Financial and Administrative Importance of the London Temple," *op. cit.*, pp. 161-162) in which she has collected the source references from each treasurer. The dates are those in which they are known to have held office.

Appendix D

A List of Markets and Fairs Granted to the English Templars

Baldock (Hertfordshire). A weekly market on Wednesday and an annual fair of four days[1] — later changed to three[2] — on the vigil, feast, morrow, and following day of St. Matthew the Apostle (September 20-23).[3]

Balsall (Warwickshire). A weekly market on Sunday[4] — later changed to Thursday[5] — and two annual fairs;[6] one on the vigil, feast, and morrow of St. George the Martyr (April 22-24); and the other on the vigil, feast, and morrow of St. Matthew the Apostle (September 20-22).

Bruer (Lincolnshire). A weekly market on Thursday — later changed to Wednesday[7] — and an annual fair on the vigil, feast, and morrow of St. James the Apostle (July 24-26).[8]

Gaddesby (Leicestershire). A weekly market on Wednesday and an annual fair on the vigil, feast, and morrow of St. Barnabas (June 10-12).[9]

Kirkeby (Lincolnshire). A weekly market on Tuesday and an annual fair on the eve, feast, and morrow of St. Jacob (July 24-26).[10]

Newburgh (Yorkshire). A weekly market on Wednesday.[11]

Rothley (Leicestershire). A weekly market on Monday and an annual fair on the vigil, feast, and morrow of St. Barnabas (June 10-12).[12] Both the market and the fair were discontinued in 1306.[13]

Southcave (Yorkshire). A weekly market on Monday and an annual fair on the vigil, feast, morrow, and following day of the Holy Trinity (June 2-5).[14]

Walnesford (Essex.) A weekly market on Sunday[15] — changed to Tuesday or Thursday in 1227[16] — and an annual fair on the vigil, feast, and morrow of the Decollation of St. John the Baptist (August 28-30).[17] Both the market and the fair were discontinued in 1240.[18]

Werriby (Essex). A weekly market on Thursday and an annual fair on the vigil, feast, and morrow of the birth of St. John the Baptist (June 23-25).[19]

Wetherby (Yorkshire). A weekly market on Sunday and an annual fair on the vigil, feast, and morrow of St. Jacob (July 24-26).[20]

Witham (Essex). A weekly market on Sunday[21] – later changed to Tuesday.[22]

Wyham (Lincolnshire). A market.[23]

---

[1] Granted by Stephen, *ca.* 1153-54: Lees, p. 152. Confirmed by John: *Rotuli Cartarum*, 1 John (1199), part II, m. 3 – cited in *VCH: Hertfordshire*, III, 68; also confirmed by Henry III: *CChR*, 11 Hen. III (1227), p. 5. Cf. Dugdale, VII, 838.

[2] Cf. *CPatR*, 6 Ed. II (1312), pp. 536, 537.

[3] The calendar dates given in this appendix are derived from information found in the *Handbook of British Chronology*, ed. F. M. Powicke (London, 1939).

[4] Granted by Henry III, probably in his first year (1216-17): Dugdale, VII, 838.

[5] Cf. *CChR*, 52 Hen. III (1268), p. 112.

[6] Granted by Henry III, probably in his first year (1216-17): Dugdale, VII, 838. Cf. *CChR*, 52 Hen. III (1268), p. 112.

[7] *Ibid.*, 43 Hen. III (1259), p. 19.

[8] Originally granted by Henry II but not used by the Templars till 1259: *ibid.*

[9] This grant, made in 1306, was to replace the market and fair at Rothley, in the same county, which was discontinued: *ibid.*, 34 Ed. I (1306), p. 71; *Rot. Parl.*, I, 182a.

[10] Granted by Henry III, probably in his first year (1216-17): Dugdale, VII, 838.

[11] *Ibid.*

[12] Granted by Edward I in 1284: *CChR*, 12 Ed. I (1284), p. 276; Dugdale, VII, 839.

[13] *CChR*, 34 Ed. I (1306), p. 71.

[14] Granted by Edward I in 1291: *ibid.*, 19 Ed. I (1291), p. 404; Dugdale, VII, 839.

[15] Granted by Henry III, probably in his first year (1216-17): *ibid.*, 838. This is a reinstatement of a grant made by John: *Rotuli Cartarum*, p. 188 – cf. *CChR*, 11 Hen. III (1227), p. 5, 22.

[16] *Ibid.*

[17] See above, n. 15. A fourth day was apparently added at a later date – cf. *ClR*, 25 Hen. III (1240), p. 250.

[18] *CChR*, 25 Hen. III (1240), p. 255; *ClR*, 25 Hen. III (1240), p. 250.

[19] This grant, made in 1240, was to serve as a replacement for the market and fair at Walnesford, in the same county, which was discontinued: *CChR*, 25 Hen. III (1240), p. 255; *ClR*, 25 Hen. III (1240), p. 250.

[20] Granted by Henry III, probably in his first year (1216-17): Dugdale, VII, 838.

[21] Granted by Stephen and confirmed by John: Cf. *CClR*, 11 Hen. III (1227), p. 8; *CChR*, 11 Hen. III (1227), pp. 5, 8.

[22] James L. Cate, "The Church and Market Reform in England during the Reign of Henry III," *Medieval and Historiographical Essays in Honor of James Westfall Thompson*, ed. James L. Cate and Eugene N. Anderson (Chicago, [1938]), p. 60; *VCH: Essex*, II, 177.

[23] This market is known only through a royal pardon of a sum exacted by the officials of the Exchequer in 1293: *CClR*, 21 Ed. I (1293), p. 288.

Notes to Chapters

Footnotes

Abbreviations

Bain	Bain (ed.), *Calendar of Documents relating to Scotland*
Bliss	Bliss (ed.), *Calendar of Entries in the Papal Registers relating to Great Britain and Ireland*
CChanWar	*Calendar of Chancery Warrants*
(C)ChR	*(Calendar of) Charter Rolls*
(C)ClR	*(Calendar of) Close Rolls*
(C)LibR	*(Calendar of) Liberate Rolls*
(C)PatR	*(Calendar of) Patent Rolls*
CRR	*Curia Regis Rolls*
Dugdale	Dugdale, *Monasticon Anglicanum*
DuPuy	DuPuy, *Histoire de l'ordre militaire des Templiers*
Hosp. Rpt.	Larking (ed.), *The Knights Hospitallers in England: . . . the Report of Prior Philip de Thame*
Jaffé, RP	Jaffé and Wattenbach (eds.), *Regesta Pontificum Romanorum*
Lees	Lees (ed.), *The Inquest of 1185*
Pat. Lat.	Migne (ed.), *Patrologiae . . . Latina*
Pipe R	*Ripe Roll*
Quo. War.	*Placita de Quo Warranto*
Règle	Curzon (ed.), *Le Règle du Temple*
Rot. Hund.	*Rotuli Hundredorum*
Rot. Parl.	*Rotuli Parliamentorum*
RLC	*Rotuli Litterarum Clausarum*
RLP	*Rotuli Litterarum Patentium*
RS	Rolls Series: *Rerum Britannicarum medii aevi scriptores*
Rymer	Rymer and Sanderson (eds.), *Foedera, Conventiones, Litterae et . . . Acta Publica*
VCH	*The Victoria History of the Counties of England*
Wilkins	Wilkins (ed.), *Concilia Magnae Britanniae et Hiberniae*

Preface

[1] *Records of the Templars in England in the Twelfth Century: the Inquest of 1185, with illustrative Charters and Documents,* "Records of the Social and Economic History of England and Wales," Vol. IX (London, 1935).

[2] "The History of the Knights Templars in England" (unpublished Ph.D. dissertation, Department of History, Harvard University, 1908).

[3] *The History of the Temple, London, from the Institution of the Order of the Knights of the Temple to the Close of the Stuart Period* (London, 1924), chaps. I-IV.

Chapter One

[1] Among the general histories of the Templars are the following: C. G. Addison, *The Knights Templars* (American ed.; New York, 1874); G. A. Campbell, *The Knights Templars, their Rise and Fall* (London, 1937); Pierre DuPuy, *Histoire de l'Ordre militaire des Templiers, ou Chevaliers du Temple de Jérusalem, depuis son Etablissement jusqu'à sa Decadence et sa Suppression* (Brussels, 1751); Hans Prutz, *Entwicklung und Untergang des Tempelherrenordens* (Berlin, 1888) and *Die geistlichen Ritterorden: ihre Stellung zur kirchlichen, politischen, gesellschaftlichen, und wirtschaftlichen Entwicklung des Mittelalters*

(Berlin, 1908); Amand Rastoul, *Les Templiers, 1118-1312* (4th ed.; Paris, 1908); and Edith Simon, *The Piebald Standard, A Biography of the Knights Templars* (Boston, 1959).

The most complete work in English is that of Addison. The best brief but thorough study of the Templars is Prutz' *Entwicklung*. DuPuy's work is a collection of valuable documents preceded by a general historical essay on the Templars. Rastoul's book is too brief for serious purposes. Both Campbell's and Simon's works are brief, informative, accurate, and readable in the popular sense. Both also lack specific documentation and are clearly written for the general public.

Specific histories of the Templars in individual countries are largely lacking although a number of histories and collections of charters do exist for a number of separate regions in France. Some excellent work has been done on the Templars in England by Lees, Perkins, and Williamson, as referred to in the Preface. Perkins has also written "The Knights Templars in the British Isles," *English Historical Review*, XXV (1910), 209-30.

[2] See chap. IV below.

[3] Thomas Walsingham, *Historia Anglicana, 1292-1422*, in *Chronica monasterii sancti Albani*, ed. Henry T. Riley (RS, No. 28; 2 vols.; London, 1863-76), I, 457: "... ubi plura munimenta, quae juridici in custodia habuerunt, igne consumpta sunt." Walsingham referred to "Temple Barre," but he clearly meant New Temple. This destruction was also noted in *Chronicon Henrici Knighton, vel Cnitthon, monachi Leycestrensis*, ed. Joseph R. Lumby (RS, No. 92; London, 1889), I, 135. Cf. Williamson, *op cit.*, p. 90, n. 1.

[4] William of Tyre, *Historia rerum in partibus transmarinis gestarum*, ed. A. Beugnot and A. Le Provost, in *Recueil des Historiens des Croisades: les Historiens Occidentaux*, (Paris, 1844), Vol. I, Part I, *Lib.* xii, *cap.* 7; Matthew Paris, *Chronica Majora*, ed. Henry R. Luard (RS, No. 57; 7 vols.; London, 1872-83), II, 144-45 and *Historia Anglorum sive Historia Minor*, ed. Frederick Madden (RS, No. 44; 3 vols.; London, 1866-69), I, 222 and III, 182; Roger of Wendover, *Chronica sive Flores Historiarum*, ed. Henry O. Saxe (5 vols.; London, 1841-44), II, 195-96; Jacques de Vitry, *History of Jerusalem*, tr. Aubrey Stewart, "Palestine Pilgrims' Text Society," Vol. XI, No. 2 (London, 1896), chap. LXV. None of these men lived at the time of the actual founding of the order. William of Tyre (*ca.* 1130-90) is our best source. Born, raised, and spending most of his life in the Holy Land, he was a man of talent, experience, and reliability. He served as royal tutor and advisor, Chancellor of the Kingdom of Jerusalem, and Archbishop of Tyre. As a historian (cf. August C. Krey, "William of Tyre: the Making of an Historian in the Middle Ages," *Speculum*, XVI [1941], 149-66; Emily A. Babcock and August C. Krey, Introduction [pp. 28-34] to their translation of William of Tyre, [*A History of Deeds Done Beyond the Sea*, "Records of Civilization," No. 35; 2 vols.; N. Y., 1943] William was critical of his sources and usually based his statements not upon the account of a single chronicler but upon a careful comparison and consideration of all sources available to him. Jacques de Vitry was only briefly in the Holy Land; and Roger of Wendover took his remarks from the account of William of Tyre.

[5] Addison, Campbell, Perkins, Prutz, and Williamson, cited in no. 1 above, accept the account of William of Tyre without question.

[6] William of Tyre, *op. cit., Lib.* xii, *cap.* 7.

[7] *Ibid.*

[8] DuPuy, no. 4.

[9] Henri de Curzon (ed.), *La Règle du Temple* (Paris, 1886), pp. iii and x.

[10] William of Tyre, *op. cit., Lib.* xii, *cap.* 7; DuPuy (no. 5) reproduces the pertinent parts of the *acta* of the council.

[11] "Liber de laude novae militiae ad milites Templi," ed. Jacques P. Migne, *Patrologiae cursus completus . . . series Latina* (221 vols.; Paris, 1878-90), CLXXXII, 922-37.

[12] *Op. cit., Lib.* xii, *cap.* 7.

13 *Chronica Majora*, RS, IV, 291.

14 Prutz, *Entwicklung,* chap. III; Perkins, "The Knights Templars in England," *op. cit.,* chap. II. Both of these works contains numerous examples and citations of references to papal privileges. Cf. also DuPuy, nos. 6 (documents of twelve different popes), 21, 22, 27, 35, 36, 38.

15 Perkins (*op. cit.,* p. 13, n. 1) cites more than thirty references to this type of exemption. Cf. *Calendar of Entries in the Papal Registers relative to Great Britain and Ireland,* ed. William H. Bliss (3 vols.; London, 1893-95), I, 229, 232, 268, 429, 432, 444, 551. Very frequently other orders — e.g., Hospitallers, Teutonic Knights, Carthusians, and Cistercians — as well as the Templars are included in certain of these exemptions and privileges. The great charter of privileges of the Templars is *Omne datum optimum* which was first issued in 1162 by Pope Alexander III, was republished in 1172, and was subsequently confirmed by most popes for well over a century. Copies of this bull can be found in Thomas Rymer and Robert Sanderson (eds.), *Foedera, conventiones, litterae et cujuscunque generis acta publica inter reges Angliae et alios quovis imperatores, reges, pontifices, principes, vel communitates* (rev. ed.; 5 vols.; London, 1816), I, 37-38; *Pat. Lat.,* CCI, 1195; DuPuy, no. 21. Cf. also Philipp Jaffé and William Wattenbach (eds.), *Regesta pontificum Romanorum ab condita ecclesia ad annum post Christum natum MCXCVIII* (2 ed.; 2 vols.; Leipzig, 1885-88), no. 14117. In addition, the Rule of the Templars (*Règle,* art. 58), approved in essence by the Council of Troyes and Pope Honorius II, authorized the Templars to receive tithes.

16 J. Delaville le Roulx (ed.), *Documents concernant les Templiers; Extraits des Archives de Malte* (Paris, 1882), no. 1. Cf. Jaffé, *RP,* nos. 8821, 8829, and others.

17 *Ibid.,* no. 9193 *et passim.* Cf. Perkins, *op. cit.,* p. 11, n. 3.

18 A bull of Eugenius III, dated 1145 or 1146, first gave the Templars this privilege: Prutz, *op. cit.,* p. 27 and n. 1, and pp. 259-60, nos. 3 and 10. Perkins, *op. cit.,* p. 9, n. 2, cites fifty-eight instances in which this privilege was in substance repeated.

19 *Omne datum optimum,* as cited in n. 15 above. Cf. also a bull of Innocent III (1139) in Guigues A. M. J. d'Albon (ed.), *Cartulaire général de l'Ordre du Temple, 1119-1150* (Paris, 1913), p. 375; Prutz, *op. cit.,* p. 260, no. 1, p. 261, no. 16, p. 265, no. 54, p. 266, no. 72.

20 *Omne datum optimum* emphasized the subservience of the Templars to the papacy alone.

21 Rymer, I, 334; Delaville le Roulx, *op. cit.,* no. 27; Prutz, *op. cit.,* p. 267, nos. 83 and 84, p. 269, no. 104, and p. 271, no. 122. Cf. Perkins, *op. cit.,* p. 12.

22 Prutz, *op. cit.,* p. 259, no. 6, p. 262, no. 23, p. 263, no. 32, p. 270, nos. 108 and 110, p. 274, no. 152, and p. 279, no. 201.

23 Perkins (*op. cit.,* pp. 12, 25) cites a goodly number of these. See also, the registers of individual popes.

24 Cf. Jaffé, *RP,* nos. 11076, 11814; Delaville le Roulx, *op. cit.,* nos. 29, 30, 32. Perkins (*op. cit.,* p. 12, n. 3) gives twelve examples. Also, Prutz, *op. cit.,* chaps. III and IV, discusses additional privileges to those cited here.

25 Cf. Perkins, *op. cit.,* pp. 17-18. The bull of Alexander IV, dated 1255 (DuPuy, no. 35), is an especially good example of this.

26 Cf. *ibid.,* nos. 23, 29; Jaffé, *RP,* no. 15842; and decree of the Lateran Council of 1179 in Roger of Wendover, *op. cit.,* RS, I, 119, and in William of Newburgh, *Historia rerum Anglicarum,* in *Chronicles of the Reigns of Stephen, Henry II, and Richard I,* ed. Richard Howlett (RS, No. 82; 4 vols.; London, 1884-89), I, 221. Cf. Prutz, *op. cit.,* pp. 40-41.

27 Some discussion of the attitudes toward the Templars in England will be indicated in chapter IV below. Numerous citations could be made showing instances of praise and instances of criticism. The works of Matthew Paris, Jacques de Vitry, William Tyre, and others are filled with references, sometimes favorable and sometimes unfavorable, to the Templars.

²⁸ Cf. David Knowles and R. Neville Hadcock, *Medieval Religious Houses, England and Wales* (London, 1953), p. 234.

²⁹ The officials and the basic organization of the Templars, as they existed in the Holy Land, are to be found in the Rule of the order, the best edition of which is that of Curzon (*op. cit.*). The original rule was most likely written in French; but a Latin version, attributed to or inspired by St. Bernard was appended to the records of the Council of Troyes. The Latin version can be found in Curzon, DuPuy, no. 5, and Giovanni D. Mansi (ed.), *Sacrorum conciliorum nova, et amplissima collectio* (new ed.; 31 vols.; Venice, 1759-98), XXI, 358-71. The earliest copies of the rule which survive are two manuscripts of the thirteenth and fourteenth centuries. Both the French and the Latin versions are given in Curzon and are discussed in his introduction. The original rule was apparently quite brief, consisting of seventy-two articles. But in time extensive additions were made until the rule grew to six hundred and eighty articles. Most of the information on the organization and procedure of the order comes from these additional articles.

³⁰ *Règle*, arts. 79-98 deal with the power of the Grand Master (called Master in the Rule); arts. 198-223 set down the procedure for the election of a Grand Master: On the death of the Grand Master, the Marshall is to summon the Commanders of the Holy Land and to meet and choose a temporary Grand Commander to govern until a new Grand Master has been elected. A date for the election is set far enough in the future so that all the commanders of overseas provinces may participate in person. On the appointed day, the temporary Grand Commander singles out two or three of the most distinguished men of the order from whom the chapter chooses by voice vote a "Commander of the Election." Then one of the knights is selected to serve as his assistant. These two men proceed to choose two more persons; the four then choose an additional two; and so the matter proceeds until twelve men (eight knights and four sergeants) have been selected. Then as a thirteenth member, a brother chaplain is added. These men constitute the "Council of Election" which, meeting apart from the others, and under the presidency of the Commander of the Election, proceed to examine the positions and records of various dignitaries of the order. Finally, by simple majority vote, they elect a new Grand Master. After the electors have rejoined the other Templars, the Commander of the Election calls upon all those present to swear to obey the new master, whoever he may be. Thereupon he turns to the one chosen and says: *"Et nos, el nom dou Pere et dou Fis et dou Saint Esperit, nos avons esleu a Maistre et elisons vos, frere - - - -."*

³¹ *Ibid.*, arts. 99-100.

³² *Ibid.*, arts. 101-09, 173-76.

³³ *Ibid.*, arts. 110-19.

³⁴ *Ibid.*, arts. 120-24. Other lesser officials existed, too. Cf. arts. 125-81 for their titles and duties.

³⁵ Direct information on the provincial organization of the Templars is largely lacking in the Rule and must be gained from a study of documents from the individual provinces. Altogether the Templar realm was divided into eighteen provinces. The eastern provinces were: Jerusalem, Tripoli, Antioch, Romania (Morea and Thessaly), and Cyprus; and the western provinces were: England, Normandy, France, Poitou, Aquitaine, Alvernia (Provence), Aragon, Castille, Portugal, Apulia, Lombardy, Germany, and Hungary. In the Rule itself, reference is made to only nine provinces: three in the east and six in the west.

³⁶ More will be written in the next chapter on this provincial and local organization as it is found in England.

³⁷ *Règle*, art. 96.

³⁸ *Ibid.*, art. 36.

³⁹ *Ibid.*, arts. 36, 85, 87, 92, 106, 125.

⁴⁰ *Ibid.*, p. xxviii.

⁴¹ *Ibid.*, arts. 45, 48, 389, 396-404. The holding of frequent "chapters of faults"

was common among many religious communities, and perhaps the Templars were especially influenced by the Cistercian practice.

[42] *Ibid.*, arts. 406, 416-656.

[43] *Ibid.*, arts. 87, 586, 661. The Rule speaks of the provinces of Jerusalem, Antioch, and Tripoli. Later, additional provinces (cf. n. 35 above) were established. The Rule does not speak specifically of local chapters, but such records as exist, especially in reference to the trial — see chap. IV below — prove their existence.

[44] This is also inferred from other records and is in harmony with the content and intent of the Rule.

[45] *Règle*, art. 17 *et passim*. During their first decade or so, the Templars had no distinctive habit. The Council of Troyes and Pope Honorius II (1128) authorized them to wear a white mantle, symbolic of purity and innocence. The influence of the white garb of the Cistercians whose great leader, Bernard of Clairvaux, was their special sponsor, may help to explain the choice. Some twenty years later, when the Second Crusade was being preached, Pope Eugenius III authorized the Templars to add a red cross to their mantle. (Cf. William of Tyre, *op. cit., Lib.* xii, *cap.* 7.) Very likely the pope and the Templars selected the red cross because of its association with crusaders since 1095. As the badge and seal of devotion and martyrdom, it clearly proclaimed the Templars' dedication of their lives to the defense of the Holy Land and Christian pilgrims. Cf. remarks of Fucher of Chartres, *Historia Iherosolymitana*, I, iv and Robert the Monk, *Historia Iherosolimitana*, I, 2 in *Recueil des Historiens des Croisades: les Historiens Occidentaux*, Vol. III (Paris, 1866). Karl Erdmann (*Die Entstehung des Kreuzzugsgedankens* [Stuttgart, 1935], p. 49) in his chapter on "Heilige Fahnen" also states that the red cross on a white flag had by the mid-twelfth century become a religious symbol: "... hatte die rot-weisse Kreuzfahne den Charakter eines rein religiösen symbols ..." Members of the order other than Knights, though strictly forbidden to wear the white mantle, were permitted to add the red cross to their black or brown robes.

[46] *Règle*, arts. 51, 57, *et passim* (poverty); 70, 71, 675, *et passim* (chastity); and 39, 98, 436, 457, *et passim* (obedience). Only in the case of married men joining the order is it specifically stated that a part of the initiate's property must be given to the order — art. 69. It would not be surprising to find other brothers surrendering their property to the order upon initiation, however.

[47] *Ibid.*, art. 429. The Benedictine and Augustinian orders are specifically mentioned as religious houses which former Templars might join. Normally, the only persons to leave the order were those who had been expelled for some serious offense. In a letter of St. Bernard to Pope Eugenius III (DuPuy, no. 11), a Templar is specifically refused permission to enter the Cistercian order.

[48] The number of Templars at any one time was apparently small though the influence of the order was great. There seems to be no real way of estimating the numbers of the Templars; and most modern historians — e.g., Prutz, Addison, Lea, and others — mindful of the uncertain reliability of statistics found in medieval documents or in the writings of medieval historians, wisely avoid committing themselves. In chapter IV below, however, some comment on the number of known Templars in England at the time of the dissolution of the order will be made. This matter of the size of Templar membership is a problem which could well be looked into in more detail. Checking over some thirty or more references dealing with the Templars in the Holy Land, one gathers that the Templars were able to muster only between one and four hundred knights for any given campaign or battle. The number of Templars outside the Holy Land at any one time is even harder to estimate. Matthew Paris (*Chronica Majora*, RS, IV, 291), writing in reference to the serious Christian losses in the east at the time of the Battle of Gaza (1244), says, probably referring to their financial ability rather than their actual numbers, that the Temple could easily have raised nine thousand soldiers from its houses outside the Holy Land and equipped them for war at the expense of the order. William of Tyre (*op. cit., Lib.* xii, *cap.* 7), writing in the second half of the twelfth

century, says that there were in his own day three hundred knights and count-less lesser members.

[49] *Règle*, art. 673: "... l'on li puet demander se il est fiz de chevalier et de dame, et que ses peres soit de lignage de chevaliers; et se il est de loial mariage." Cf. also, *ibid.*, arts. 337, 431, *et passim.*

[50] *Ibid.*, art. 445.

[51] *Ibid.*, art. 68 *et passim.*

[52] *Ibid.*, arts. 143, 152, 171, 180.

[53] *Ibid.*, arts. 135, 181.

[54] Cf. *ibid.*, art. 64.

[55] *Ibid.*, arts. 268-71. The papal bull of Alexander III, *Omne datum optimum*, and bulls of his successors not only authorized but guaranteed the Templars their own priests independent of all ecclesiastical authority save that of Rome – cf. n. 19 above.

[56] *Règle*, arts. 175, 319, 321, *et passim.*

[57] *Ibid.*, arts. 22, 65, 66, 69, 632, *et passim.*

[58] *Ibid.*, art. 70. On at least one occasion, however, a married woman seems to have been admitted in England. A certificate of reception of a sister (Lees, p. 210, chapter no. 5) dating from the period 1189-93 is addressed to Geoffrey Fitz Stephen, then Master of the Temple in England.

[59] *Règle*, arts. 14, 56, 70.

[60] *Ibid.*, arts. 10, 15, 16, 279-84 *et passim* (prayer); 8, 31, 32, 42 (silence); 26, 27, 28, 30 (food and drink). Realizing the danger of immoderate abstinence and the needs of military life, the Templar Rule permitted two regular meals daily and a third at the discretion of the Master, meat three times a week, and wine. Fasting was not emphasized to the degree it was in many another religious order. Also, special care and consideration were given to the old and sick – arts. 33, 60, 61, 190-97.

[61] *Ibid.*, arts. 148-55, 161-63, 285, 286, 319, 320, 336-84.

[62] *Ibid.*, art. 57: "... et poés avoir terres et homes et vilains et chans tenir et governer justement ... "

[63] *Ibid.*, art. 58: "... nos éguardons a vos qui vivés de vie communal diesmes avoir."

[64] The brief survey of Templar history given in the next few pages relies on the following standard works: Steven Runciman, *A History of the Crusades* (3 vols.; Cambridge, 1951-54), Kenneth M. Setton (ed.), *A History of the Crusades*, Vol. I: *The First Hundred Years*, ed. Marshall W. Baldwin (Philadelphia, 1955); and René Grousset, *Histoire des Croisades et du Royaume franc de Jérusalem* (3 vols.; Paris, 1939).

[65] Cf. Campbell, *op. cit.*, p. 40; Runciman, *op. cit.*, II, 183-84.

[66] Cf. Campbell, *op. cit.*, p. 50; Grousset, *op. cit.*, II, 250-70; and Runciman, *op. cit.*, II, 282-86. Some commentators suggested the Templars had been bribed by the Moslems to give Louis and Conrad bad advice which led to the failure of the Christian effort.

[67] DuPuy, no. 10.

[68] For a brief but thorough discussion of this battle, consult R. C. Smail, *Crusading Warfare (1097-1193)*, "Cambridge Studies in Medieval Life and Thought," No. 3, N.S. (Cambridge, 1956) pp. 189-97.

[69] Campbell (*op. cit.*, pp. 155-66), Grousset (*op. cit.*, III, 311-14, 318-21), and Runciman (*op. cit.*, III, 182-87) tell the story of Frederick II and his dealings with the Templars. Cf. the letter to Richard of Cornwall (DuPuy, no. 34) in which Frederick makes known his views on the conduct of the Templars. Grousset is especially severe in his discussion of the Templars' dealings with Frederick.

[70] Jean Sire de Joinville, *Histoire de Saint Louis*, ed. Natalis de Wailly (Paris, 1868), p. 135.

[71] Cf. the pertinent remarks of Smail (*op. cit.,* pp. 60-61, 98-101, 205-15) on the importance of the fortresses.

[72] This was late in May. Cf. Campbell, *op. cit.,* p. 196; Runciman, *op. cit.,* III, 420; and Grousset, *op. cit.,* III, 751-62.

[73] For an excellent analysis of disinterest in further crusades, consult Palmer A. Throop (*Criticism of the Crusade: a Study of Public Opinion and Crusade Propaganda* [Amsterdam, 1940], especially pp. 284-88) who argues that a variety of factors are involved: for example, the unwillingness of the ruling classes in the west to sacrifice their own interests for a distant holy war, the decline in interest and suspicion of papal projects arising from the papacy's diversion of crusades from war against the infidel to campaigns against political enemies in Europe, the new nationalism which led people to support their king and his policies rather than those of the pope, and the resentment against being asked to forego material comforts at home for dangerous and distant wars which had become characterized by repeated Christian defeat.

[74] Prutz (*op. cit.,* pp. 14-20, 58-73) discusses the establishment and development of the Templars in these various areas.

Chapter Two

[1] The works of Addison, Campbell, and Williamson, *op. cit.,* are of little value on the origins of the Templars in England. The best and most thorough discussion of this problem is to be found in Lees, pp. xxxviii-xlvii.

[2] *The Anglo-Saxon Chronicle,* ed. and trans. Charles Plummer (2 vols.; Oxford, 1892-99), *sub anno* 1128, I, 259; Roger of Hoveden, *Chronica,* ed. William Stubbs (RS, No. 51; 4 vols.; London, 1868-71), I, 184; Henry of Huntingdon, *The History of the English from A.D. 55 to A.D. 1154,* ed. Thomas Arnold (RS, No. 74; London, 1879), p. 250. Cf. Paris, *Chronica Majora,* RS, I, 208.

[3] Lees, pp. 145-46; D'Albon, *op. cit.,* no. 124.

[4] Lees, p. xli. Cf. also, pp. xxxix-xl.

[5] *Op. cit.,* RS, I, 53: "Denique multo plura sub brevitate temporis, quo Stephanus regnavit, vel potius nomen regis obtinuit, quam centum retro annis servorum et ancillarum Dei monasteria initium in Anglis sumpsisse noscuntur." Using the data to be found in David Knowles' and R. Neville Hadcock's work (*Medieval Religious Houses, England and Wales,* 3 vols. [London, 1953-59], Vol. I *passim*), it would appear that in the century before 1135 there were 297 monasteries and nunneries established, plus 42 hospitals and 61 secular colleges, for a total of 400 religious houses. Under Stephan (1135-54), there were 253 monasteries and nunneries established, plus 44 hospitals and 5 secular colleges, for a total of 302 religious houses. Cf. also, David Knowles, *The Religious Orders in England* (vols. I-II; Cambridge, 1950-55), II, 256.

[6] Lees, p. 176; D'Albon, *op. cit.,* no. 179; Lees, p. 148; D'Albon, *op. cit.,* no. 256; William Dugdale, *Monasticon Anglicanum,* new ed. John Caley, Henry Ellis, and Bulkeley Badinel (7 vols.; London, 1856), VII, 843.

[7] Lees, pp. 148, 177-78; D'Albon, *op. cit.,* nos. 208, 256.

[8] *Ibid.,* nos. 258, 271; Lees, pp. 212-13.

[9] *Ibid.,* pp. 178-79. Though this is the only charter which can be positively assigned to the Empress Matilda, one cannot rule out the possibility that she made additional grants to the Templars. At least one reference in the Inquest of 1185 (Lees, p. 61) can be found to land granted to the Templars by a supporter of Matilda.

[10] "The Sandford Cartulary," ed. Agnes Leys, *Oxfordshire Record Society Publications,* XIX (1937), 1-177 and XXII (1940), 179-328, nos. 1, 6, 25, 39, 74, 89, 164, *et passim;* Lees, pp. 178, 180, 181, 207, 227-29.

[11] *Ibid.,* pp. 198-99.

[12] *Ibid.,* pp. 149-50.

[13] *Ibid.,* p. 156.

[14] *Ibid.,* pp. 203-04.

138   *The Knights Templars in England*

¹⁵ *Ibid.,* p. 137.

¹⁶ For comparative purposes, see Prutz, *op. cit.,* chaps. I-II, where the evolution of the order in France, the western state for which the most information in available, is discussed.

¹⁷ Cf. Lees, pp. lx-xiv.

¹⁸ See above, Chap. I.

¹⁹ "The Knights Templars in the British Isles," *op. cit.,* pp. 222-24. Knowles and Hadcock (*op. cit.,* p. 27), without citing their evidence, suggest that the number of Templars in England in 1308 was 165, including 6 knights and 118 sergeants; and Knowles, *op. cit.,* p. 256, suggests that the total number of the military orders in England was over 600.

²⁰ *Calendar of Patent Rolls of Edward I, 1272-1307,* ed. under the superintendence of the Deputy Keeper of the Records (4 vols.; London, 1893-1901), III, 391, 483 [27-28 Ed. I (1298-99)].

²¹ See Appendix A below for an incomplete list.

²² Addison (*op. cit.,* p. 494) says that the masters in the provinces were appointed by the Grand Master of the order and could be removed at his discretion.

²³ A royal order (*Close Rolls of the Reign of Henry III, 1216-1272,* ed. under the superintendence of the Deputy Keeper of the Records (14 vols.; London, 1902-38), III, 183 [19 Hen. III (1235)] and *Calendar of Documents Relating to Ireland,* ed. H. S. Sweetman, Vols. I-V [London, 1875-86], I, no. 2264) instructs the justiciar in Ireland to protect the new master there whom the "council and brethren have chosen." If the Master of Ireland — the Preceptor of Ireland (see below, n. 29) was known as master rather than preceptor — was thus chosen, it would seem logical that the Master of England was similarly chosen. This order of royal protection is unique in that the new master was being protected from the old master who was at the time a fugitive from his order. Ordinarily, the election of a master must have proceeded without any need for royal protection.

²⁴ Cited by Addison, *op. cit.,* p. 496. This is a copy of the oath taken by the Master in France. No copy of an oath for England survives.

²⁵ Cf. *ClR,* 21 Hen. III (1237), p. 440. This is only one of many references to the Templars' headquarters and chapter meetings at New Temple, London.

²⁶ Cf. Lees, p. lxv.

²⁷ Cf. *ClR,* 16 Hen. III (1231), p. 8; *CPatR,* 21 Ed. I (1293), p. 26. These two entries are typical of the phraseology in hundreds of such grants to the Templars.

²⁸ Cf. Lees, pp. lxvii-lxxi. The Rule, which is overwhelmingly concerned with the east, does not speak of subordinate provincial officials.

²⁹ *CPatR,* 25-29 Ed. I (1297-1301), pp. 313, 391, 483, 572; *ibid.,* 30-35 Ed. I (1302 13), pp. 31, 138, 222, 384, 499.

³⁰ See below, the section of this chapter where an indication of the preceptories is given in the survey of Templar holdings in England and Appendix B.

³¹ Perkins ("The Knights Templars in England," *op. cit.,* Appendix D) cites only eighteen known preceptors among the prisoners at the time of the Templars' trial. Addison (*op cit.,* p. 426) refers to the Preceptor of Denney and Dokesworth in Cambridgeshire and the Preceptor of Sandford and Bistlesham in Oxfordshire.

³² Cf. Lees, pp. 169, n. 8; 170, n. 7; 231, n. 1; 238, n. 10, 244.

³³ If Jacques de Molay, the Grand Master of the order was illiterate — as he himself affirmed at his second interrogation in 1309 (DuPuy, no. 82) — then, it can hardly be expected that many of the other Templars, excluding the chaplains, were literate. Cf. *Règle,* p. xxvi.

³⁴ In the corrody payments authorized by Edward II while the Templar properties were in his hands, references are found to chaplains and clerks attached to Templar houses — e.g., chaplains: 2 at New Temple, and 1 each at Temple Bruer, Eagle, Wetherby, Upleden, and Garewy; clerks: 5 at New Temple, 2 at

Temple Bruer, and 1 each at Temple Dinsley, Stocton, and Garewy (*CC1R*, 5-6 Ed. II [1312-13], pp. 388, 410, 429-30, 482, 512; *ibid.*, 8 Ed. II [1315], pp. 232, 269, 270; and *ibid.*, 5-6 Ed. II [1311-13], pp. 388, 409, 422-23, 473, 482, 483, 492, 510, 516). The task of these chaplains and clerks is not indicated, but they most likely rendered religious and clerical services respectively. There is no way of knowing whether or not this is a complete list of these persons.

³⁵ Lees, pp. 175, 248, 250.

³⁶ *Op. cit.*, pp. 494-95.

³⁷ Cf. Lees, pp. 158, 166, 170, 217, 245, 246, 248; *Règle*, p. xxviii, arts. 11, 36, 328, *et passim; CPatR*, 50 Hen. III (1266), p. 86.

³⁸ Lees, pp. 169, n. 8; 170; 171; 217, n. 12; 226.

³⁹ Cf. *ibid.*, p. lxv.

⁴⁰ Pp. lxx-lxxi.

⁴¹ Cf. *ibid.*, p. lxxxiii – e.g., Finchingfield in Essex.

⁴² *Ibid.*, pp. lxxx, cxvi – e.g., Cressing-Witham and Cowley on the honour of Boulogne.

⁴³ *Ibid.*, pp. xcvi-vii, cv-vi, cxxii, cxxxvi, clxxii, ccvi, ccx-xii – e.g., the fees of Lacy, Clare, Mowbray, *et al.*

⁴⁴ *Ibid.*, pp. cxix, cxlvii, cli, clxxv, cxcix, ccii-v, ccx – e.g., the lands of Harcourt, Basset, Vilers, *et al.*

⁴⁵ *Ibid.*, pp. xcvi, 25, 164 – e.g., the benefactions of the Archbishop of Canterbury, of the monks of Bermondesey, *et al.*

⁴⁶ *Ibid.*, pp. xxvi, cli.

⁴⁷ "The Sandford Cartulary," *op. cit.*, nos. 24, 50, 52, 53, 56, 64, 66, 69, 72, 73, 77, 78, 85, 86, 120, 125, 180-83, 187-91, 193-96, 200-02, 231, 232, 234, 235, 242; Lees, pp. 196, 204, 223, 273.

⁴⁸ *Ibid.*, p. 197; "The Sandford Cartulary," *op. cit.*, nos. 185, 306, 328, 410, 446, 468.

⁴⁹ E. A. Kosminsky, *Studies in the Agrarian History of England in the Thirteenth Century*, "Studies in Medieval History," Vol. VIII, ed. Geoffrey Barraclough, trans. Ruth Kisch (Oxford, 1956), pp. 98, 270.

⁵⁰ *Ibid.*, pp. 112, 116: 20% large, 14% medium, and 66% small.

⁵¹ *Ibid.*, pp. 113, 116.

⁵² *Ibid.*, p. 104.

⁵³ *Ibid.*, – citing *Rot. Hund.*, II, 581.

⁵⁴ Some data of a comparative sort can be obtained by examination of certain entries in the Domesday Book, the Inquest of 1185, and the Hospitaller Report of 1338. Some idea of the methods used in the administration of medieval estates can be gotten from N. Denholm-Young, *Seignorial Administration in England* (Oxford, 1937), especially chaps. II and IV.

⁵⁵ See the Inquest, *sub verbis.*

⁵⁶ Cf. Kosminsky, *op. cit.*, pp. 55-56.

⁵⁷ Lees, pp. 117-34.

⁵⁸ *Ibid.*, pp. 13-16.

⁵⁹ Cf. *Ibid.*, pp. lxxi, lxxxiv, 75-76, 83-84, 86-90, 92, 95-97 *et passim.*

⁶⁰ *Ibid.*, pp. 11-12 – as at Finchingfield in Essex.

⁶¹ *Ibid.*, also at Finchingfield.

⁶² *Ibid.*, p. 34 – in Leicestershire.

⁶³ *Ibid.*, p. 36 – in Warwickshire.

⁶⁴ *Ibid.*, p. 65 – in Hertfordshire.

⁶⁵ *Ibid.*, p. 125 – in Yorkshire.

⁶⁶ E. Lipson, *An Introduction to the Economic History of England*, Vol. I: *The Middle Ages* (London, 1915), pp. 89-103; W. Cunningham, *The Growth of English Industry and Commerce during the Early and Middle Ages*, 5th ed.,

Vol. I (Cambridge, 1910), pp. 233-34; W. J. Ashley, *An Introduction to English Economic History and Theory,* Vol. I, 4th ed. (London, 1923), Part I, pp. 20-23, 46-48.

[67] *Op. cit.,* pp. 44, 164, 191-92, 276.

[68] *Ibid.,* pp. 31, 44, 164, 167.

[69] *Ibid.,* pp. 240, 327. Cf. also, the same author's "Services and Money Rents in the Thirteenth Century," *Economic History Review,* V (1935), 24-25; and Hans Nabholz, "Medieval Agrarian Society in Transition," *Cambridge Economic History of Europe from the Decline of the Roman Empire,* Vol. I, ed. J. H. Clapham and Eileen Power (Cambridge, 1941), pp. 504, 508.

[70] *Ibid.,* p. 503.

[71] E.g., *CClR,* 5-6 Ed. II (1311-12), pp. 388, 397, 429, 430 *et passim.*

[72] E.g., *ibid.,* pp. 385, 388, 397, 409, *et passim.*

[73] E.g., *ibid.,* 5 Ed. II (1312), pp. 409, 413, 423, *et passim.*

[74] E.g., *ibid.,* pp. 397, 409, 422, *et passim.*

[75] E.g., *ibid.,* pp. 385, 388, 397, 409, *et passim.*

[76] Cf., *ibid.,* pp. 393, 413, 423, 468, 476, 493, *et passim.*

[77] "Corrodia petita de domibus Templariorum — annis I° et II° Edwardi II[i] et aliis annis sequentibus," ed. Henry Cole, *Documents illustrative of English History in the Thirteenth and Fourteenth Centuries, selected from the Records of the Department of the Queen's Remembrancer of the Exchequer* (London, 1844), pp. 139-230.

[78] Cf. Addison, *op. cit.,* p. 475.

[79] Williamson, *op. cit.,* p. 8.

[80] Léopold Delisle (ed.), *Receuil des actes de Henri II, roi d'Angleterre et duc de Normandie, concernant les provinces françaises et les affaires de France* (3 vols.; Paris, 1916-27), I, 312.

[81] It is often assumed that the Templars did not move to their new headquarters at New Temple until 1185, the date of the dedication of their round church there. However, Williamson (*op. cit.,* p. 9, n. 4) suggests that the date must have been earlier, sometime after 1163, the date of the sale of Holborn church, and before 1185.

[82] The New Temple Church was restored in 1829. For a picture and a sketch of the church, see *ibid.,* frontispiece, and Dugdale, VII, opposite p. 817.

[83] Roger of Wendover, *op. cit.,* RS, I, 133-36; Ralph de Diceto, *Opera Historica,* ed. William Stubbs (RS, No. 68; 2 vols.; London, 1876), II, 27, 32. (The Patriarch of Jerusalem had left the Holy Land with the Grand Prior of the Hospitallers and the Grand Master of the Templars, but only he and the Grand Prior arrived in England since the Grand Master had died at Verona, Italy.)

[84] Henry had summoned his Great Council to meet at the Hospitallers' house of Clerkenwell at this time: Roger of Wendover, *op. cit.,* RS, I, 135.

[85] For details of the Templar buildings in London at the time of the dissolution, see Williamson, *op. cit.,* pp. 70-72.

[86] Cf. *ibid.,* p. 9.

[87] *Ibid.*

[88] Sir Edward Coke, *The Second Part of the Institutes of the Laws of England,* Vol. II (London, 1797), p. 431.

[89] Lees, p. 137.

[90] *Ibid.,* p. 138.

[91] *Ibid.,* pp. 139-40.

[92] *Calendar of Charter Rolls preserved in the Public Record Office,* ed. under the superintendence of the Deputy Keeper of the Records (6 vols.; London, 1903-54), I, 4 [11 Hen. III (1227)] — a confirmation of John's charter.

[93] *Rotuli Litterarum Clausarum in Turri Londinensi asservati,* ed. Thomas D. Hardy (2 vols.; London, 1833-44), II, 171 [11 Hen. III (1227)]; *CChR,* 11

Hen. III (1227), p. 4; Dugdale, VII, 844; and cf. *ClR,* 14 Hen. III (1230), pp. 391-92.

[94] *CChR,* 9 Ed. I (1280), pp. 237-38.

[95] Cf. Lees, p. lxxi.

[96] Cf. Richard Fitzneale, *Dialogus de Scaccario,* ed. and trans. Charles Johnson (London, [1950]), p. 51 (1178); *ClR,* 48 Hen. III (1264), pp. 358-59; *ibid.,* 36 Hen. III (1252), p. 190 in reference to a local grant in Hereford; Johannes de Oxenedes, *Chronica,* ed. Henry Ellis (RS, No. 13; London, 1859), p. 235 (1168).

[97] Lees, pp. 138 (charter of Henry II, 1154-55), 139-40 (charter of Richard I, 1189); Rymer, I, 49 (charter of Richard I); *CChR,* 9 Ed. I (1280), p. 237 (confirmation of grant of 37 Hen. III).

[98] *RLC,* 4 Hen. III (1220), I, 428b; *CChR,* 9 Ed. I (1280), p. 237 – confirmation of the charter of 37 Hen. III.

[99] *Ibid.,* 19 Hen. III (1235), pp. 192-93; *ClR,* 30 Hen. III (1246), p. 412; *ibid.,* 37 Hen. III (1252), p. 428; *CClR,* 32 Ed. I (1304), pp. 145, 202; *CChR,* 9 Ed. I (1280), p. 237.

[100] *ClR,* 13-15 Hen. III (1228-31), pp. 131, 548; *ibid.,* 18 Hen. III (1234), p. 404; *CChR,* 26 Hen. III (1242), p. 267; *ClR,* 36-37 Hen. III (1252), pp. 170-71, 267-68, 384; *CPatR,* 47 Hen. III (1263), p. 281; *Cal. Doc. rel. to Ire.,* I, nos. 312, 2101; *Chartularies of St. Mary's Abbey, Dublin: with the Register of its House at Dunbrody, and the Annals of Ireland,* ed. John T. Gilbert (RS, No. 80; 2 vols.; London, 1884), I, 269 (1192).

[101] *RLC,* 8 Hen. III (1224), p. 594b.

[102] *CChR,* 51 Hen. III (1267), p. 62; *CPatR,* 53 Hen. III (1269), p. 330; *Annales de Burton,* ed. Henry R. Luard, in *Annales Monastici* (RS, No. 36; 5 vols.; London, 1864-69), I, 325 (1254); *Annales Monasterii de Wintonia, ibid.,* II, 104 (1266); *Annales Monasterii de Waverleia, ibid.,* II, 373 (1266); *Chronicles of the Mayors and Sheriffs of London,* trans. Henry T. Riley (London, 1863), p. 162 (1272); *Cal. Doc. rel. to Ire.,* III, no. 873; Bliss, I, 432 (Clement V, 1266), 444 (Gregory X, 1272), 551-52 (Nicholas V, 1291).

[103] *CClR,* 29 Ed. I (1301), p. 471; *CPatR,* 29 Ed. I (1301), p. 598; Statutes of Westminster, 3 Ed. I (1275), in the *Register of Malmesbury Abbey,* ed. J. S. Brewer (RS, No. 72; 2 vols.; London, 1879), I, 504.

[104] *Les Registres d'Innocent IV publiés ou analysés d'après les manuscrits originaux du Vatican et de la Bibliothèque nationale,* ed. Elie Berger (3 vols.; Paris, 1884-97), nos. 2053, 3551.

[105] *ClR,* 21 Hen. III (1239), pp. 566-67, 569.

[106] *CClR,* 18 Ed. I (1290), p. 67; *The Book of Fees commonly called Testa de Nevill* (3 vols.; London, 1920-31), II, 832 [1242-43, Oxfordshire]; *Magna Carta* in Rymer, I, 131-32.

[107] *ClR,* 48 Hen. III (1264), p. 359.

[108] *CChR,* 11 Hen. III (1227), p. 4; *ibid.,* 9 Ed. I (1280), pp. 237-38 – a confirmation of the grant of 37 Hen. III (1253).

[109] *RLC,* 17 John (1215), I, 238; *ibid.,* 8 Hen. III (1224), I, 599b; *PatR,* 9 Hen. III (1225), p. 517; *ibid.,* 10-12 Hen. III (1226-28), pp. 24, 105, 196-97; *ibid.,* 14 Hen. III (1230), p. 368, 374-75.

[110] *RLC,* 15-17 John (1213-14), I, 148b, 214; *ibid.,* 8 Hen. III (1224), I, 609; *ibid.,* 9-10 Hen. III (1225-26), II, 51, 110; *ClR,* 15 Hen. III (1231), p. 519; Rymer, I, 115; *Cal. Doc. rel. to Ire.,* no. 1276.

[11] *ClR,* 46-47. Hen. III (1262), pp. 160-61; *CClR,* 21-22 Ed. I (1293), pp. 289, 339; *Cal. Doc. rel. to Ire.,* II, no. 1672; *CChR,* 9 Ed. I (1280), p. 237.

[112] *Ibid.,* 32-37 Hen. III (1248-53), pp. 331, 414, 415; *ibid.,* 31 Ed. I (1303), p. 33; *Placita de Quo Warranto temporibus Edw. I, II, et III in Curia receptae Scaccarij Westm. asservata* (London, 1818), pp. 281, 291.

[113] *CChR,* 11 Hen. III (1227), p. 5; *ibid.,* 9 Ed. I (1280), p. 237 – confirmation

of the grant of 37 Hen. III; Rymer, I, 49 (charter of Richard I, 1189); Lees, p. 139 (charter of Richard I, 1189).

[114] *CClR*, 9 Ed. I (1280), p. 237.

[115] *ClR*, 35 Hen. III (1252), p. 534.

[116] *RLC*, 7 Hen. III (1222), I, 558. This grant refers to the privilege as dating back to the time of John. Cf. Assize Roll, p. 325 — cited in *The Victoria History of the County of Hertford*, ed. William Page, Vols. II-IV (London, 1908-14), III, 10.

[117] *Calendar of Documents preserved in France illustrative of the History of Great Britain and Ireland*, ed. J. Horace Round, Vol. I (London, 1899), pp. 91-92 [1 Ric. I (1189)]; Lees, p. 139; *CChR*, 9 Ed. I (1280), p. 237.

[118] *ClR*, 16 Hen. III (1232), p. 92; *CClR*, 25 Ed. I (1297), p. 10; *CChR*, 9 Ed. I (1280), p. 237.

[119] Lees, pp. 137-39; *CChR*, 9 Ed. I (1280), pp. 237-38.

[120] Rymer, I, 49; Lees, p. 139; *ClR*, 36 Hen. III (1251-52), pp. 10, 69.

[121] Lees, p. 140; Rymer, I, 74; *CChR*, 9 Ed. I (1280), pp. 237-38; *Assize Roll*, p. 325 — cited in *VCH: Hertfordshire*, III, 10.

[122] Lees, pp. 137-40; Rymer, I, 49, 78; *RLC*, 7 Hen. III (1223), I, 558; *CChR*, 9 Ed. I (1280), pp. 237-38.

[123] *ClR*, 55-56 Hen. III (1271-72), pp. 397, 427, 553, 562, 563, *CClR*, 9-16 Ed. I (1279-88), pp. 111, 299, 344-45, 364, 407, 413, 471, 539; *ibid.*, 17-22 Ed. I (1288-93), pp. 29, 262, 263, 270, 271, 274, 378; *ibid.*, 30 Ed. I (1302), p. 599.

[124] *Cal. Docs. in France*, p. 92, (10 Ric. I [1198]), *ClR*, 19 Hen. III (1235), p. 110, Cf. *Rotuli de Oblatis et Finibus in Turri Londinensi asservati, tempore Regis Johannis*, ed. Thomas D. Hardy ([London], 1835), p. 175; *Calendar of Fine Rolls preserved in the Public Record Office*, ed. A. E. Bland, Vol. I (London, 1911), p. 95; and *Cal. Docs. rel. to Ire.*, I, no 168.

[125] *CChR*, 9 Ed. I (1280), p. 238.

[126] Cf. Lees, pp. 137-39; *CChR*, 9 Ed. I (1280), pp. 237-38.

[127] Coke, *op. cit.*, p. 431. Cf. Lees, p. 256 (Lincolnshire charter no. 14).

[128] Coke (*op. cit.*, p. 431) stated that the thirty-third chapter of the Statute of 13 Ed. I (1285) prohibited unauthorized use of the Templar cross on penalty of forfeiture of land to the superior lord or to the king. *Statutes of the Realm*, I, 87. Cf. *Historic and Municipal Documents of Ireland,, A.D. 1172-1320, from the Archives of the City of Dublin*, ed. J. T. Gilbert (RS No. 53; London, 1870), p. 255.

[129] The best example of the appeal of the Templars is found in the *Rotuli Parliamentorum; ut et Petitiones et Placita in parliamento tempore Edwardi R. I.* ([London], 1767), p. 2b [5 Ed. 1 (1276)]. Information on other appeals is gained indirectly from royal and papal orders as cited in nn. 130 and 131 below.

[130] Cf. *RLC*, 11 Hen. III (1227), p. 587; *ClR*, 22 Hen. III (1238), p. 76; *CPatR*, 50 Hen. III (1266), p. 587; *Calendar of Chancery Warrants preserved in the Public Record Office, A.D. 1244-1326*, prepared under the superintendence of the Deputy Keeper of the Records, Vol. I (London, 1927), I, 235 *et passim* [32 Ed. I (1304)].

[131] Rymer, I, 37 (Lucius III, 1183), 189 (Gregory IX, 1228), 333 (Alexander IV, 1255), 335 (Alexander IV, 1256), 497 (Gregory X, 1272).

[132] *Selected Letters of Pope Innocent III concerning England (1198-1216)*, ed. C. R. Cheney and W. H. Semple (London, [1953]), p. 96.

[133] Cf. *Rotuli Curiae Regis: Rolls and Records of the Court held before the King's Justiciar or Justices, from the Sixth Year of King Richard I to the Accession of King John*, ed. Francis Palgrave (2 vols.; [London,] 1835), II, 266 [1 John (1199)]; *Curia Regis Rolls of the Reigns of John and Henry III preserved in the Public Record Office*, ed. C. T. Fowler *et al.* (11 vols.; London, 1922-55), II, 128 [4 John (1202)]; *ibid.*, 8 John (1206), p. 279; *ibid.*, 4 Hen. III (1220),

p. 182; *CIR*, 21 Hen. III (1237), p. 515; *ibid.*, 36 Hen. III (1251), pp. 10, 220; *CCIR*, 21 Ed. I (1293), p. 294.

[134] The Pipe Rolls published thus far cover the reigns of Henry II, Richard, and John to the fourteenth year. The Pipe Rolls for the reigns of Henry III, Edward I, and Edward II, since they as yet exist in manuscript form only, have not been used here.

[135] *The Great Roll of the Pipe for the Fifth Year of the Reign of King John*, ed. Doris Stenton, "Publications of the Pipe Roll Society," Vol. XVI N.S. (London, 1938, p. 203 [5 John (1203)]; *ibid.*, 9 John (1207), pp. 59, 63. Cf. also, *Pipe R*, 12 Hen. II (1165-66), p. 121; *ibid.*, 1 Ric. I (1189), pp. 126, 184, 185; *CCIR*, 21-22 Ed. I (1293), pp. 289, 339. (These citations, and the subsequent ones, give only a few references by way of illustration and do not pretend to be complete.)

[136] *Pipe R*, 6 Hen. II (1159-60), p. 34; *The Chancellor's Roll for the eighth Year of the Reign of King Richard the First, Michaelmas 1196*, ed. Doris M. Stenton, "Publications of the Pipe Roll Society," Vol. VII N.S. (London, 1930), p. 35 [8 Ric. I (1196)]; *RLC*, 3 Hen. III (1219), I, 398; *CChR*, 11 Hen. III (1227), p. 5.

[137] *Pipe R*, 9 Ric. I (1197), p. 47; *Chancellor's R*, 8 Ric. I (1196), p.233.

[138] *Pipe R*, 3-4 Ric. I (1191-92), p. 14.

[139] *Ibid.*, pp. 187, 272, 290; *ibid.*, 7 Ric. I (1195), p. 9.

[140] *Ibid.*, 6 Ric. I (1194), p. 229.

[141] *Ibid.*, 24 Hen. II (1177-78), pp. 85, 96; *ibid.*, 1 John (1199), p. 11; *ibid.*, 14 Hen. III (1230), p. 255; *CPatR*, 21 Ed. I (1293), p. 56.

[142] *Pipe R*, 3-4 Ric. I (1191-92), p. 278.

[143] See below, n. 163.

[144] *Pipe R*, 14 Hen. III (1230), p. 279.

[145] *Ibid.*, 2 Ric. I (1190), p. 127; *ibid.*, 33 Hen. II (1186-87), p. 79.

[146] *Chancellor's R*, 8 Ric. I (1196), pp. 57, 180.

[147] *Pipe R*, 6 Ric. I (1194), p. 161; *ibid.*, 7 Ric. I (1195), pp. 89, 90.

[148] *Ibid.*, 16 Hen. II (1169-70), p. 133; *ibid.*, 22 Hen. II (1175-76), p. 29; *ibid.*, 31 Hen. II (1184-85), pp. 51, 59, 140; *ibid.*, 2 Ric. I (1190), p. 127; *ibid.*, 10 Ric. I (1198), pp. 73, 164; *ibid.*, 1 John (1194), pp. 156, 175, 257.

[149] *Ibid.*, 5 Ric. I (1193), p. 152; *ibid.*, 1 John (1199), p. 101.

[150] *Ibid.*, 5 Ric. I (1193), p. 51; *ibid.*, 6 Ric. I (1194), p. 112.

[151] See below, n. 162.

[152] *Rot. de Oblatis*, 1 John (1199), p. 73; *ibid.*, 2 John (1200), p. 101; *Pipe R*, 2 John (1200), p. 154; *Rot. de Oblatis*, 1 John (1199), p. 13.

[153] *Ibid.*, 3 John (1201), p. 175; *Pipe R*, 3 John (1201), p. 263.

[154] *Ibid.*, 11 John (1209), p. 30.

[155] *Annales Monasterii de Waverleia, op. cit.*, RS, II, 264; *Annales Monasterii de Bermundeseia, ibid.*, RS, III, 452; Paris, *Chronica Majora*, RS, II, 530.

[156] *Rot. de Oblatis*, 17-18 John (1216), p. 576.

[157] *PatR*, 10 Hen. III (1226), p. 17; *CIR*, 29 Hen. III (1244), pp. 265-66.

[158] *Taxatio ecclesiastica Angliae et Walliae auctoritate P. Nicholai IV, circa A.D. 1291* (London, 1802), pp. 61b, 62b, 167b.

[159] Cf. *ibid.*, pp. 59b, 61, 63b, 299, 310b.

[160] *RLC*, 4 Hen. III (1220), I, 428b.

[161] *Ibid.*

[162] Scutage: *Pipe R*, 14 Hen. III (1230), p. 148; *The Memoranda Roll of the King's Remembrancer for Michaelmas 1230 — Trinity 1231*, ed. Chalfant Robinson, "Publications of the Pipe Roll Society," Vol. XI (Princeton, 1933), pp. 16, 36, 42, 62, 73 [14-15 Hen. III (1230-31)]; *Pipe R*, 9 John (1207), p. 214. Tallage: *ibid.*, 10 Ric. I (1198), p. 7; *ibid.*, 1 John (1199), p. 26; *Memoranda*

R, 1 John (1199), pp. 20, 39; *Pipe R,* 2 John (1199), pp. 100, 126; *ibid.,* 3 John (1201), p. 29; *ibid.,* 8 John (1206), p. 118.

[163] Scutage: *Pipe R,* 3-4 Ric. I (1191-92), p. 151; *Memoranda R,* 1 John (1199-1200), p. 38. Tallage: *Pipe R,* 20 Hen. II (1173-74), p. 23; *ibid.,* 7 Ric. I (1195), p. 110; *ibid.,* 1 John (1199), p. 144; *ibid.,* 3 John (1201), pp. 287, 288; *ibid.,* 7 John (1205), pp. 99, 118; *ibid.,* 8 John (1206), p. 1.

[164] Scutage: *CClR,* 18 Ed. I (1289), p. 67. Tallage: *ClR,* 39 Hen. III (1255), p. 83.

[165] *Ibid.; Ibid.,* 45 Hen. III (1261), p. 389; *ibid.,* 52 Hen. III (1268), p. 483.

[166] *RLC,* 8 Hen. III (1224), I 594b.

[167] Bartholomew de Cotton, *Historia Anglicana,* ed. Henry R. Luard (RS, No. 16; London, 1859), pp. 208-09.

[168] *CPatR,* 40 Hen. III (1256), p. 511; *ibid.,* 44 Hen. III (1259-60), pp. 99, 112.

[169] Bliss, pp. 429 (Clement IV, 1265), 432 (Clement IV, 1266), 444 (Gregory X, 1272), 551-52 (Nicholas V, 1291); *Annales de Burton, op. cit.,* RS, I 325 (1254); Johannes de Oxenedes, *op. cit.,* RS, p. 232; *Annales Monasterii de Wintona, op. cit.,* RS, II, 104 (1266); *Annales Monasteria de Waverleia, op. cit.,* RS, II, 373 (1266); *Chronicles and Memorials of the Mayors and Sheriffs of London,* p. 162 (1272).

[170] *CPatR,* 40 Hen. III (1256), p. 524. Cf. *Reg. d'Inn. IV,* nos. 2777, 5131. A statute of Westminister of 1274 (*Register of Malmesbury Abbey,* RS, I, 504) stated, with regard to the grant by Parliament of a fifteenth to Edward I, that, though the Templars were exempted from the payment, their men, free or villein, were to be taxed.

[171] *CClR,* 17 Hen. III (1233), pp. 284, 293, 300, 301, 303; *CPatR,* 29 Ed. I (1301), p. 606.

[172] *PatR,* 10 Hen. III (1226), p. 17; *CClR,* 34 Ed. I (1306), p. 221.

[173] *CRR,* 8 John (1206), p. 279.

[174] *CClR,* 21 Ed. I (1293), p. 288.

[175] *CPatR,* 6 Ed. II (1312), pp. 536, 538-39, 541, 545-46.

[176] Cf. *ibid.,* 26-27 Hen. III (1242), p. 333.

[177] *CChanWar,* 26 Ed. I (1298), I, 93.

[178] Cf. *ClR,* 24 Hen. III (1240), p. 203 where the Templars' tenants are to help with the construction of a wall, and *ClR,* 35 Hen. III (1251), p. 534 where they are exempted from such service.

[179] *Pipe R,* 17 Hen. II (1170-71), p. 108; *ibid.,* 23 Hen. II (1176-77), p. 43; *Cal. Docs. rel. to Ire.,* I, no. 168; *Rot. de Oblatis,* p. 175; *Pipe R,* 3 John (1201), p. 263.

[180] *ClR,* 37 Hen. III (1252), p. 428; *ibid.,* 38 Hen. III (1254), p. 113; *ibid.,* 48 Hen. III (1264), pp. 357-58; *CClR,* 22 Ed. I (1293), p. 339. Cf. *Cal. of Fine Rolls,* 6 Ed. I (1278), p. 95 where the king orders his sheriff in Yorkshire to proceed against the Templars despite their claim of immunity from prosecution except before the king or his chief justice.

[181] *CPatR,* 1-9 Hen. III (1217-24), pp. 87, 436, 500; *ibid.,* 14-15 Hen. III (1230-31), pp. 338, 433; *ibid.,* 43-50 Hen. III (1259-66), pp. 47, 78, 598; *ibid,* 55 Hen. III (1271), p. 542; *ibid.,* 5-8 Ed. I (1277-80), pp. 233, 381; *ibid.,* 10-20 Ed. I (1282-91), pp. 19, 20, 463; *ibid.,* 32-35 Ed. I (1304-07), pp. 222, 501.

[182] *PatR,* 13 Hen. III (1229), p. 239; *CPatR,* 20 Hen. III (1236), p. 147; *ibid.,* 51 Hen. III (1267), p. 76; *ibid.,* 25 Ed. I (1297), p. 238.

[183] *CClR,* 25 Ed. I (1297), p. 16.

[184] Lees, p. 1.

[185] Cf. *ibid.,* pp. xxx, lvi.

[186] Cf. *ibid.,* p. lxxxiii.

[187] Cf. *ibid.,* pp. lxxix, lxxxiii, cviii, clxxii. Probably the commonest sizes were 240 acres for a carucate; 120, for a hide; 30, for a virgate; and 24, for a bovate. Cf. Ashley, *op. cit.,* Part I, pp. 7-8; Kosminsky, *op. cit.,* pp. 35-36.

[188] *The Knights Hospitallers in England: Being the Report of Prior Philip de Thame to the Grand Master Elyan de Villanova for A.D. 1338*, ed. Lambert B. Larking, "Camden Society Publications," Vol. LXV (London, 1857), pp. 133-99.

[189] Cf. John Kemble in the introduction to the report, *ibid.*, p. lxix.

[190] Cf. *ibid.*, pp. 212-13.

[191] For example, lands in the counties of Surrey, Hertford, Norfolk, Suffolk, Berkshire, and Nottingham are omitted.

[192] The Victoria County Histories, *passim*, and Perkins, "Knights Templars in England," *op. cit.*, Appendix E, provide data taken from the manuscripts. Also very valuable is the list of Templar houses in England and Wales in Knowles and Hadcock, *op. cit.*, pp. 235-39.

[193] *VCH: Yorkshire*, III, 257. Cf. E. J. Martin, "The Templars in Yorkshire," *Yorkshire Archaeological Journal*, XXIX (1930), 366-85 and XXX (1931), 135-56.

[194] Dugdale, VII, 817, 838; Lees, pp. 270-71. Cf. H. E. Chetwynd-Stapylton, "The Templars at Templehurst," *Yorkshire Archaeological and Topographical Journal*, X (1889), 276-86 and 431-43.

[195] *VCH: Yorkshire*, III, 258-60.

[196] *Ibid.*, p. 259. Cf. however, Lees, pp. 263-64.

[197] *Ibid.*, p. 260.

[198] Dugdale, VII, 838; *VCH: Yorkshire*, III, 258. Cf. R. V. Taylor, "Ribston and the Knights Templars," *Yorkshire Archaeological and Topographical Journal*, VII (1882), 429-52; VIII (1884), 259-99; IX (1886), 71-98; and Alfred Brett, "The Manor of Wetherby and Lands within the Manor," *Yorkshire Archaeological Journal*, XXX (1931), 261-73; Knowles and Hadcock, *op. cit.*, pp. 237, 239. Cf. *CChR*, 11 Hen. III (1227), p. 27.

[199] *VCH: Yorkshire*, III, 257.

[200] *Ibid.*, II, 428. Knowles and Hadcock (*op. cit.*, pp. 236, 239) suggest Foulbridge had come into existence by 1226 and Whitley by 1248.

[201] *VCH: Yorkshire*, III, 257-58.

[202] There is no general agreement on the exact income accruing to the crown in 1308. The figures given here and in the following paragraphs, usually in terms of the average net income while in the hands of the king, are taken from Perkins, "The Knights Templars in England," *op. cit.*, Appendix E; Knowles and Hadcock, *op. cit.*, pp. 235-39; and pertinent sections of the Victoria County Histories.

[203] *VCH: Yorkshire*, III, 257.

[204] *Hosp. Rpt.*, pp. 135-43; *VCH: Yorkshire*, III, 257.

[205] Dugdale, VII, 835; *VCH: Lincolnshire*, II, 211.

[206] *Ibid.*, pp. 35, 210-13; Dugdale, VII, 804, 835-36.

[207] *Ibid.*, p. 835; *VCH: Lincolnshire*, II, 211-12.

[208] Lees, pp. 250-51; *VCH: Lincolnshire*, II, 212.

[209] *Ibid.*, p. 312.

[210] *Ibid.*

[211] Lees, p. clxxix.

[212] Dugdale, VII, 801-05; *Hosp. Rpt.*, pp. 144-62.

[213] Cf. Perkins, "Knights Templars in England," *op. cit.*, Appendix E; *VCH: Lancashire*, II, 102; Knowles and Hadcock, *op. cit.*, pp. 235-39; *Hosp. Rpt.*, p. 133.

[214] *Ibid.*, p. 199.

[215] Dugdale, VII, 817. Cf. Addison, *op. cit.*, p. 485.

[216] *VCH: Worcestershire*, III, 31, 117, 377, 505-06; IV, 444-45; *CClR*, 56 Hen. III (1272), p. 556.

[217] *Hosp. Rpt.*, p. 195; Perkins, "Knights Templars in England," *op. cit.*, Appendix E.

²¹⁸ Dugdale, VII, 838; *Hosp. Rpt.,* pp. 183-85.

²¹⁹ *Ibid.,* pp. 187-88; Lees, pp. cxxiii, cxxviii, 206-10. Rockley dates back to the late 1150's and was a gift of John Marshall.

²²⁰ Lees, pp. 60-62.

²²¹ *Hosp. Rpt.,* pp. xx-xxii, 133, 179, 183-88, 195, 199; Knowles and Hadcock, *op. cit.,* pp. 235-39.

²²² Lees, p. 145; D'Albon, *op. cit.,* no. 124; Dugdale, VII, 817, 820, 838.

²²³ Granted by Stephen and confirmed by Henry II: Lees, pp. 141, 149-53; D'Albon, *op. cit.,* nos. 482-84; Dugdale, VII, 821, 838; *VCH: Essex,* II, 177.

²²⁴ Lees, p. 148; *VCH: Essex,* II, 177.

²²⁵ Lees, p. 174; *VCH: Kent,* II, 175; *Rotuli Hundredorum temp. Hen. III & Edw. I in Turr' Lon' et in curia receptae scaccarij Westm asservati,* ed. W. Illingworth (2 vols.; London, 1812-18); I, 222.

²²⁶ Perhaps the Templars owned Shipley as early as 1125 or 1139 — cf. Lees, p. 227; *VCH: Sussex,* II, 92.

²²⁷ Dugdale, VII, 817, 820, 834, 840; Lees, pp. 227-28, 232-40; *VCH: Sussex,* II, 92-93.

²²⁸ Cf. Lees, pp. 134-35; *Hosp. Rpt.,* pp. 166-67.

²²⁹ *VCH: Surrey,* III, 358; IV, 149, 165.

²³⁰ Lees, pp. 203-04; Dugdale, VII, 819; *VCH: Berkshire,* II, 133; III, 73, 139, 145-46; IV, 315.

²³¹ Dugdale, VII, 836, 843; *VCH: Hampshire,* II, 105; III, 7, 10; V, 117, 163. *CChR,* 24 Hen. III (1240), p. 251.

²³² *Hosp. Rpt.,* p. 213.

²³³ *Ibid.,* pp. 168-70, 173-75.

²³⁴ Dugdale, VII, 833, 838, 843; Lees, pp. 176-78; D'Albon, *op. cit.,* nos. 178-79; *VCH: Oxfordshire,* II, 106-07.

²³⁵ Dugdale, VII, 833, 834; Lees, pp. 184-89, 190-94; *VCH: Oxfordshire,* II, 106.

²³⁶ *Ibid.;* Dugdale, VII, 833, 842; "The Sandford Cartulary," *op. cit.,* VI, nos. 3, 6, 25, 74; *VCH: Oxfordshire,* II, 106-07.

²³⁷ Dugdale, VII, 823, 836; *VCH: Gloucestershire,* II, 113; Lees, pp. 47-49.

²³⁸ Cf. *ibid.,* p. cxxxii.

²³⁹ *Ibid.; Hosp. Rpt.,* pp. 182-84.

²⁴⁰ Dugdale, VII, 817; *VCH: Leicestershire,* II, 31-32; *CChR,* 15 Hen. III (1231), p. 135.

²⁴¹ *Hosp. Rpt.,* pp. 176-78; *VCH: Leicestershire,* II, 31-32.

²⁴² Lees, pp. cv-cviii; *Hosp. Rpt.,* pp. 179-81; *VCH: Warwickshire,* II, 99.

²⁴³ The original grant at Balsall goes back to Roger Mowbray in the reign of Stephen: Dugdale, VII, 817, 834. Cf. *VCH: Warwickshire,* II, 99-100.

²⁴⁴ Dugdale, VII, 818; Lees, p. lxxxv-lxxxix, 157, 166-68, 172; *Hosp. Rpt.,* p. 95. Cf. *CChR,* 21-22 Hen. III (1237-38), pp. 227, 234.

²⁴⁵ Dugdale, VII, 817, 833; *Rot. Hund.,* II, 454-56; *VCH: Cambridgeshire,* II, 259-63. Grants at Denney go back to 1176-77: Lees, pp. 224-25. Cf. *CChR,* 11 Hen. III (1227), p. 1.

²⁴⁶ Dugdale, VII, 817, 819-20, 832-33; Lees, pp. 211-18; *VCH: Hertfordshire,* III, 10, 18, 66, 68, 174, 176; IV, 445-46.

²⁴⁷ Dugdale, VII, 833; Lees, pp. cxxxvii and n. 6, cxxxviii.

²⁴⁸ *Hosp. Rpt.,* p. 162. Cf. Lees, pp. 79, 87, n. 4.

²⁴⁹ *VCH: Northhamptonshire,* II, 11.

²⁵⁰ Dugdale, VII, 835; *Rot. Hund.,* II, 634, 636, 654; *VCH: Huntingdonshire,* III, 53, 57, 137, 142, 174-75, 198, 218-20, 229.

²⁵¹ Dugdale, VII, 820; Lees, pp. 219-21; *Hosp. Rpt.,* pp. 170-72.

²⁵² *Rot. Hund.,* I 43, 45; *CChR,* 11-12 Hen. III (1228), pp. 5, 77, 79; Dugdale,

VII, 823, 834; *VCH: Buckinghamshire,* I, 346, 391; III, 73, 90, 92, 124, 129, 196, 280; IV, 132, 310.

[253] For the transfer of most of these lands to the Hospitallers, see the *Hosp. Rpt.,* pp. 176, 179, 189-95 (for the first group of counties), 163-67, 172-73 (for the second group), and 162 (for the third group).

[254] Lees, p. 142; Perkins, "Knights Templars in England," *op. cit.,* Appendix E.

[255] *Ibid.* Cf. David E. Easson, *Medieval Religious Houses, Scotland* (London, 1957), pp. 131-32.

[256] Perkins, "The Knights Templars in England," *op. cit.,* Appendix E.

[257] Balsall (Warwickshire) included 560 acres; Upleden (Herefordshire), 740 acres; and Cressing (Essex), 800 acres. These figures (*Hosp. Rpt.* [1308], pp. 168, 179, 195) refer to arable lands and do not include meadows, pastures, forests, gardens, and the like. In such areas as Lincolnshire and Yorkshire, where Templar holdings were greatest, the expression used may be one *"manerium"* (e.g., Ribston, Bruer, and Eagle) or so many carucates — which might be 120, 160, or 240 acres — of land (e.g., Copmanthorp, 3; Eagle, 4; Langenok, 4; and South Witham, 8). Cf. *ibid.,* pp. 136, 143, 154, 160, 172. Hence, the actual area of many estates cannot be given precisely.

[258] Temple Guiting (Gloucestershire), £206; Ribston-Wetherby (Yorkshire), £270; and Temple Bruer (Lincolnshire), £325 — Perkins, "The Knights Templars in England," *op. cit.,* Appendix E.

[259] Cf. tables of holdings of the various religious orders as given in Knowles and Hadcock, *op. cit.* Kosminsky (*op. cit.,* p. 150) also credits the Hospitallers with larger holdings than the Templars in the thirteenth century.

[260] See above, Chap. I, especially the section on "Classes of Membership," and nn. 48 and 49.

[261] *Règle,* arts. 657-86.

[262] *Ibid.* arts. 77-80, 99-100, 101-03, 110, 120, 125, 130, 132, 138, 169, 173, 177, 180-81.

[263] Cf. *ibid.,* arts. 169-72.

[264] Cf. letter of appeal of Terric, Grand Master of the Templars, to the West — Roger of Hoveden, *op. cit.,* RS, II, 324-25.

[265] Charles W. Oman, *A History of the Art of War in the Middle Ages* (London, 1898), pp. 126-28, 510-14; Smail, *op. cit.,* pp. 107-09.

[266] *Ibid.,* pp. 116-20, 199. Smail points out that the foot soldiers played a far more important part in crusading warfare than most authors have attributed to them. No doubt the Templars had some foot soldiers, too — cf. *Règle,* art. 161; Oman, *op. cit.,* p. 309 — but whether or not they actually took an active part in the fighting is not known. Each Templar knight was assigned one or two squires to stand before him and to carry his lance and to stand behind him to lead a spare horse — cf. *Règle,* arts. 51, 77, 99, 101, 110, 120, 130, 132, 138, 140, 143, 157, 180, 181.

[267] Oman, *op. cit.,* pp. 103-04; Smail, *op. cit.,* pp. 111-12.

[268] Smail (*op. cit., passim*) has carefully studied the tactics and strategy, the organization, and the equipment of the Crusaders during the twelfth century and has pointed out many errors and dubious interpretations of scholars who have written in this field. He has concluded (pp. 112, 201) that the Christian forces — presumably this includes the Templars — did not greatly alter their tactics and strategy in view of their actual experiences. They did, however, learn to exercise more restraint and caution in warfare; and they did introduce certain modifications in their organization and in their ways of fighting. The greatest of these changes and modifications was the creation of the Turcopole units which played a very important part in all subsequent operations and whose commander, in the case of the Templars, became one of the chief officers of the order — cf. *Règle,* arts. 169-71.

[269] Cf. above, n. 86.

270 Paris, *Chronica Majora*, RS, IV, 88 (1241); *CPatR*, 18 Hen. III (1234), p. 70; *ibid.*, 27 Hen. III (1243), pp. 722-23.

271 *Règle*, arts. 190-97.

272 *VCH: Cambridgeshire*, II, 260, Lees, p. clxxx.

273 *VCH: Cambridgeshire*, II, 260.

Chapter Three

1 *RLC*, 17 John (1215), I, 231b, 238, 241, 242.

2 *CPatR*, 18-22 Hen. III (1234-38), pp. 47, 105, 161, 172, 184, 189, 230, 233; *LibR*, 14-22 Hen. III (1230-38), pp. 160, 215, 333.

3 For some years after the disgrace of Ralph Neville, Chancellor and Keeper of the Seal (1238), King Henry III entrusted the seal, on a temporary basis, to a number of men of whom Roger the Templar was one. Cf. *Annales de Theokesberia in Annales Monastici*, ed. Henry R. Luard (RS No. 36, 5 vols.; London, 1864-69), I, 110; F. M. Powicke, *King Henry III and the Lord Edward* (2 vols.; Oxford, 1947), II, 780-83; and L. B. Dibben, "Chancellor and Keeper of the Seal under Henry III," *English Historical Review*, XXVII (1912), 42.

4 *Chronica Majora*, RS, III, 629.

5 *Ibid.*, V, 364-65.

6 *Ibid.*, IV, 88. Cf. also *Calendar of Liberate Rolls preserved in the Public Record Office* (3 vols.; London, 1916-37), III, 91 [26 Hen. III (1241)] where John is instructed what to do with certain royal alms. For other instances of the use of Templars to announce royal prohibitions of tournaments, see *CPatR*, 18 Hen. III (1234), p. 70; and *ibid.*, 27 Hen. III (1243), pp. 722-23.

7 Cf. *Calendar of Documents relating to Scotland preserved in Her Majesty's Public Record Office*, ed. Joseph Bain (vols. I-III; Edinburgh, 1881-88), I, no. 2013.

8 Adam of Eynsham, *Magna Vita Sancti Hugonis Episcopi Lincolniensis*, ed. James F. Dimock (RS No. 37; London, 1864), pp. 358-59, 364.

9 *CPatR*, 20 Hen, III (1236), p. 161.

10 Cf. *RLC*, 6 John (1205), I, 27b; *CRR*, 7-9 Hen. III (1223-24), no. 2284; *ClR*, 22 Hen. III (1238), p. 55; *LibR*, 26 Hen. III (1242), p. 94; *CPatR*, 36 Hen. III (1251), p. 118; *ClR*, 36 Hen. III (1252), p. 192; *CPatR*, 47 Hen. III 1243), pp. 722-23; *CLibR*, 36-39 Hen. III (1252-55), pp. 15, 201.

11 Cotton MS, Claud B, fol. 26 – cited by Robert W. Eyton, *Court, Household, and Itinerary of Henry II* (London, 1878), p. 68.

12 *Ibid.*, p. 217.

13 *PatR*, 8 Hen. III (1224), pp. 484-85; Rymer, I, 174.

14 *PatR*, 9 Hen. III (1225), p. 558, Rymer, I, 176.

15 Paris, *Chronica Majora*, RS, III, 335; Rymer, I, 219; *Treaty Rolls*, 19 Hen. III (1235), nos. 23, 24, 26, 89. Cf. *ibid.*, 21 Hen. III (1237), no. 48.

16 *ClR*, 36 Hen. III (1252), pp. 108, 186-87; *CPatR*, 36 Hen. III (1252), pp. 133, 159, 161; Walter W. Shirley (ed.), *Royal and Other Historical Letters illustrative of the Reign of Henry III* (RS No. 27, 2 vols.; London, 1862-66), II, 69-72, 76-81, 83, 92, 391-92. Cf. Powicke, *op. cit.*, I, 227-30. Cf. *CLibR*, 38 Hen. III (1254), p. 173.

17 *ClR*, 38 Hen. III (1254), p. 273; *CLibR*, 38 Hen. III (1254), p. 169. Cf. *ibid.*, 42 Hen. III (1257), p. 406.

18 *ClR*, 38 Hen. III (1254), p. 320.

19 *Ibid.*, 42 Hen. III (1258), p. 326; Paris, *Chronica Majora*, RS, VI, 410-16. Cf. Powicke, *op. cit.*, I, 241-48.

20 *CPatR*, 46-49 Hen. III (1261-65), pp. 189, 275, 366, 476-77.

21 *Ibid.*, 47 Hen. III (1263), p. 239.

22 Roger of Wendover, *op. cit.*, RS, III, 80-83. Cf. Powicke, *op. cit.*, I, 136.

23 Roger of Wendover, *op. cit.*, RS, III, 108.

[24] Roger of Hovedon, *op. cit.*, RS, I, 218; Ralph of Diceto, *op. cit.*, RS, I, 303; William of Newburgh, *op. cit.*, RS, I, 159.

[25] Delisle, *op. cit.*, II, 276 (no. 660).

[26] Roger of Hovedon, *op. cit.*, RS, III, 58; Benedict of Peterborough, *op. cit.*, RS, II, 129; Walter of Coventry, *Historical Collections*, ed. William Stubbs (RS No. 58, 2 vols.; London, 1872-73), I, 412.

[27] Roger of Hovedon, *op. cit.*, RS, I, 221-22; Gervase of Canterbury, *Historical Works*, ed. William Stubbs (RS No. 73, 2 vols.; London, 1879-80), I, 177, 230; Anonymous Life of Thomas Becket, No. I, *Materials for the History of Thomas Becket, Archbishop of Canterbury*, ed. James C. Robertson and J. Brigstocke Sheppard (RS No. 67, 7 vols.; London, 1879-85), IV, 35; Benedict of Peterborough, *op. cit.*, RS, I, 31-33; Delisle, *op. cit.*, I, 585-86; Roger of Wendover, *op. cit.*, RS, II, 36.

[28] Cf. *RLC*, 5 John (1204), I, 17; *LibR*, 5 John (1204), p. 81.

[29] Roger of Wendover, *op. cit.*, RS, II, 68; John de Oxenedes, *op. cit.*, RS, p. 128; Walter of Coventry, *op. cit.*, RS, II, 210; Paris, *Hist. Angl.*, RS, II, 134.

[30] *ClR*, 14 John (1213), p. 148. This sum was subsequently repaid, nine silver marks for the gold mark: *RLC*, 15 John (1213), I, 148b.

[31] Paris, *Chronica Majora*, RS, II, 589-90, 598. For a good edition of *Magna Carta*, see William S. McKechnie, *Magna Carta: A Commentary on the Great Charter of King John* (2d ed.; Glasgow, 1914).

[32] Especially arts, 1, 60, and 63; Rymer, I, 131-32; Paris, *Chronica Majora*, RS, II, 598; Continuation of William of Newburgh, *op. cit.*, RS, III, 519.

[33] Paris, *Chronica Majora*, RS, V, 544.

[34] Cf. *PatR*, 8-9 Hen. III (1224-25), pp. 484, 558; Paris, *Chronica Majora*, RS, III, 235; *ClR*, 36 Hen. III (1252), pp. 159, 161, 186-87.

[35] Rymer, I, 18.

[36] Ralph of Diceto, *op. cit.*, RS, I, 352; Roger of Wendover, *op. cit.*, RS, II, 368; Benedict of Peterborough, *op. cit.*, RS, I, 32.

[37] Roger of Hovedon, *op. cit.*, RS, II, 299; Roger of Wendover, *op. cit.*, RS, I, 134-35.

[38] Rymer, I, 47; Gervase of Canterbury, *op. cit.*, RS, I, 298; Delisle, *op. cit.*, II, 219-20 (no. 613).

[39] Cf. Roger of Hoveden, *op. cit.*, *RS*, III, 179. For the story of Richard on the Third Crusade, see *Itinerarium peregrinorum et Gesta regis Ricardi* in *Chronicles and Memorials of the Reign of Richard I*, ed. William Stubbs (RS No. 38, 2 vols.; London, 1864-65), Vol. I; Runciman, *op. cit.*, III, 34-75; and Grousset, *op. cit.*, III, 60-120.

[40] Roger of Wendover, *op. cit.*, RS, I, 218; Ralph of Coggeshall, *Chronicon Anglicanum*, ed. Joseph Stevenson (RS No. 66; London, 1875), p. 54.

[41] Gervase of Canterbury, *op. cit.*, RS, I, 513; Ralph of Coggeshall, *op. cit.*, RS, pp. 54-56; *Itinerarium . . . Ricardi, op. cit.*, RS, I, 441-45. Cf. also the interesting biography of Kate Morgate: *Richard the Lion Heart* (London, 1924), pp. 264-84.

[42] *Op. cit.*, RS, I, 399.

[43] Cf. Roger of Wendover, *op. cit.*, RS, II, 68, 113, 114; *RLC*, 16 John (1215), I, 196, 196b, 198, 198b, 199, 199b for John; and *ibid.*, 8-10 Hen. III (1225-26), II, 18-21, 70b, 104; *PatR*, 3-9 Hen. III (1219-25), pp. 189, 202-06, 287-88, 435-37, *et passim* for Henry.

[44] Dugdale, VII, 818; *PatR*, 15 Hen. III (1231), p. 439; *CClR*, 21 Hen. III (1237), p. 6. The £8 for chaplains at New Temple were continued by Edward I — *Issues of the Exchequer; being a Collection of Payments made out of His Majesty's Revenue from King Henry III to King Henry VI inclusive*, ed. and trans. Frederick Devon, Vol. VIII (London, 1837), 88-89 [3 Ed. I (1276)].

[45] *Flores Historiarum*, ed. Henry R. Luard (RS No. 95; 3 vols.; London, 1890), III, 28. Cf. Williamson, *op. cit.*, p. 21.

[46] *CPatR*, 36 Hen. III (1252), p. 158.

[47] *Flores Historiarum,* RS, II, 405; John of Oxenedes, *op. cit.,* RS, p. 199; Paris, *Chronica Majora,* RS, V, 478.

[48] *Ibid.,* IV, 640; VI, 142.

[49] *The Parliamentary Writs and Writs of Military Summons,* ed. Francis Palgrave (2 vols.; London, 1827-30), II, 304 [26 Ed. I (1297)].

[50] Thomas Walsingham, *op. cit.,* RS, I, 76; William Rishanger, *Chronica et Annales regnantibus Henrico Tertio et Edwardo Primo, A.D., 1259-1307,* ed. Henry T. Riley (RS No. 28; London, 1865), p. 188; Continuation of William of Newburgh, *op. cit.,* RS, III, 583; *Flores Historiarum,* RS, III, 104; *The Chronicles of London from 44 Hen. III to 17 Edw. III,* trans. Edmund Goldsmid (3 vols.; Edinburgh, 1885), I, 51-52.

[51] Bain, III, nos. 508, 823; Rymer, I, 773.

[52] *CClR,* 1 Ed. II (1307), p. 50.

[53] Paris, *Chronica Majora,* RS, III, 186; Roger of Wendover, *op. cit.,* RS, II, 375; *Parl. Writs,* pp. 28, 30, 47, 56, 84, 90, 112, 138, 170; *CClR,* 23-24 Ed. I (1295-96), pp. 444, 459; *ibid.,* 25-30 Ed. I (1297-1303), pp. 128, 374, 375, 408, 409, 583, 592, 598; *ibid.,* 32 Ed. I (1304), p. 225.

[54] Letters dated at New Temple: *RLC,* 16 John (1215), I, 196, 196b, 198, 198b, 199, 199b (30 letters); *ibid.,* 3 Hen. III (1219), I, 400, 400b, 401 (32 letters); *ibid.,* 9-10 Hen. III (1225-26), II, 18-21, 70b, 104 (52 letters); *ClR,* 27 Hen. III (1243), p. 91 (1 letter); *PatR,* 3-9 Hen. III (1219-25), pp. 189, 202-06, 287-88, 435-37, 480, 508-11 (35 letters); *ibid.,* 11 Hen. III (1227), p. 137 (1 letter); *CPatR,* 27 Hen. III (1243), p. 720 (1 letter); *ibid.,* 1-4 Ed. I (1272-76), pp. 1-3, 6-7, 15, 31-32, 136-37 (35 letters). Cf. also, *ibid.,* 22 Ed. I (1294), p. 102 and *Fines in the Tower of London,* pp. 496-97. Letters dated at Temple Bruer: *ClR,* 14-20 Hen. III (1230-36), pp. 283, 319; *CPatR,* 20 Hen. III (1236), p. 159; *ibid.,* 4 Ed. I (1276), pp. 137, 176; *CChanWar,* 12 Ed. I (1284), I, 18; *CPatR,* 12 Ed. I (1284), pp. 114-15; *CChanWar,* 33 Ed. I (1305), I, 245 (25 letters). Letters dated at Temple Dinsley: *ClR,* 33-35 Hen. III (1249-51), pp. 196, 426-27; *ibid.,* 36 Hen. III (1252), pp. 151, 248; *CLibR,* 35 Hen. III (1251), p. 344; *CPatR,* 36 Hen. III (1252), p. 149; *CChanWar,* 21-25 Ed. I (1293-97), I, 37, 75; *CPatR,* 22 Ed. I (1294), p. 110 (10 letters). Letters dated at Temple Cowton; *CPatR,* 28 Ed. I (1300), p. 551; *CChanWar,* 30 Ed. I (1302), I, 160-61 (3 letters).

[55] *Annales de Wintonia, op. cit.,* RS, II, 99.

[56] *Flores Historiarum,* RS, III, 28; Thomas Walsingham, *Ypodigma Neustriae,* ed. Henry T. Riley (RS No. 28; London, 1876), pp. 166-67; Rymer I, 497.

[57] *CClR,* 27 Ed. I (1299), p. 318.

[58] Cf. *Chronicon Abbatiae Ramesiensis a Saec. X usque ad an. circitur 1200,* ed. W. Dunn Macray (RS No. 83; London, 1886), pp. 400-1; *PatR,* 2-7 Hen. III (1218-23), pp. 135, 481-82; *Flores Historiarum,* RS, III, 124.

[59] Paris, *Chronica Majora,* RS, V, 524-27, 532; VI, 315; *Annales de Burton, op. cit.,* RS, I, 360; *Registrum Epistolarum Fratris Johannis Peckham, Archiepiscopi Cantuariensis,* ed. Charles T. Martin (RS No. 77, 3 vols.; London, 1882-85), I, 256-57; II, 507-09, 537, 594; Gervase of Canterbury, *op. cit.,* RS, II, 299; *CPatR,* 5 Ed. I (1277), p. 210; *ibid.,* 27 Ed. I (1299), pp. 450-51.

[60] Benedict of Peterborough, *op. cit.,* RS, II, 238; Roger of Hoveden, *op. cit.,* RS, III, 187; *ClR,* 19 Hen. III (1235), p. 55; Paris, *Chronica Majora,* RS, V, 509; *CLibR,* 39 Hen. III (1255), p. 245.

[61] *Flores Historiarum,* RS, II, 269; Paris, *Chronica Majora,* RS, IV, 284, 379, 420, 561. William E. Lunt (*Financial Relations of the Papacy with England to 1327* [Cambridge, 1939], p. 581) suggests that the general collectors of papal revenue also stayed at New Temple.

[62] *ClR,* 39 Hen. III (1255), pp. 114, 116, 117, 212.

[63] Paris, *Chronica Majora,* RS, III, 43, 201; IV, 136, 493. The first Earl serves as an example of those persons who joined the order just before their death — in his case in accordance with a vow taken while on a crusade in his earlier

years. Cf. Williamson, *op. cit.*, pp. 19-20 citing an old French chronicle, "L'histoire de Guillaume le Marechal."

[64] Shirley, *op. cit.*, I, 119-20.

[65] *CPatR*, 31 Hen. III (1246), p. 495.

[66] *ClR*, 34 Hen. III (1250), p. 283. For other valuables deposited in New Temple, see below.

[67] *CPatR*, 19-20 Hen. III (1234-36), pp. 81, 143; *ClR*, 52 Hen. III (1267), p. 407; *CClR*, 17-20 Ed. I (1289-91), pp. 56, 245-46.

[68] *LibR*, 17 Hen. III (1233), p. 215; *ibid.*, 26 Hen. III (1241), p. 91; *ibid.*, 32 Hen. III (1248), p. 160; *ClR*, 27 Hen. III (1243), p. 42; *ibid.*, 32-34 Hen.III (1247-50), pp. 10, 263-64; *ibid.*, 36 Hen. III (1252), p. 50.

[69] Cf. *ClR*, 42 Hen. III (1258), pp. 331-32; *ibid.*, 51 Hen. III (1267), pp. 386-88, 391-92. (These agreements covered such matters as payments of money and transfer of lands.)

[70] E.g., *PipeR*, 5 Hen. II (1158), pp. 28, 29, 32, 34, 35, 36, 38, 40 *et passim; ibid.*, 12 John (1210), pp. 18, 42, 43, 65, 69, 76, *et passim*. (Over a thousand references can be found in the Pipe Rolls.)

[71] *RLC*, 6-7 Hen. III (1221-23), I, 477, 512, 565; *LibR*, 11-23 Hen. III (1227-38), pp. 55, 104, 149, 244, 297, 347; *ibid.*, 26-28 Hen. III (1241-44), pp. 93, 160; *CLibR*, 30 Hen. III (1246), pp. 42, 48; *CClR*, 9 Ed. I (1280), p. 70. Once (*RLC*, 15 John [1213], I, 153) the same sum was granted by John.

[72] Cf. *ibid.*, 15 John (1214), I, 141; *ibid.*, 8 Hen. III (1224), I 618-43; *ClR*, 16 Hen. III (1232), p. 90; *ibid.*, 33 Hen. III (1249), p. 189.

[73] *RLC*, 15 John (1214), I, 141; *ibid.*, 9 Hen. III (1225), II, 21b; *ClR*, 19-21 Hen. III (1235-37), pp. 94, 266, 440; *ibid.*, 22-26 Hen. III (1238-42), pp. 54, 160, 190, 301, 426; *ibid.*, 27-30 Hen. III (1243-46), pp. 22, 149, 182, 192, 273, 307, 422; *CLibR*, 26-28 Hen. III (1242-44), pp. 142, 245.

[74] *RLC*, 8 Hen. III (1224), I, 618-43; *ClR*, 15 Hen. III (1231), p. 501; *ibid.*, 16-18 Hen. III (1232-34), pp. 90, 428; *ibid.*, 19-21 Hen. III (1235-37), pp. 88, 134, 135, 272, 440, 441. Except for his twenty-third and twenty-fifth years, similar entries are found for all the remaining years of Henry III's reign. Only one entry (*CClR*, 14 Ed. I [1286], p. 392) is found for Edward I. It cannot be said positively, however, that additional grants were not made by Edward I.

[75] E.g., *ClR*, 28 Hen. III (1243), p. 149; *ibid.*, 49 Hen. III (1264), p. 4.

[76] E.g., *ibid.*, 24 Hen. III (1239), p. 160.

[77] *Ibid.*, 15 Hen. III (1231), p. 510; *ibid.*, 19-20 Hen. III (1235-36), pp. 45, 227; *ibid.*, 24-29 Hen. III (1239-45), pp. 163, 229, 287, 330; *CPatR*, 19 Ed. I (1291), p. 442.

[78] *ClR*, 24 Hen. III (1239), p. 160; *LibR*, 24 Hen. III (1240), p. 443.

[79] *Ibid.*, p. 179.

[80] *Ibid.*, 22 Hen. III (1238), p. 56.

[81] *RLC*, 6 John (1205), I, 17b.

[82] *CPatR*, 27 Hen. III (1243), p. 371.

[83] Cf. comments on the inquest in Chap. II above.

[84] Clarence Perkins, "The Wealth of the Templars in England," *American Historical Review*, XV (1909), 252-63 at p. 253.

[85] *Règle*, arts. 135, 181; Lees, p. lxxxii.

[86] Cf. *ibid.*, p. lxi.

[87] We know, for example, that at Evesham (Knowles, *op. cit.*, I, 287 — citing the *Evesham Chronicle*, p. 285) that Benedictine lay brothers managed the manors of that house.

[88] For additional comments on land and personnel, see section section of Chap. II above.

[89] Lees, p. lxxi.

[90] The figures given here are taken from the extracts of several keepers' reports

published in the *Gentleman's Magazine and Historical Review* ("Original Documents relating to the Knights Templars"), III N.S. (1857), 250, 520-25.

[91] J. E. T. Rogers, *A History of Agriculture and Prices in England,* Vol. I (Oxford, 1866), p. 21.

[92] Norman S. B. Gras, *The Evolution of the Corn Market from the Twelfth to the Eighteenth Century,* "Harvard Economic Studies," Vol. XIII (Cambridge, 1915), pp. 22-24, 30.

[93] *Ibid.,* p. 12. Cf. also, W. H. Beveridge, "The Yield and Price of Corn in the Middle Ages," *Economic History,* I (1927), 155-67. D. L. Farmer ("Some Grain Price Movements in Thirteenth Century England," *Economic History Review,* X (1957-58) 3rd S, 207-20) adversely criticizes the methods and conclusions of Rogers, Gras, and Beveridge, and feels that Gras' price schedule is far too high; nonetheless, he definitely agrees that the general trend of grain prices in the thirteenth century was upwards and that landlords found it profitable to sell their surplus.

[94] *The Pipe Roll of the Bishopric of Winchester for the Fourth Year of the Pontificate of Peter des Roches, 1208-1209,* "Studies in Economic and Political Science," Vol. XI (London, 1913), pp. xliii-xlv. Cf. Kosminsky, *op. cit.,* pp. 324-25.

[95] *Ibid.*

[96] This involves royal permission to the Master of the Temple in Ireland to ship his grain for trading purposes where he will without payment of customs fees: *Doc. rel. to Ire.,* I, no. 1276.

[97] Cf. Lees, pp. 15, 39, 77 *et passim; Hosp. Rpt.,* pp. 144 ,145, 146, 154 *et passim.*

[98] Lees, pp. 15, 39, 77.

[99] *VCH: Bedfordshire,* III, 66; *VCH: Worcestershire,* IV, 444-45; *VCH: Leicestershire,* II, 32, 171, 173; *CPatR,* 5 Ed. II (1312), pp. 466, 467; "Original Documents relating to the Knights Templars," *op. cit.,* pp. 520-25; Perkins, "Wealth of the Templars in England," *op. cit.,* p. 256, n. 23.

[100] Pp. 136, 157, 168, 183, 184, 187.

[101] R. A. Pelham, "Fourteenth-Century England," *Historical Geography of England before A.D. 1800,* ed. H. C. Darby (Cambridge, 1936), p. 240, n. 3.

[102] *CChanWar,* 26 Ed. I (1298), p. 93.

[103] Lord Treasurer's Remembrancer, Enrolled Accounts, Misc. Roll 20, m. 15-17 — cited by Perkins, "Knights Templars in England," *op. cit.,* p. 255, n. 16.

[104] Lees, pp. 2, 72, 73.

[105] "Original Documents relating to the Knights Templars," *op. cit.,* pp. 520-25; *VCH: Bedfordshire,* III, 66; *VCH: Leicestershire,* II, 171.

[106] Hugh H. L. Bellot, *The Inner and Middle Temple* (London, 1902), p. 17

[107] Lees, pp. 80, 81, 131 *et passim.* Cf. *CRR,* 9-10 Hen. III (1225-26), no. 2376.

[108] *Ibid.,* p. 132.

[109] *Ibid.,* pp. 50, 127.

[110] Eleanora Carus-Wilson, "The Woollen Industry," *Cambridge Economic History of Europe,* Vol. II: *Trade and Industry in the Middle Ages.,* ed. M. M. Postan and E. E. Rich (Cambridge, 1952), p. 409. Miss Wilson ("An Industrial Revolution of the Thirteenth Century," *Economic History Review,* XI [1941], 39-60 at p. 45) even goes so far as to say it is "conceivable" that the Templars may have introduced the fulling mill to England.

[111] E. Lipson, *An Introduction to the Economic History of England,* Vol. I: *The Middle Ages* (London, 1915); Eileen Power, *"The Wool Trade in English Medieval History"* (London, 1942); W. Cunningham, *"Growth of English Industry and Commerce,* Vol. I (5th ed.; Cambridge, 1910); L. Salzman, *English Industry of the Middle Ages* (Oxford, 1923) and *English Trade in the Middle Ages* (Oxford, 1931); Carus-Wilson, "The Woollen Industry," *op. cit.,* pp. 355-428; Herbert Heaton, *The Yorkshire Woollen and Worsted Industries from the earliest Times up to the Industrial Revolution* (Oxford, 1920); and E. Lipson, *History of the Woollen and Worsted Industries* (London, 1921).

[112] Cf. Chap. II above.

[113] Nellie Nielson, "Medieval Agrarian Society in its Prime: England," *Cambridge Economic History of Europe,* Vol. I: *The Agrarian Life of the Middle Ages,* ed. J. H. Clapham and Eileen Power (Cambridge, 1941), p. 465.

[114] *CPatR,* 26 Ed. I (1298), p. 332. The stone as a unit of weight varied during the Middle Ages from 8 to 24 pounds, but was decreed by statute of Edward III (1357) to weigh 14 pounds with 26 stones making one sack — Denholm-Young, *op. cit.,* p. 57. Cf. Power, *op. cit.,* p. 23.

[115] *CPatR,* 26 Ed. I (1298), p. 332.

[116] *CChanWar,* 26 Ed. I (1298), p. 93.

[117] *CPatR,* 26 Ed. I (1298), p. 332.

[118] Cf. Coburn V. Graves, "The Economic Activities of the Cistercians in Medieval England, 1128-1307," *Analecta Sacri Ordinis Cisterciensis,* XIII (1957), fasc. 1-2, at p. 26; A. Schaube, "Die Wollsausfuhr Englands von Jahre 1273," *Vierteljahrschrift für Social- und Wirtschaftsgeschichte,* VI (1908), 39-72 and 159-85, at p. 174.

[119] Cf. Robert J. Whitwell, "English Monasteries and the Wool Trade in the Thirteenth Century," *Vierteljahrschrift für Social- und Wirtschaftsgeschichte,* II (1940), p. 17; and *CClR,* 32 Ed. I (1304), pp. 172-73 for sale to the Mozzi of Florence of wool worth 700 marks.

[120] *RLC,* 15 John (1213), I, 104, 148b, 214; *ibid.,* 8 Hen. III (1224), I, 609; *ClR,* 15 Hen. III (1231), pp. 518-19; Rymer, I, 115.

[121] Cf. *CPatR,* 55 Hen. III (1271), pp. 594-95.

[122] Carus-Wilson, "The Woolen Industry," *op. cit.,* p. 402. The tax set in 1275 was accepted by those involved in the sale and export of wool as reasonable, but there was much opposition to the very high rates of 5 and 3 marks (66s. 8d. and 40s.) set by Edward briefly in view of his great need for increased revenue during the last decade of the thirteenth century. Cf. Power, *op. cit.,* p. 78.

[123] *Ibid.,* pp. 22-23, 33. References in primary sources to the Templars as producers and sellers of wool, though few in number, are such as to suggest that the complete omission or merest mention of them by writers of secondary accounts (cf. n. 111 above) does not do them justice.

[124] Cf. *PatR,* 10-11 Hen. III (1226-27), pp. 13-14, 24, 105; *CPatR,* 26-27 Hen. III (1242), pp. 309, 330, 333; *ClR,* 14-15 Hen. III (1230-31), pp. 368, 477; *ibid.,* 26 Hen. III (1242), p. 505.

[125] *RLC,* 17 John (1215), I, 214; *PatR,* 9 Hen. III (1224), pp. 492, 517; *ibid.,* 14 Hen. III (1230), pp. 368, 370, 374; *ClR,* 14 Hen. III (1230), p. 368. Cf. *RLC,* 15 John (1213), I, 136b; *ibid.,* 8 Hen. III (1224), I, 599b; *ClR,* 14-15 Hen. III (1230-31), pp. 291, 477. Cf. Jules Piquet, *Les Templiers: étude de leurs opérations financières* (Paris, 1939), pp. 3, 30, 31 where reference to the "fleet" is made.

[126] *PatR,* 14 Hen. III (1230), p. 368; *ClR,* 15 Hen. III (1231), p. 477.

[127] Cf. *RLC,* 10 Hen. III (1226), II, 112.

[128] *PatR,* 11-12 Hen. III (1227-28), pp. 105, 197. Cf. *CPatR,* 21 Ed. I (1293), p. 20.

[129] Cf. *ibid.,* 26-27 Hen. III (1242), p. 333.

[130] *RLC,* 17 John (1215), I, 214; *ibid.,* 10-11 Hen. III (1226-27), II, 114, 115, 169; *PatR,* 9 Hen. III (1225), pp. 492, 517; *ibid.,* 10 Hen. III (1226), pp. 24, 113; *ibid.,* 14 Hen. III (1230), pp. 368, 370; *ClR,* 14-15 Hen. III (1230-31), pp. 291, 368, 477.

[131] *CPatR,* 26-27 Hen. III (1242), p. 333.

[132] *RLC,* 15-17 John (1213-16), I, 159, 229b, 238, 268b; *ibid.,* 10-11 Hen. III (1226-27), II, 114, 169; *PatR,* 9 Hen. III (1225), p. 540.

[133] *Ibid.,* 12-14 Hen. III (1228-30), pp. 197, 368; *CPatR,* 26-27 Hen. III (1242), pp. 330, 333.

[134]*RLC*, 17 John, (1215), I, 229b, 238; *ibid.*, 9-10 Hen. III (1225-26), II, 51, 110, 112, 113, 113b, 114, 114b, 115, 117; Bain, I. no. 935.

[135] *RLC*, 17 John (1215), I, 229b, 238; *PatR*, 9 Hen. III (1225), p. 540.

[136] *Ibid.*, pp. 505, 540, 542; *ibid.*, 10 Hen. III (1226), pp. 13, 14; *RLC*, 10-11 Hen. III (1226-27), II, 94b, 160, 183.

[137] See below, Appendix D for the references in the source materials for each of these markets and fairs.

[138] Cf. Léopold Delisle, *Mémoires sur les opérations financières des Templiers*, "Académie des Inscriptions et Belles-Lettres, Mémoires," Vol. XXXIII (Paris, 1889); Piquet, *op. cit.*; Agnes Sandys, "The Financial and Administrative Importance of the London Temple in the Thirteenth Century," *Essays in Medieval History presented to Thomas Frederick Tout*, ed. A. G. Little and F. M. Powicke (Manchester, 1925), pp. 147-62; Eleanor Ferris, "The Financial Relations of the Knights Templars to the English Crown," *American Historical Review*, VIII (1902), 1-17.

[139] Cf. Thomas F. Tout, *Chapters in the Administrative History of Medieval England*, "University of Manchester Publications," No. XCCVII, Vols. I-II (Manchester, 1920), II, 74; S. B. Chrimes, *An Introduction to the Administrative History of Medieval England* (Oxford, 1952), p. 28. Even today, safekeeping (e.g., safe deposit boxes) is still an important function of banks.

[140] *Rotuli litterarum patentium in Turri Londinensi asservati*, ed. Thomas D. Hardy (London, 1835), 5-6 John (1204-05), I, 139.

[141] *PatR*, 16 Hen. III (1232), p. 490.

[142] *CPatR*, 26 Hen. III (1242), p. 281.

[143] *ClR*, 38 Hen. III (1254), p. 62.

[144] *CPatR*, 56 Hen. III (1272), p. 627; Rymer, I, 410.

[145] *Ibid.*, p. 435.

[146] *CPatR*, 17 Hen. III (1232), pp. 2, 5; *ClR*, 17 Hen. III (1233), p. 199; Bain, I, no. 1163. Cf. Paris, *Chronica Majora*, RS, III, 221, 232-33.

[147] *CPatR*, 26 Hen. III (1242), p. 270.

[148] *Ibid.*, 43 Hen. III (1259), pp. 21-22.

[149] Cf. *CClR*, 62 Hen. III (1278), p. 447.

[150] Cf. *CLibR*, 22 Hen. III (1238), pp. 326, 330; *ibid.*, 35 Hen. III (1251), pp. 326, 374.

[151] Cf. *CPatR*, 41 Hen. III (1257, pp. 587-88; *ibid.*, 4 Ed. I (1276), pp. 140-41; *ibid.*, 14 Ed. I (1286), pp. 231-32, 244.

[152] Cf. *RLC*, 9-10 Hen. III (1225), II, 40, 75, 76, 82, 84; *PatR*, 9 Hen. III (1225), pp. 534, 535, 538, 546-49; *ibid.*, 10-11 Hen. III (1226), pp. 1, 2, 8, 9, 93.

[153]Cf. *CPatR*, 54-56 Hen. III (1270-72), pp. 439, 448, 466, 487, 493, 494, 498, 508, 513, 517, 524, 538-40, 542, 547, 557, 570, 572, 578, 579, 639-40, 655-56, 682-83, 710; *CClR*, 13 Ed. I (1285), pp. 350-51.

[154] *ClR*, 22 Hen. III (1238), p. 52; *CPatR*, 22-26 Hen. III (1238-42), pp. 221, 222, 230, 275, 78; *ibid.*, 11 Ed. I (1283), p. 70; *LibR*, 22-24 Hen. III (1238-40), pp. 325-26, 330, 333, 446.

[155] *ClR*, 16 Hen. III (1232), pp. 155-56; Roger of Wendover, *op. cit.*, RS, III, 41; Paris, *Chronica Majora*, RS, III, 232; Rymer, I, 207.

[156] *Book of Fees*, I, 290, 291, 331, 1439-45; *PatR*, 9 Hen. III (1225), pp. 505, 506, 508.

[157] *ClR*, 34 Hen. III (1250), p. 321; *CPatR*, 18 Hen. III (1234), p. 75; *ibid.*, 39 Hen. III (1255), pp. 400, 401; *ibid.*, 2-3 Ed. I (1274-75), pp. 52, 83, 84, 99, 100.

[158] *ClR*, 37 Hen. III (1253), p. 448; *RLC*, 2 Hen. III (1218), I, 367.

[159] E.g., *ibid.*, 8 Hen. III (1224), I, 593, 630.

[100] *CLibR*, 32-35 Hen. III (1248-51), pp. 184, 332, 358. Cf. *ibid.*, 37 Hen. III (1252), p. 52.

[161] *CPatR*, 31 Hen. III (1247), p. 500; *ClR*, 34-35 Hen. III (1250-51), pp. 318, 500.

[162] Rymer, I, 87; *CClR*, 15 Hen. III (1231), p. 593; *CPatR*, 26 Hen. III (1242), pp. 277, 281, 282, 287.

[163] *Ibid.*, 41 Hen. III (1257), pp. 568, 605; *ibid.*, 43 Hen. III (1259), p. 30; *ibid.*, 4 Ed. I (1276), pp. 140, 147.

[164] *CClR*, 24 Hen. III (1239-40), pp. 153-54, 171-72; *CPatR*, 55-56 Hen. III (1272), pp. 657, 680-81.

[165] *RLC*, 16 John (1214), I, 175b.

[166] Bliss, I, 74-75 (Honorius III, 1220), 383 (Urban IV, 1262), 423 (Clement IV, 1266), 444 (Gregory X, 1272); *Reg. de Grég.* IX (1238), nos. 4268-72; *RLC*, 3 Hen. III (1219), I, 396b; *Select Letters of Innocenct III*, pp. 159-60 (1213); *Records of Anthony Bek, Bishop and Patriarch (1283-1311)*, ed. C. M. Fraser ("Publications of the Surtees Society," Vol. CLXII; London, 1947), no. 407 (1294). Cf. Lunt, *op. cit.*, pp. 243-45.

[167] Bliss, I, 75 (Honorius III, 1220), Rymer, I, 266-67 (Innocent IV, 1246-48); *CLibR*, 22-23 Hen. III (1237-39), pp. 295, 408; Paris, *Chronica Majora*, RS, IV, 557, 560-61, 577 (Innocent IV, 1245-46); *Reg. de Grég. IX* (1272), no. 193.

[168] Bliss, I, 75, 383, 384, 423; *Select Letters of Innocent III*, pp. 159-60.

[169] *CPatR*, 22 Hen. III (1238), p. 221.

[170] Walter of Hemingway, *op. cit.*, II, 273-74.

[171] Paris, *Chronica Majora*, RS, III, 221, 232-33; *Annales Londoniensis, op. cit.*, RS, I, 31; *Flores Historiarum*, RS, p. 291; Shirley, *op. cit.*, RS, I, 525; *CPatR* 17 Hen. III (1233), p. 2.

[172] Cf. *ibid.*, 26 Hen. III (1242), p. 270.

[173] Cf. *ClR*, 38 Hen. III (1254), p. 62. In this reference, the king orders an inventory of royal treasures made; but we are not told the results.

[174] Paris, *Chronica Majora*, RS, V, 704.

[175] *Ibid.*

[176] *Annales de Dunstaplia, op. cit.*, RS, III, 222 give the sum as £1,000; Gervase of Canterbury, *op. cit.*, RS, II, 222 gives it as £10,000. The latter figure is so large a sum of money for this period that the smaller figure is more likely to be correct. Gervase says the money was taken "de thesauro multorum magnatum terrae et mercatorium." This act so enraged Londoners that riots immediately broke out and Edward and his supporters found it necessary to flee.

[177] Cf. original papal document given by William E. Lunt, "A Papal Tenth levied in the British Isles from 1274 to 1280," *English Historical Review*, XXXII (1917), 48-89, at pp. 75-76.

[178] *Ibid.; CPatR*, 61 Hen. III (1277), pp. 326, 354.

[179] Rymer, II, 823.

[180] Walter of Hemingburg, *op. cit.*, II, 273-74. Hubert de Burgh's money was stored in strong boxes under double lock and key. Cf. above, n. 171.

[181] Cf. *CPatR*, 41 Hen. III (1257), p. 568.

[182] For a fuller discussion of the difference between these two types of deposit, see Usher, "The Origins of Banking," *op. cit.*, pp. 412-13.

[183] Piquet, *op. cit.*, pp. 46-48.

[184] *Ibid.*, p. 50.

[185] Cf. above, n. 171.

[186] Cf. Piquet, *op. cit.*, p. 48.

[187] *Ibid.*, p. 58. Cf. more general comment of Raymond A. DeRoover, "New Interpretations of the History of Banking," *Journal of World History*, II (1954), 38-76, at p. 54.

[188] Piquet, *op. cit.*, pp. 31-32, 36-38; Delisle, *op. cit.*, p. 15.

[189] *Ibid.*, p. 20; Piquet, *op. cit.*, pp. 50-51; Usher, "The Origins of Banking," *op. cit.*, p. 415; Abbott P. Usher, *The Early History of Deposit Banking in Mediterranean Europe*, "Harvard Economic Studies," Vol. LXXV (Cambridge, 1943), p. 6.

[190] Cf. DeRoover, "New Interpretations of the History of Banking," *op. cit.*, p. 40, who says there was no law against doing so though some theologians disapproved; Noonan, *op. cit.*, p. 172; DeRoover, *L'evolution de la Lettre de Change*, p. 22, and *Money, Banking and Credit in Medieval Bruges*, pp. 41-42.

[191] Cf. *ibid.*, p. 40; Usher, "Origins of Banking," *op. cit.*, p. 413.

[192] Rymer, I, 47; *Itinerarium . . . Ricardi*, *op. cit.*, RS, I, 26.

[193] The mark at this time was worth 13s. 4d. or two-thirds of a pound: cf. *CPatR*, 16 Hen. III (1232), pp. 514-15; Power, *op. cit.*, p. 23. Hence 20,000 marks equal £13,333.

[194] *RLC*, 14-16 John (1212-15), I, 124b, 134, 136b, 141, 198b, 221b; *PatR*, 16 John (1214), p. 107.

[195] *RLC*, 14-15 John (1212-14), I, 124b, 136b; Rymer, I, 108, 165, 173; *RLP*, 15 John (1214), I, 104b, 107.

[196] *CPatR*, 2-4 Ed. I (1274-76), pp. 52, 83, 99, 100, 114, 140; *CClR*, 4 Ed. I (1276), pp. 264, 410.

[197] *PatR*, 9 Hen. III (1225), pp. 544-45; *ibid.*, 10 Hen. III (1226), p. 54; *ClR*, 30 Hen. III (1246), pp. 470-71.

[198] *PatR*, 8 Hen. III (1224), p. 467.

[199] *RLC*, 6 Hen. III (1221), I, 483.

[200] *Ibid.*, 7 Hen. III (1223), I, 558.

[201] *CPatR*, 31 Hen. III (1247), p. 507.

[202] *LibR*, 28 Hen. III (1244), pp. 229, 238; *CPatR*, 31 Hen. III (1247), p. 497.

[203] *PatR*, 8 Hen. III (1224), p. 436.

[204] *Ibid.*, 11 Hen. III (1226), pp. 40-41; *LibR*, 24 Hen. III (1240), p. 452.

[205] Rymer, I, 232.

[206] *RLC*, 6 Hen. III (1222), I, 486b; *LibR*, 23 Hen. III (1239), p. 408; *CLibR*, 30-34 Hen. III (1246-50), pp. 115, 142, 285.

[207] *PatR*, 9 Hen. III (1225), p. 325.

[208] *CPatR*, 29 Hen. III (1245), pp. 449, 453; *CLibR*, 34-35 Hen. III (1250-51), pp. 310-11, 382; *ClR*, 34 Hen. III (1250), p. 32.

[209] *PatR*, 8 Hen. III (1224), pp. 436, 438-39.

[210] *ClR*, 19 Hen. III (1235), p. 110.

[211] *Ibid.*, 29 Hen. III (1224), pp. 270, 274.

[212] *PatR*, 10 Hen. III (1225), p. 534; Rymer, I, 232; *CPatR*, 22 Hen. III (1238), p. 222; *ClR*, 29 Hen. III (1245), p. 339.

[213] *PatR*, 14 Hen. III (1230), p. 322; Rymer, I, 196; *LibR*, 14 Hen. III (1229), p. 160.

[214] *RLC*, 5 Hen. III (1221), I, 471b; *PatR*, 6-9 Hen. III (1222-24), pp. 328, 497.

[215] *ClR*, 15 Hen. III (1231), p. 544.

[216] Paris, *Chronica Majora*, RS, V, 704; *ClR*, 43 Hen. III (1258), pp. 341-42, 418-19, 446-47, 471; *CPatR*, 43 Hen. III (1258-59), pp. 4, 15. Cf. Powicke, *op. cit.*, I, 384-85.

[217] *CPatR*, 29 Hen. III (1245), p. 453.

[218] Paris, *Chronica Majora*, RS, III, 233; Roger of Wendover, *op. cit.*, RS, III, 41; *Cal. of Doc. rel. to Scot.*, I, no. 1163; *CPatR*, 17 Hen. III (1233), p. 2

[219] *RLC*, 10 Hen. III (1226), II, 214.

[220] Paris, *Chronica Majora*, RS, V, 704.

[221] *Annales de Dunstaplia*, *op. cit.*, RS, III, 222; Gervase of Canterbury, *op. cit.*, RS, II, 222.

[222] Cf. Rymer, I, 616.

[223] *CClR*, 4 Ed. I (1278), pp. 446-47, 462; Walter of Hemingburg, *op. cit.*, II, 273; Rymer, II, 7. Cf. *The Chronicle of Walter of Guisborough previously edited as the Chronicle of Walter of Hemingford or Hemingburgh*, ed. Harry Rothwell ("Publications of the Camden Society," Vol. LXXXIX; London, 1957), p. 382.

[224] Bliss, I, 117.

[225] *CPatR*, 2 Hen. III (1218), p. 168; *RLC*, 4 Hen. III (1220), I, 415.

[226] *ClR*, 18 Hen. III (1234), p. 556.

[227] *Ibid.*, 50 Hen. III (1266), p. 239.

[228] *CPatR*, 37 Hen. III (1253), p. 195.

[229] *Ibid.*, 54 Hen. III (1270), p. 407.

[230] *CChR*, 41 Hen. III (1256), p. 454.

[231] *CPatR*, 41 Hen. III (1257), p. 569.

[232] *Ibid.*, 53 Hen. III (1296), p. 358.

[233] *Chronicles of the Mayors and Sheriffs of London*, RS, p. 117.

[234] *RLC*, 10 Hen. III (1226), II, 122b.

[235] *PatR*, 11 Hen. III (1227), p. 141.

[236] *CPatR*, 37 Hen. III (1253), p. 174.

[237] *ClR*, 41 Hen. III (1257), p. 122.

[238] *CPatR*, 43 Hen. III (1259), p. 33.

[239] Cf. *ClR*, 43 Hen. III (1258), pp. 341-42, 418-19; 446-47, 471; *CPatR*, 43-45 Hen. III (1258-60), pp. 4, 15, 66, 96, 126.

[240] *ClR*, 54 Hen. III (1270), p. 258.

[241] *Ibid.*, 56 Hen. III (1271), p. 559; *CClR*, 10 Ed. I (1282), p. 184.

[242] *CPatR*, 43 Hen. III (1259), p. 41.

[243] Paris, *Chronica Majora*, RS, VI, 220-21.

[244] *Cal. of Doc. in France*, I, 336 (no. 1041).

[245] *ClR*, 55 Hen. III (1271), p. 410.

[246] *CClR*, 18 Ed. I (1290), p. 118.

[247] E.g., *PatR*, 6 Hen. III (1221), pp. 317-18, 321-22; *ClR*, 45 Hen. III (1261), pp. 463-64; *CClR*, 28 Ed. I (1300), p. 392.

[248] Cf. contract cited by Paris, *Chronica Majora*, RS, III, 329.

[249] *PatR*, 16 Hen. III (1232), pp. 514-15; *CPatR*, 32 Hen. III (1247), p. 1; Rymer, I, 365; *CPatR*, 42 Hen. III (1258), pp. 629, 631; *ibid.*, 43-44 Hen. III (1259-60), pp. 16, 30, 71; *ibid.*, 50 Hen. III (1266), p. 675; *ibid.*, 52 Hen. III (1268), p. 277.

[250] *Ibid.*, 41 Hen. III (1257), p. 562.

[251] *Historic and Municipal Documents of Ireland*, p. 168 (1266); Paris, *Chronica Majora*, RS, VI, 220-21; *Records of Anthony Bek*, no. 8 (1288).

[252] E.g., *CPatR*, 37 Hen. III (1253), p. 228.

[253] Over forty such cases can be cited for the years from 1249 to 1272. Cf. *ClR*, 33 Hen. III (1249), p. 230; *ibid.*, 41 Hen. III (1257), p. 115; *ibid.*, 44-45 Hen. III (1260-61), pp. 161, 213, 463-64; *ibid.*, 51 Hen. III (1267), pp. 378-81, 393, 398; *ibid.*, 52 Hen. III (1268), pp. 243-45, 280-81, 501-02, 513-14, 520-22, 532, 559; *ibid.*, 53-56 Hen. III (1269-72), pp. 98, 107, 130, 139, 145, 248, 251, 266, 285-86, 474, 558, 561, 562; *CPatR*, 37 Hen. III (1253), p. 227; *ibid.*, 50 Hen. III (1266), pp. 656-57; *ibid.*, 52 Hen. III (1268), pp. 282-84; *CRR*, 4 Hen. III (1220), p. 287.

[254] *ClR*, 52 Hen. III (1268), pp. 520-21.

[255] *Ibid.*, 51 Hen. III (1267), p. 374.

[256] Cf. *CPatR*, 52 Hen. III (1268), pp. 280-83.

[257] Cf. *ibid.*

²⁵⁸ E.g., *CClR,* 40 Hen. III (1256), p. 442; *ibid.,* 51-52 Hen. III (1267-68), pp. 379, 381, 442, 514, 521, 522, 542, *ibid.,* 53 Hen. III (1269), p. 107; *ibid.,* 10 Ed. I (1282), p. 184; *CPatR,* 54 Hen. III (1270), p. 446.

²⁵⁹ Cf. Delisle, *op. cit.,* p. 15; DeRoover, *Money, Banking, and Credit,* p. 215.

²⁶⁰ The details of the contracts of Italian, French, and Flemish merchants which survive in large number in notarial archives, can be used for comparative purposes. Cf. Robert S. Lopez and Irving W. Raymond (eds.), *Medieval Trade in the Mediterranean World,* "Records of Civilization," No. 52 (New York, 1955); Louis Blanchard (ed.), *Documents inédits sur le commerce de Marseilles au moyen âge: contrats commerciaux du xiii*ᵉ *siècle* (2 vols.; Marseilles, 1884-85); Renée Doehaerd (ed.), *Les relations commerciales entre Gênes, la Belgique, et L'Outremont d'après les archives notarial génoises aux xiii*ᵉ *et xiv*ᵉ *siècles,* "Institut belge de Rome, Etudes d'histoire économique et sociale" (Vols. II-IV; Brussels, 1941); Federico Patetta and Mario Chiaudano (eds.), *Documenti e studi per la storia del commercio e del diritto commerciale italiano* (22 vols.; Turin, 1933-42).

²⁶¹ *RLP,* 5-7 John (1204-06), pp. 41-42, 51-52, 65; *PatR,* 5 John (1204), p. 41.

²⁶² *RLC,* 7 John (1206), I, 144; *RLP,* 7 John (1206), pp. 41b, 65.

²⁶³ *RLC,* 7 John (1215), I, 194 where the sum is ordered repaid.

²⁶⁴ *Ibid.,* 17 John (1216), I, 197; *RLP,* 17 John (1216), pp. 152-53.

²⁶⁵ *RLC,* 17 John (1216), I, 141, 177. To get the loan from the Templars of Poitou, John had to put up collateral in gold worth 2,000 marks — cf. Piquet, *op. cit.,* p. 84.

²⁶⁶ *RLC,* 16 John (1215), I, 194; *RLP,* 17 John (1216), pp. 135, 141.

²⁶⁷ *RLC,* 17 John (1216), I, 197.

²⁶⁸ Cf. *PatR,* 1-4 Hen. III (1217-20), pp. 51, 232.

²⁶⁹ *Ibid.:* 300 of the remaining 500 marks still unpaid were to be paid by Easter (1221), and the balance would have to be gotten from the revenues of Bordeaux.

²⁷⁰ *RLC,* 6 Hen. III (1221), I, 479.

²⁷¹ *Ibid.,* 8 Hen. III (1224), I, 612; *PatR,* 8 Hen. III (1224), pp. 453, 456, 497.

²⁷² *CPatR,* 10 Hen. III (1225), p. 537.

²⁷³ *Ibid.,* 18 Hen. III (1234), p. 47.

²⁷⁴ *Ibid.,* 19 Hen. III (1235), pp. 116-17; Rymer, I, 218.

²⁷⁵ *LibR,* 24 Hen. III (1239), p. 433.

²⁷⁶ *CPatR,* 27 Hen. III (1243), p. 378; *LibR,* 28 Hen. III (1244), p. 213.

²⁷⁷ *CPatR,* 31 Hen. III (1247), p. 378.

²⁷⁸ *Ibid.,* 32 Hen. III (1247), p. 2; Shirley, *op. cit.,* RS, II, 50.

²⁷⁹ *CPatR,* 32 Hen. III (1248), p. 20.

²⁸⁰ *Ibid.,* 44 Hen. III (1260), p 114

²⁸¹ *Ibid.,* 46-47 Hen. III (1262), p. 731.

²⁸² *Issues of the Exchequer,* III, 86.

²⁸³ Rymer, II, 514; *CPatR,* 3 Ed. I (1275), pp. 83, 114; *ibid.,* 8 Ed. I (1279), p. 353. Cf. Delisle, *op. cit.,* p. 18.

²⁸⁴ *CPatR,* 28 Ed. I (1299), p. 419. Cf. *ibid.,* 8 Ed. I (1280), p. 375.

²⁸⁵ Cf. Robert J. Whitwell, "Italian Bankers and the English Crown," *Transactions of the Royal Historical Society,* XVII NS (1903), 175-233, at pp. 173, 178, 217. It is possible, though the evidence is not conclusive, that the Templars, being conservative in the granting of loans, were not opposed to the transfer of royal borrowing to the Italian merchants — cf. Piquet, *op. cit.,* pp. 52-53, 90-92.

²⁸⁶ Shirley, *op. cit.,* RS, I, 525.

²⁸⁷ *CPatR,* 5 Ed. I (1277), p. 208.

²⁸⁸ *CClR,* 33 Ed. I (1305), p. 343.

²⁸⁹ *Ibid.,* 34 Ed. I (1306), p. 429.

²⁹⁰ *Ibid.,* p. 444.

²⁹¹ *Ibid.,* 35 Ed. I (1307), p. 535.

[292] Cf. G. LeBras, "L'usure: la doctrine écclésiastique de l'usure à l'époque classique (xiie – xve siècles), *Dictionnaire de théologie catholique*, ed. A. Vacant, E. Mangenot, and E. Amman, IX (1950), cols. 2335-72; Benjamin N. Nelson, *The Idea of Usury: from Tribal Brotherhood to Universal Otherhood*, "History of Ideas Series," No. 3 (Princeton, 1949); John M. Baldwin, *Medieval Theories of Just Price; Romanists, Canonists, and Theologians in the Twelfth and Thirteenth Centuries*, "Transactions of the American Philosophical Society," Vol. XLIX, Part 4 (Philadelphia, 1959); T. P. McLaughlin, "The Teaching of the Canonists on Usury (XII, XIII, and XIV Centuries)," *Medieval Studies*, I (1939), 81-147; II (1940), 1-22; Noonan, *op. cit.;* Edgar Salin, "Usury," *Encyclopedia of the Social Sciences*, XV (1935), 193-97; Raymond A. De-Roover, *Money, Banking, and Credit in Medieval Bruges; ibid., L'évolution de la Lettre de Change; ibid.*, "New Interpretations of the History of Banking," *op. cit.;* Ashley, *op. cit.*, I, Part I, 148-63.

[293] *CClR*, 32 Ed. I (1204), pp. 172-73.

[294] Cf. Usher, *Early History of Banking*, p. 78; Noonan, *op. cit.*, p. 6.

[295] *Decretum, Distinctio* XLVI, cap. 9; XLVII, cap. 1-4; *Causa* XIV, *quest.* 3-6. Cf. Baldwin, *op. cit.*, pp. 32-33. The application of usury to cases of buying and selling at a profit and to all speculative transactions made for the sake of gain is not pertinent to the present discussion. Cf., however, Gratian, *Causa* XIV, *quest.* 4, cap. 9; Baldwin, *op. cit.*, pp. 32, 35; and McLaughlin, "Teachings of the Canonists," *op. cit.*, p. 82.

[296] Panatorius: *Usura solum in mutua cadit.* Albertus Magnus: *Usura est lucrum ex mutuo.* (Cited by DeRoover, *Money, Banking, and Credit*, p. 353.) Cf. De-Roover, *Lettre de Change*, p. 19; *ibid., Money, Banking, and Credit*, p. 54; *ibid.*, "New Interpretations," *op. cit.*, p. 42; Baldwin, *op. cit.*, pp. 32, 37; McLaughlin, "Teachings of the Canonists," *op. cit.*, p. 81, n. 1, 98-100; Noonan, *op. cit.*, pp. 80-81.

[297] *Ibid.;* McLaughlin, "Teachings of the Canonists," *op. cit.*, pp. 100, 103.

[298] *Ibid.*, p. 112.

[299] *Ibid.*, p. 143; Noonan, *op. cit.*, pp. 104-05.

[300] *Ibid.*, p. 107; McLaughlin, "Teachings of the Canonists," *op. cit.*, pp. 140-41.

[301] *Digesta*, 13:4:2:8; *Codex*, 7:47:1 – cited by Noonan, *op. cit.*, p. 106, nn. 32-33. Cf. McLaughlin, "Teachings of the Canonists," *op. cit.*, pp. 145-46; Ashley, *op. cit.*, I, Part I, 196-97, Part II, 395-405; Whitwell, "Italian Bankers and the English Crown," *op. cit.*, p. 185.

[302] Noonan, *op. cit.*, p. 106; Ashley, *op. cit.*, I, Part II, 399. Cf. Frank H. Knight, "Interest," *Encyclopedia of the Social Sciences*, VIII (1932), 131-44.

[303] Noonan, *op. cit.*, p. 110.

[304] Cf. DeRoover, *Money, Banking, and Credit*, pp. 27, 32-35, 54, 62, 126, 305; *ibid., Lettre de Change*, p. 20; *ibid.*, "New Interpretations," *op. cit.*, p. 50; Doehaerd, *op. cit.*, II, 116-18; Piquet, *op. cit.*, 52-53. Lopez and Raymond (*op. cit.*, documents no. 66-71) cite specific notarial contracts illustrating usury and interest.

[305] *Op. cit.*, p. 52.

[306] *Chronica Majora*, RS, III, 329.

[307] Noonan, *op. cit.*, p. 107; Lopez and Raymond, *op. cit.*, doc. no. 66.

[308] Cf. *PatR*, 3 Hen. III (1219), p. 203.

[309] *CPatR*, 8 Hen. III (1225), pp. 453, 456; *RLC*, 8 Hen. III (1224), I, 612.

[310] McLaughlin, "Teachings of the Canonists," *op. cit.*, pp. 113-14; DeRoover, *Money, Banking, and Credit*, p. 9.

[311] *CPatR*, 44 Hen. III (1260), p. 114.

[312] *Ibid.*, p. 71. *Donum* is the standard word found in Italian documents – cf. Lopez and Raymond, *op. cit., passim.*

[313] Rymer, I, 514. Cf. remarks of Delisle, *op. cit.*, p. 87.

[314] *CPatR*, 25 Hen. III (1241), p. 250.

[315] Shirley, *op. cit.*, RS, I, 336-37.

[316] *CPatR,* 19 Hen. III (1235), pp. 116-17.

[317] *Ibid.,* 22 Hen. III (1238), p. 222.

[318] *Ibid.,* 38 Hen. III (1254), pp. 320, 364, 367, 369; *CLibR,* 38 Hen. III (1254), pp. 159, 168, 177, 180. Cf. Piquet, *op. cit.,* p. 63.

[319] CPatR, 37-38 Hen. III (1254), p. 326. Cf. Piquet, *op. cit.,* p. 63.

[320] *CPatR,* 39 Hen. III (1255), pp. 405, 412-13.

[321] Cf. *RLC,* 8 Hen. III (1224), I, 590, 594b; *ClR,* 12 Hen. III (1228), pp. 116-17; *LibR,* 13 Hen. III (1228), p. 108.

[322] Cf. Delisle, *op. cit.,* p. 22.

[323] Cf. *ibid.,* pp. 20-24; Piquet, *op. cit.,* chap. II; DeRoover, *Money, Banking, and Credit,* p. 9; Sandys, "Financial and Administrative Importance of the London Temple," *op. cit.,* pp. 147-62; Ferris, "Financial Relations of the Knights Templars to the English Crown," *op. cit.,* p. 12; R. G. Hawtrey, "Credit," *Encyclopedia of the Social Sciences,* IV (1931), 545-50; Julius Landmann, "History of Commercial Banking to the Close of the Eighteenth Century," *ibid.,* II (1930), 423-31; M. M. Postan, "Private Financial Instruments in Medieval England, *"Vierteljahrschrift für Social- und Wirtschaftsgeschichte,* XXIII (1930), 39-90; André E. Sayous, "Le capitalisme commercial et financier dans les pays chrétiens de la Méditeranée occidentale depuis la première croisade jusqu'à la fin du moyen âge," *ibid.,* XXIX (1936), 270-95; M. M. Postan, "Credit in Medieval Trade," *Economic History Review,* I (1928), 234-61; Jacob Strieder, "Origin and Evolution of early European Capitalism," *"Journal of Economic and Business History,* II (1929), 1-19; Heaton, *op. cit.,* chap. IX. The views of Cunningham (*op. cit.,* I, 362) on the general absence of the use of credit in the Middle Ages have been shown to be incorrect.

[324] The most thorough and up-to-date discussion of these problems is to be found in DeRoover, *Money, Banking, and Credit,* and *Lettre de Change* where the ideas of earlier writers such as Adolf Schaube, André Sayous, and Levin Goldschmidt are carefully examined. Cf. also Usher, *Early History of Banking;* Doehaerd, *op. cit.,* introductory remarks to vol. II; Margaret W. Hall, "Early Bankers in Genoese Notarial Records," *Economic History Review,* VI (1935), 73-79; Robert L. Reynolds, "A Business Affair in Genoa in the Year 1200, Banking, Bookkeeping, a Broker (?), and a Lawsuit," in *Studi di storia e diritto in onore di Enrico Besta* (Milan, 1938), II, 167-81; Yves Renouard, *Les hommes d'affaires italiens du moyen âge* (Paris, 1949).

[325] *CPatR,* 39 Hen. III (1255), p. 405.

[326] *CClR,* 32 Ed. I (1304), p. 172.

[327] *RLP,* 14 John (1213), pp. 103, 141; *RLC,* 14 John (1213), I, 221b.

[328] *PatR,* 2 Hen. III (1218), p. 168; *ClR,* 4 Hen. III (1220), p. 415.

[329] *RLC,* 5 Hen. III (1221), I, 465.

[330] *Ibid.,* p. 471b.

[331] *CPatR,* 5 Hen. III (1221), p. 303.

[332] *RLC,* 10 Hen. III (1226), II, 122b.

[333] *CPatR,* 8 Hen. III (1224), p. 439; *RLC,* 8 Hen. III (1224), I, 594b.

[334] *Ibid.,* 19 Hen. III (1235), pp. 116-17; Rymer, I, 218.

[335] *ClR,* 19 Hen. III (1235), p. 110; Rymer, I, 373.

[336] *ClR,* 26 Hen. III (1242), p. 402; *CPatR,* 26 Hen. III (1242), p. 277; Delisle, *op. cit.,* pp. 13-14. Cf. Rymer, I, 616.

[337] *ClR,* 50 Hen. III (1266), p. 239.

[338] *Chronicles of the Mayors and Sheriffs of London,* RS, p. 117.

[339] Cf. DeRoover, *Lettre de Change,* introduction and chap. I; Delisle, *op. cit.,* pp. 20-24; Ferris, "Financial Relations of the Templars to the English Crown," *op. cit.,* p. 12. Usher ("Origins of Banking," *op. cit.,* p. 415), when he states, no doubt correctly, that extensive use of non-negotiable bills of exchange came only in the last half of the fourteenth century, fails to give adequate considera-

tion to the long evolution and the selective use of bills of exchange in the preceding century. Actually, G. Sayles ("A Dealer in Wardrobe Bills," *Economic History Review*, III [1931], 267-73) has shown (pp. 270-71) that Wardrobe bills were negotiated with the appearance of usualness before the mid-fourteenth century — cf. *CClR*, 20-22 Ed. III (1346-49), p. 76. Moreover, Piquet, (*op. cit.*, pp. 50-51) has pointed out that letters from clients to the Templars instructing them to pay a given sum to a named person, or his representative, considerably facilitated the mobility and transferability of funds and may be looked upon as fulfilling the economic function of a check. For fifteenth century authorizations for the drawing up of bills of exchange, see *CClR*, 7-10 Hen. IV (1409-13), pp. 439-51; *ibid.*, 1-7 Hen. VI (1422-29), pp. 477-87. Cf. also, n. 324 above.

[340] For critical examination of these forms of exchange, see DeRoover, *Lettre de Change*, p. 24 *(cambium minutum)*, 28-32 *(instrumentum)*, 14-20, 24-26, 40-43, 54, 61 *(cambium per litteras); ibid., Money, Banking, and Credit*, pp. 49-54, 57, 61-62, and "New Interpretations," *op. cit.*, pp. 41-42, 49.

[341] *Early History of Banking*, p. 6.

[342] Cf. Delisle, *op. cit.*, p. 20; Piquet, *op. cit.*, p. 64.

[343] William of Newburgh, *op. cit.*, RS, I, 158; Roger of Hoveden, *op. cit.*, RS, I, 218.

[344] Rymer, I, 383.

[345] *RLP*, 17 John (1215), p. 181; *RLC*, 6 Hen. III (1221), I, 480; *CPatR*, 4 Hen. III (1220), p. 243; Rymer, I, 137.

[346] *RLP*, 15 John (1214), pp. 119, 121.

[347] *CClR*, 12 Hen. III (1228), p. 72; Bain, I, nos. 1003, 1005.

[348] *LibR*, 23 Hen. III (1239), p. 381.

[349] *CChR*, 39 Hen. III (1255), pp. 438-39.

[350] *ClR*, 33-35 Hen. III (1248-51), pp. 33, 41, 526; *ibid.*, 43 Hen. III (1258-59), pp. 341-42, 418-19, 446-47, 471; *CPatR*, 43 Hen. III (1258-59), pp. 4, 15, 22; *ibid.*, 44-46 Hen. III (1260-62), pp. 66, 96, 126, 218; *ClR*, 52 Hen. III (1268), p. 542; *CPatR*, 54 Hen. III (1270), p. 446.

[351] *ClR*, 44 Hen. III (1260), p. 28.

[352] *Cal. of Doc. in France*, RS, I, 382-83.

[353] *RLP*, 16 John (1214), pp. 116b, 121b.

[354] Rymer, I, 196, 269, 365; *RLC*, 7-8 Hen. III (1223-24), I, 544, 581, 594; II, 118, 126. Cf. Ferris, "Financial Relations of the Knights Templars to the English Crown," *op. cit.*, p. 13.

[355] *CPatR*, 43 Hen. III (1258), pp. 3, 4, 9, 12.

[356] *Reg. of Malmesbury Abbey*, RS, I, 428.

[357] *LibR*, 11 Hen. III (1227), p. 19; *CPatR*, 42 Hen. III (1257-58), pp. 605, 622; Bliss, I, 117.

[358] A detailed discussion of the material in this paragraph is to be found in Piquet, *op. cit.*, pp. 115-43, 203-11 and Delisle, *op. cit.*, pp. 73-86. Both Piquet and Delisle give extracts from the Journal.

[359] Abbott P. Usher, "The Origins of Banking: the primitive Bank of Deposit, 1200-1600," *Economic History Review*, IV (1934), 399-428, at pp. 411-12.

[360] Cf., Delisle, *op. cit.*, p. 2.

[361] *Munimenta Gildhallae Londoniensis: Liber Albus, Liber Custumarum, et Liber Horn*, ed. Henry T. Riley (RS No. 12, 3 vols.; London, 1859-62), II, 654.

[362] Benedict of Peterborough, *op. cit.*, RS, II, 31.

[363] *Ibid.*, pp. 47-48; Walter of Coventry, *op. cit.*, RS, I, 360.

[364] *LibR*, 22 Hen. III (1238), pp. 309, 333, 334; *ClR*, 22 Hen. III (1238), pp. 52, 119; *LibR*, 24 Hen. III (1240), p. 446; *CPatR*, 26 Hen. III (1242), p. 277.

[365] *Ibid.*, 22 Hen. III (1238), p. 221.

[366] *Ibid.*, 26 Hen. III (1242), p. 277; *ibid.*, 34 Hen. III (1250), p. 68; *ibid.*, 8-9 Ed. I (1281), pp. 212, 379.

[367] *Ibid.,* 37 Hen. III (1253), p. 312; *ibid.,* 7 Ed. I (1279), p. 298; *Cal. of Doc. rel. to Ire.,* I, no. 2157; II, nos. 238, 881, 1485.

[368] Shirley, *op. cit.,* RS, pp. 91-92 (no. 491).

[369] *CPatR,* 13 Ed. I (1285), p. 184.

[370] *Ibid.,* 22 Ed. I (1294), p. 88. Cf. Rogers Ruding, *Annals of the Coinage of Great Britain and its Dependencies,* 3rd ed. (3 vols.; London, 1840), I, 198-99. The reference here appears to be to Edward's decision to call in clipped and counterfeit coins and to issue new coins in their place.

[371] *LibR,* 22-24 Hen. III (1238-40), pp. 326-27, 452; *CPatR,* 25-26 Hen. III (1241-42), pp. 249, 278.

[372] *ClR,* 26 Hen. III (1242), p. 172; Paris, *Chronica Majora,* RS, III, 495, 543.

[373] *RLC,* 17 John (1215-16), I, 228-31, 233-34, 236-40, 252, 255.

[374] *Ibid.,* 5-10 Hen. III (1221-26), I, 471b; II, 14, 33, 44, 45, 69, 92, 94, 98, 112. Cf. *ibid.,* p. 303.

[375] *CPatR,* 22 Hen. III (1238), pp. 176, 196, 211, 214, 223, 231.

[376] Tout, *op. cit.,* I, 51, 229-32, 315-16; Chrimes, *op. cit.,* pp. 100-06; Sandys, "Financial and Administrative Importance of the London Temple in the Thirteenth Century," *op. cit.,* pp. 149-51.

[377] *Ibid.;* Chrimes, *op. cit.,* p. 137.

[378] *PatR,* 9 Hen. III (1225), pp. 505, 506, 508; *RLC,* 9 Hen. III (1225), II, 21, 26b.

[379] E.g., *ibid.,* 7 Hen. III (1222-23), I, 486b, 549.

[380] E.g., *ClR,* 26 Hen. III (1242), p. 415; *ibid.,* 35 Hen. III (1251), p. 455; *CPatR,* 26 Hen. III (1242), p. 282; *ibid.,* 34-39 Hen. III (1250-55), pp. 67, 100, 113, 398; *ibid.,* 43-44 Hen. III (1259-60), pp. 21, 22, 68; *ibid.,* 3 Ed. I (1275), p. 83.

[381] *PatR,* 10 Hen. III (1225), pp. 2, 8, 9, 10.

[382] *CPatR,* 31 Hen. III (1247), p. 497.

[383] *Ibid.,* 54-56 Hen. III (1270-71), pp. 439, 448, 466, 513.

[384] *Ibid.,* 4 Ed. I (1276), p. 141.

[385] *RLC,* 3 Hen. III (1219), I, 396b; cf. also, *ibid.,* pp. 558, 581.

[386] For Hugh of Stocton: *ClR,* 22-26 Hen. III (1237-42), pp. 46, 115, 119, 153, 171, 172, 389; *CPatR,* 18-26 Hen. III (1234-42), pp. 209, 212, 217, 218, 282, 287. For Robert of Sicklinghall: *ibid.,* 30 Hen. III (1246), p. 474; *ClR,* 34 Hen. III (1250), p. 326; Rymer, I, 380. For a list of the known treasurers of New Temple and the dates they held that office, see Appendix C.

[387] Cf. remarks regarding the Hospitallers in Benjamin Bromberg, "The Financial and Administrative Importance of the Knights Hospitallers to the English Crown," *Economic History,* IV (1940), 307-11

[388] Delisle, *op. cit.,* pp. 41-60; Piquet, *op. cit.,* pp. 181-89, 193-224.

[389] Delisle, *op. cit.,* pp. 40-41, 58-59.

[390] *Op. cit.,* p. 182.

[391] *Ibid.,* pp. 182, 185; Delisle, *op. cit.,* pp. 60-61.

[392] Cf. Piquet, *op. cit.,* p. 184.

Chapter Four

[1] *History of the Inquisition of the Middle Ages* (3 vols.; New York, 1887), III, 238.

[2] The specific charges, which were essentially the same from country to country, will be discussed in some detail below in the section dealing with the trial in England. Some picture of the conditions at the time of the attack on the Templars can be seen in Pierre du Bois' *The Recovery of the Holy Land* (trans. Walther I. Brandt; "Records of Civilization," No. 51; New York, 1956), *passim.* DuBois himself proposed the consolidation of the military orders (pp. 8,

40, 56, 81, 200) and the confiscation of their property (pp. 40, 56, 81, 82, 201, 204, 207).

³ Cf. Lea, *op. cit.,* III, 254; Campbell, *op. cit.,* p. 238; Thomas Fuller, *Historie of the Holy Warre* (London, 1840), p. 246; Perkins, "The Trial of the Knights Templars in England," *op. cit.,* p. 432; Konrad Schottmüller, *Der Untergang des Templer-ordens* (2 vols.; Berlin, 1887), I, 63-68, 532.

⁴ For a fuller discussion, see: Heinrich Finke, *Papsttum und Untergang des Templerordens* (Münster, 1907), chaps. III-V; Schottmüller, *op. cit.,* chaps. IV-VII; Lea, *op. cit.,* III 252-98; Campbell, *op. cit.,* chaps. XIV-XVI; Prutz, *op. cit.,* chaps. VI-IX; E. Boutaric, "Clement V, Phillippe le Bel, et les Templiers," *Revue des questions historiques,* X (1871), 301-42 and XI (1872), 5-40; J. Delaville le Roulx, "La Suppression des Templiers," *ibid.,* XLVIII (1890), 29-61; and Charles V. Langlois, "Le Procès des Templiers," *Revue des deux mondes,* CIII (1891), 382-421. The documents for the trial of the Templars in France can be found in: M. Michelet (ed.), *Le Procès des Templiers* (2 vols.; Paris, 1841-51); François J. M. Raynouard (ed.), *Monumens historiques relatifs à la Condemnation des Chevaliers du Temple, et à l'Abolition de leur Ordre* (Paris, 1813); DuPuy; Georges Lizerand (ed.), *Le Dossier de l'Affaire des Templiers* (Paris, 1923).

⁵ DuPuy, no. 42. Cf. Campbell, *op. cit.,* p. 246.

⁶ DuPuy, nos. 43, 56.

⁷ *Ibid.,* nos. 50, 57.

⁸ *Ibid.,* no. 50.

⁹ Michelet (*op. cit.,* I, 90-96) cites the charges. The testimony taken at the interrogations forms the bulk of the two volumes.

¹⁰ *Ibid.,* I, 36, 37, 75, *et passim.*

¹¹ Boutaric, "Clement V, Philippe le Bel, et les Templiers," *op. cit.,* p. 336; Campbell, *op. cit.,* p. 265.

¹²Rymer, II, 16; DuPuy, no. 58.

¹³ *Ibid.,* nos. 56; 71.

¹⁴ *Ibid.,* nos. 80-83.

¹⁵ *Ibid.,* no. 93.

¹⁶ *Ibid.,* no. 91.

¹⁷ Michelet, *op. cit.,* I, 81ff.

¹⁸ DuPuy, no. 95. The 54 Templars referred to here were burned in May, 1310. In later months, 46 additional Templars, of whom only 2 recanted, were handed over to the state to be burned at Paris as heretics. Cf. John Capgrave, *The Chronicle of England,* ed. Francis C. Hingeston (RS, No. 1; London, 1858), p. 177.

¹⁹ Though official records of the council insofar as they pertain to the Templars are almost wholly lacking, considerable information on the council and Templars can be gained from the writings of contemporary chroniclers. DuPuy (nos. 111 and 113A) quotes extensively from two of these: the *Chronique* of William de Nangis and the *Histoire écclésiastique* of Abbot Fleury.

²⁰Cited by Lea, *op. cit.,* III, 321-22.

²¹ Rymer, II, 167-68; DuPuy, no. 112; *Regestum Clementis Papae V ex Vaticanis archetypis,* ed. the Monks of St. Benedict (9 vols.; Rome, 1884-92), no. 7886.

²² Few of these provincial councils ever actually met. Later (December, 1319), Pope John XXII (Dugdale, VII, 848; DuPuy, no. 137) ordered that all Templars who had abandoned the ecclesiastical life, who had married, and the like, must give up their secular activities and wives, and must be assigned no more than two to a monastery, except for the houses of the Hospitallers, which might accept more than two. Apparently, the Hospitallers had already received many Templars into their order.

²³ DuPuy (nos. 118, 119) quotes the *Chronique* of William of Nangis and *Registre des Arrêts, 1299-1318.*

²⁴ Cf. Lea, *op. cit.,* III, 329.

164   *The Knights Templars in England*

25 DuPuy (nos. 123, 124) gives three agreements made between the Hospitallers and the French kings (1313, 1315, and 1317).

26 Rymer, II, 10.

27 *Ibid.*

28 *Ibid.*, II, 19; DuPuy, no. 61.

29 Rymer, II, 20; DuPuy, no. 61A.

30 Cf. the letter of Clement to Edward (August 12, 1308) in Rymer, II, 55.

31 *Ibid.*, 16-17; DuPuy, no. 58.

32 On December 26, 1307, Edward wrote Clement (Rymer, II, 24; DuPuy, no. 61B) that he would carry out the pope's wishes. Cf. *CClR*, 1 Ed. II (1307), p. 49.

33 Cf. Rymer, II, 18, 23, 24.

34 *Ibid.;* DuPuy, nos. 61C-E; *CClR*, 1 Ed. II (1307), pp. 14, 48, 49. The story of the arrest of the Templars in England is narrated by many chroniclers including: *Annales Paulini*, ed. William Stubbs, *Chronicles of the reigns of Edward I and Edward II* (RS, No. 76; 2 vols.; London, 1882-83), I, 264-65; *Commendatio lamentabilis in transitu magni regis Edwardi*, ed. William Stubbs, *ibid.*, II, 32; *Annales Prioratus de Wigornia* in *Annales Monastici*, RS, IV, 560; Thomas de Burton, *Chronica monasterii de Melsa ab fondatione usque ad annum 1406*, ed. Edward A. Bond (RS, No. 43; 3 vols.; London, 1866-68), II, 248, 313; Thomas Walsingham, *Historia Anglicana*, RS, I, 120 and *Ypodigma Neustria*, RS, VII, 242; *The French Chronicle of London A.D. 1259 to A.D. 1343*, ed. Henry T. Riley (London, 1863), p. 34; and *Chronicles of London*, ed. Charles L. Kingsford (Oxford, 1905), p. 8.

35 Cf. note 76 below. Campbell (*op cit.*, pp. 270, 282), without providing any evidence, speaks of "hundreds" of escaped Templars.

36 Rymer, II, 18; *CClR*, 1 Ed. II (1307), pp. 14, 49.

37 Cf. Rymer, II, 118, 150, 152, 173, 180, 243; *CClR*, 1 Ed. II (1307), pp. 14, 49; *ibid.*, 2 Ed. II (1308), p. 90 *et passim; ibid.*, 4 Ed. II (1310), p. 290. (There are literally scores of entries in the Close Rolls ordering the keepers of the Templar properties to make payments in support of the Templars assigned to do penance in various monasteries.) The rate of four pence per day applied to ordinary members; larger sums were authorized for chaplains (cf. *CClR*, 5 Ed. II [1312], p. 397) and for high officials (cf. *ibid.*, 6 Ed. II [1313], pp. 508, 533).

38 Rymer, II, 46, 243; DuPuy, no. 62. Cf. *CClR*, 5 Ed. II (1307-13), p. 384; *ibid.*, 6 Ed. II (1313), p. 533. When William de la More died, the king ordered the same sum allowed William to be paid to Himbert Blanke, highest remaining Templar in England: *CClR*, 6 Ed. II (1313), pp. 508, 533; *ibid.*, 7 Ed. II (1313-14), pp. 6, 39.

39 Rymer, II, 46; DuPuy, no. 62; *CClR*, 1 Ed. II (1308), pp. 35, 39. Cf. Williamson, *op. cit.*, p. 51.

40 Cf. Perkins, "The Trial of the Knights Templars in England," *English Historical Review*, XXIV (1909), 432-47, at p. 433.

41 Dugdale, VII, 844-46. Cf. DuPuy, no. 70. The actual number of charges levelled by the pope against the Templars varied from 87 to 123. The bulls *Regnans in coelis* and *Faciens misericordiam* (Rymer, II, 55; DuPuy, no. 65, 66, 67, 68A), both dated August 12, 1308, recite the evils of the Templars in considerable detail. Another version of the charges can be found in the *Annales Londonienses, op. cit.*, RS, I, 179-98.

42 Rymer, II, 55; Dugdale, VI, 844-46. Cf. Clement's instructions to the papal inquisitor in England: *Records of Anthony Bek*, no. 128.

43 Letters of safe conduct were issued for the papal representatives on September 13, 1309: Rymer, II, 88; DuPuy, no. 68C; *CPatR*, 3 Ed. II (1309), p. 190; *ibid.*, 4 Ed. II (1310), p. 289.

44 Rymer, II, 90; *CClR*, 3 Ed. II (1309), pp. 175-77, 230. Later orders had to be issued, too: *CClR*, 3 Ed. II (1309), pp. 187, 189 (Dec. 10, 14, 1309); *ibid.*, p. 189 and Rymer, II, 100 (Dec. 14, 1309); *CClR*, 3 Ed. II (1310), p. 206 and

45 Rymer, II, 105 (Mar. 12, 1310); and *ibid.*, p. 125 and *CClR*, 4 Ed. II (1311), p. 295 (Jan. 4, 1311).

45 *CClR*, 3 Ed. II (1309), pp. 175-76.

46 Rymer, II, 88; DuPuy, nos. 68A, 68B; *CClR*, 3 Ed. II (1309), pp. 179, 230.

47 Clement had apparently issued such a bull back in December, 1308 — cf. Du-Puy, no. 74.

48 The manuscript sources for the trial of the English Templars are reproduced, with some exceptions, in D. Wilkins (ed.), *Concilia Magnae Britanniae et Hiberniae, A.D. 446-1718* (Vols. I-II; London, 1737), II, 329-401. The Templars in England were ordered by the crown to be transferred from the various county prisons where they had been held since their arrest in January, 1308 to three centers: the Tower of London, the Castle of York, and the Castle of Lincoln — *CClR*, 3 Ed. II (1309), pp. 175-76, 189, 230; Rymer, II, 88, 90, 91. Later (*CClR*, 4 Ed. II [1310-11], pp. 290, 291-92, 308; Rymer, II, 119) the Templars at Lincoln were ordered sent to London. The Templars at York remained there — cf. *CClR*, 3-5 Ed. II [1310-11], pp. 206, 295, 370-71. The Templars in Scotland and Ireland (*ibid.*, 3 Ed. II [1309], p. 179) were ordered imprisoned and examined at Dublin. Cf. the orders issued by the papal commission for the examination of the Templars in England and in Scotland as given in the *Records of Anthony Bek*, nos. 144-45.

49 *Ibid.*, 334-45, gives the bulk of the testimony taken in the first phase of the examination at London. Cf. also DuPuy, no. 67B. The procedure to be followed was laid down by the provincial council which met from Oct. 8 to Nov. 24, 1309 at London: DuPuy, no. 66A. For a thorough discussion of the testimony at all of the examinations of the English Templars, see Perkins, "History of the Knights Templars in England," *op. cit.*, chap. IV. For a briefer discussion, see *ibid.*, "The Trial of the Knights Templars in England, *op. cit.*, pp. 432-47.

50 Wilkins, II, 356-57, 383. For a discussion of this problem, see Henry C. Lea, "The Absolution Formula of the Templars," *Papers of the American Society of Church History*, V (1893), 37-58. The Templars were questioned regarding their practice of confession and absolution at each of their examinations.

51 Wilkins, II, 313-14. Cf. *Decretum*, C. 23, 8, 30; X, 5, 7, 9, *et alibi*.

52 *Ibid.*, 314; Rymer, II, 100; *CClR*, 3 Ed. II (1309), p. 200; *ibid.*, 4 Ed. II (1310), pp. 279, 285. Cf. remarks of Lea, *op. cit.* (especially III, 300 and throughout chap. V), on the use of torture against the Templars.

53 Rymer, II, 104, 105.

54 Wilkins, II, 349-52.

55 Rymer, II, 104, 105; *CClR*, 3 Ed. II (1309), p. 200; *ibid.*, 4 Ed. II (1310), pp. 279, 285, 290; *CPatR*, 3 Ed. II (1310), pp. 208-09.

56 *CClR*, 4 Ed. II (1311), pp. 308-09 (Apr. 28, 1311).

57 Wilkins, II, 352-58.

58 Cotton MS, Julius B, folios 80-83 — cited by Perkins, "The Trial of the Knights Templars in England," *op. cit.*, p. 437.

59 *Reg. Clem. V*, no. 6378: ". . . *inquisitionis impedire negotium, asserebant quod contra legem seu consuetudinem patriae hoc fiebat . . .*"

60 *Ibid.*, no. 6376.

61 Rymer, II, 115, 118. Cf. *ibid.*, 100, 119, 133, 141; *CClR*, 4 Ed. II (1310), pp. 279, 290, 308-09.

62 Wilkins, II, 314.

63 Rymer, II, 117; *CClR*, 4 Ed. II (1310), pp. 285, 290, 292.

64 *Ibid.*, pp. 285, 290, 291, 308; Rymer, II, 117.

65 *Ibid.*, 133 (Apr. 28, 1311). Cf. *CClR*, 4 Ed. II (1311), p. 308.

66 *Ibid.*, p. 290.

67 *Ibid.*, pp. 291-92; Rymer, II, 120; DuPuy, no. 66E. The Templars were being concentrated in London.

⁶⁸ Wilkins, II, 349-52; DuPuy, no. 86B. A new list of questions had been drawn up by the examiners at London.

⁶⁹ *Reg. Clem. V*, no. 6670.

⁷⁰ Cf. Rymer, II, 88, 104. Archbishop Greenfield of York appears (Thomas Stubbs, *Lives of the Archbishops*, ed. James Raine, *Historians of the Church of York and its Archbishops* [RS, No. 71; 2 vols.; London, 1886], II, 413-14) to have been especially kind to the Templars in his diocese. A goodly amount of data on the trial and treatment of the Templars at York can be found in the *Register of William Greenfield, Lord Archbishop of York, 1306-1315.* "Publications of the Surtees Society," vols. CXLV, CLII, CLIII (London, 1931-38).

⁷¹ Walter of Hemingburg, *Chronicon . . . de gestis regum Angliae*, ed. Hans C. Hamilton (2 vols.; London, 1848-49), II, 287-91.

⁷² DuPuy, no. 106A.

⁷³ Wilkins (II, 358-64) gives the testimony. The three examples cited below are taken from this. Cf. also, *Annales Londonienses, op. cit.*, RS, I, 180-98.

⁷⁴ Wilkins, II, 364.

⁷⁵ *Ibid.*, 364-65; DuPuy, no. 108B.

⁷⁶ Stappelbrugge and Thoroldsby, mentioned below, were arrested in this period (*CClR*, 4 Ed. II [1310], pp. 316-17). Apparently the king's officials were so persistent that such a person as Peter Auger, a yeoman of the king's chamber, who wore a beard, found it necessary to have the king (*CPatR*, 4 Ed. II [1311], p. 330; *CChanWar*, 4 Ed. II [1311], I, 344) certify that he was not a Templar and wore a beard in fulfillment of a pilgrimage vow. In general, it would seem that few renegade Templars were found.

⁷⁷ Cf. *CClR*, 4 Ed. II (1311), pp. 308-09; *ibid.*, 5 Ed. II (1311), pp. 370-71.

⁷⁸ Wilkins, II, 383-84; DuPuy, nos. 107, 109I. Cf. *CClR*, 4 Ed. II (1311), p. 316.

⁷⁹ Wilkins, II, 384-87; DuPuy, nos. 107, 109II.

⁸⁰ *Ibid.*, nos. 107, 109III; Wilkins, II, 387-88.

⁸¹ The public records are filled with references to the disposition of Templar lands and goods. Two valuable articles have been written on the subject: Agnes M. Leys, "The Forfeiture of the Lands of the Templars in England," *Oxford Essays in Medieval History presented to Herbert Edward Salter* (Oxford, 1934), pp. 155-63, and Perkins, "The Wealth of the Knights Templars," *op. cit.*

⁸² Rymer, II, 16; DuPuy, nos. 58, 71. Cf. *ibid.*, no. 50.

⁸³ *Ibid.*, no. 53.

⁸⁴ See above, n. 34.

⁸⁵ Rymer, II, 59-60.

⁸⁶ *Ibid.*, 65.

⁸⁷ *Reg. Clem. V*, no. 5061. Cf. *Records of Anthony Bek*, nos. 147 and 150, which show that Edward did not respond to the papal suggestion.

⁸⁸ *CClR*, 1 Ed. II (1308), p. 221.

⁸⁹ *Ibid.*, 2 Ed. II (1309), p. 94. Cf. Rymer, II, 70. Documentary evidence of the surveys made at the order of the king are to be found in manuscript form in the Public Records Office at London. The detailed accounts submitted first by the sheriffs and then by the keepers for the period 1308-09 are to be found in the Lord Treasurer's Remembrancer, Enrolled Accounts, Miscellaneous, Rolls 18-21. This material has been gone through by Perkins and pertinent data can be gained from his article cited above.

⁹⁰ *CClR*, 2 Ed. II (1309), p. 94. Cf. Rymer, II, 70.

⁹¹ Cf. *CClR*, 4-5 Ed. II (1310-11), pp. 290, 365, 369; *CPatR*, 3 Ed. II (1310), p. 210.

⁹² Cf. *CClR*, 2 Ed. II (1309), p. 177; Rymer, II, 90, 91.

⁹³ *Ibid.*, 92; *CChanWar*, I, 301 (Lincolnshire), 304 (Yorkshire).

⁹⁴ *CClR*, 3 Ed. II (1309-10), pp. 184, 185; *CPatR*, 3 Ed. II (1310), p. 210; Bain, *op. cit.*, III, no. 306.

⁹⁵ The keepers were repeatedly ordered to pay certain sums out of the issues of Templar lands to the exchequer or to the king's wardrobe and were given acquittances for the sums they paid. Cf. *CClR, 5 Ed. II* (1311-12), pp. 382-83, 392, 394, 424, 438, 441, 453; *CPatR, 5 Ed. II* (1312), pp. 463, 465, 467; *ibid., 6 Ed. II* (1312-13), pp. 481, 484, 511, 523, 565, 590.

⁹⁶ *CClR, 6 Ed. II* (1313), p. 512.

⁹⁷ *Ibid., 5-6 Ed. II* (1312-13), pp. 419, 501; *ibid., 7 Ed. II* (1313), pp. 7, 13; *ibid., 10 Ed. II* (1317), p. 388.

⁹⁸ Bain, *op. cit.*, III, nos. 240, 241, 250, 253, 256, 306, 311, 315, 338, 367, 428. These grants were made in 1312-13.

⁹⁹ *CClR, 5-6 Ed. II* (1312-13), pp. 394, 408, 467, 535; *CPatR, 1 Ed. II* (1308), p. 81.

¹⁰⁰ *CClR, 5-6 Ed. II* (1312-13), pp. 409-10, 507; *CPatR, 5-6 Ed. II* (1312-13), pp. 461, 467, 486-87.

¹⁰¹ *CClR, 5-6 Ed. II* (1311-12), pp. 392-93, 408, 410, 426-27; *CPatR, 5 Ed. II* (1312), pp. 466, 467, 501, 504; and *ibid., 1 Ed. II* (1308), p. 81. This last entry is especially interesting. It contains the king's order to the justiciar in Ireland and to the treasurer at Dublin to provide for the expedition against Scotland the following items to be taken out of Templar goods: 1,000 quarters of wheat, 1,000 quarters of oats, 200 quarters of peas and beans; 300 tuns of wine, 3 tuns of honey, 200 quarters of salt, and 1,000 stockfish. It also instructs the sheriffs of thirteen counties to provide grain and livestock out of Templar goods for the same expedition.

¹⁰² *Ibid., 1-6 Ed. II* (1308-13), pp. 57, 67, 79, 93, 100, 105, 113, 134, 135, 139, 142, 202, 206, 286, 335, 341, 391, 394, 399, 403, 460, 462, 468, 482, 488, 503, 552, 555, 573, 578; *CClR, 5-6 Ed. II* (1312-13), pp. 423, 465, 532.

¹⁰³ *CPatR, 4-6 Ed. II* (1311-13), pp. 331, 381, 389, 390, 411, 412, 414, 415, 440, 442, 456, 457, 466, 514, 535, 569; *CChanWar, 4 Ed. II* (1311), I, 346. These grants sometimes involved the land only. At other times, they included livestock, grain, and implements as well. In at least one instance (*CPatR, 5 Ed. II* [1312], p. 456), Edward made the grant to a clerk who was to hold the land and receive the income from it until the amount owed him for his past service as Chamberlain of Scotland had been paid. One might suspect that Edward found this system especially useful for paying arrears of salary as well as for rewarding friends and vassals.

¹⁰⁴ *Ibid., 3-6 Ed. II* (1310-13), pp. 210, 463, 551, 552, 561-62; *CClR, 6 Ed. II* (1312), p. 480.

¹⁰⁵ *Ibid., 5-6 Ed. II* (1312-13), pp. 365, 369, 373, 375, 376, 384, 391, 422, 468, 473, 490, 497, 504, 509, 512, 518, 521, 526; *ibid., 7 Ed. II* (1313-14), pp. 10, 11, 12, 14, 15, 17, 19, 22, 24, 25, 26, 30, 35, 39. The sums were four pence per day for each Templar except de la More and Blanke who were authorized two shillings. The keepers were instructed to make these payments from the time of the arrest of the Templars on so long as Templar lands remained in the king's hands. The actual payments were made to the archbishops and bishops who had been responsible for assigning individual Templars to different monasteries. It is nowhere so indicated, but it would seem logical that the archbishops and bishops did transfer the money to the monasteries concerned.

¹⁰⁶ *Ibid., 5-7 Ed. II* (1311-12), pp. 385, 388, 409-10, 413, 421, 422, 423, 429, 430, 468, 469, 470-71, 473, 476, 480, 482-83, 490-97, 507, 510, 512, 513, 516, 517, 520. For a fuller discussion of Templar corrodies, see, Chap. II above. Between 1308 and 1310, Edward had special commissioners sent out to the counties to take testimony regarding these obligations and to decide, if possible, which claims were just. The details of this survey, including the decision whether or not a claim should be paid, can be found in the *"Corrodia petita de domibus Templariorum," op. cit.*, pp. 139-230. The Close Rolls, as cited here, agree with this survey.

¹⁰⁷ *CClR, 4-6 Ed. II* (1311-12), pp. 312, 467; *ibid., 7 Ed. II* (1313), p. 12. These authorized expenses were usually for the repair of walls, ditches, dykes, mills, and the like.

[108] *Ibid.*, 6 Ed. II (1313), p. 528.

[109] *Ibid.*, p. 508; *ibid.*, 7 Ed. II (1313), p. 17.

[110] *Ibid.*, 3-6 Ed. II (1310-13), pp. 214-15; *ibid.*, 11 Ed. II (1317), p. 502.

[111] *Ibid.*, 6 Ed. II (1313), p. 465. Cf. *ibid.*, 10 Ed. III (1336): "... all the lands which belonged to the Templars came as escheats into the hands of the late king and of other lords ... "

[112] "The Wealth of the Templars in England," *op. cit.*, pp. 252-63.

[113] *Ibid.*, pp. 257-58. Knowles and Hadcock (*op. cit.*, p. 27), without giving their evidence, state that the gross Templar revenue accruing to the crown in 1308 was £4,720.

[114] Perkins, "The Wealth of the Templars in England," *op. cit.*, p. 259.

[115] *Ibid.*, "History of the Knights Templars in England," *op. cit.*, p. 83, where the manuscript records are referred to. Cf. also, "Original Documents relating to the Knights Templars," *op. cit.*, pp. 273-80, 519-26.

[116] Cf. *CChanWar*, 6 Ed. II (1312), I, 385. Cf. Perkins, "The Wealth of the Templars in England," *op. cit.*, p. 254, n. 11.

[117] *Ibid.*, "History of the Knights Templars in England," *op. cit.*, p. 83, n. 1.

[118] *Ibid.*, p. 84, n. 6; Perkins, "The Wealth of the Templars in England," *op. cit.*, pp. 255, 257.

[119] Cf. *ibid.*, p. 255 and n. 76 above.

[120] Wilkins, II, 385.

[121] Perkins, "History of the Knights Templars in England," *op. cit.*, p. 85.

[122] *Ibid.*

[123] *Reg. Clem. V*, no. 7886; Rymer, II, 168-69; DuPuy, no. 115.

[124] What happened to New Temple, London, clearly reflects both the policy of the king and the determination of the Hospitallers to get possession of the Templar property. In December, 1312, Edward granted New Temple, along with other Templar tenements and rents in the city of London to his cousin, Aymer de Valence, in return for the latter's good service (*CChR*, 6 Ed. II [1312], p. 221). In October, 1314, it was transferred by royal order to Thomas, Earl of Lancaster (*CPatR*, 8 Ed. II [1314]) pp. 184-85), who held it until his attainder, in March, 1322, at which time it was again granted to Aymer de Valence (*CChR*, 15 Ed. II [1322], p. 441) and was held by him until his death in June, 1324 (*Annales Paulini, op. cit.*, RS, I, 302). Thereupon, it was granted to Hugh Despencer the Younger who held it until his execution in November, 1326 (*ibid.*, 319-20). Meanwhile, of course, New Temple was claimed by the Prior of the Hospitallers, but to no avail (Rymer, II, 174; *CClR*, 6 Ed. II [1313], p. 544), though Parliament in 1324 decided in favor of the Prior's claim (*CClR*, 17 Ed. II [1324], p. 91; *Rot. Parl.*, I, 431a). The king, however, had the Mayor ot London assume possession of the property at the death of Despencer — as can be determined from royal orders to the mayor regarding the repair of the property (*CClR*, 3 Ed. III [1329], p. 580; *ibid.*, 4 Ed. III [1330], p. 102). Then, in 1332, the king let New Temple to William de Langeford (cf. *CClR*, 6 Ed. III [1332], p. 431; *ibid.*, 12 Ed. III [1338], p. 416; *CPatR*, 12 Ed. III [1338], p. 99). The Prior continued to claim the property and petitioned the king in council. An inquisition was held, the findings of which supported the Prior's claim. Ultimately, in 1337 or 1338, New Temple was handed over to the Hospitallers (*CClR*, 11 Ed. III [1337], pp. 72-73; *CPatR,* 12 Ed. III [1338], p. 99).

[125] Rymer, II, 174; *CClR*, 6 Ed. II (1313), p. 544.

[126] *Ibid.*, 7 Ed. II (1313), pp. 88, 89.

[127] Rymer, II, 236-37; *CClR*, 7 Ed. II (1313), pp. 29-30; *CPatR*, 7 Ed. II (1313), p. 52.

[128] Rymer, II, 243; *CClR*, 8 Ed. II (1314), p. 243; DuPuy, nos. 125, 126.

[129] *CPatR*, 7 Ed. II (1313), pp. 44-45.

[130] *CClR*, 8-10 Ed. II (1315-17), pp. 234, 388; *ibid.*, 12 Ed. II (1318), p. 25.

[131] *Ibid.*, 17-19 Ed. II (1324-25), pp. 126, 203. Some of the Templar records had been delivered to the king: *CClR*, 19 Ed. II (1325), p. 561; *CPatR*, 8 Ed. II (1314), p. 184.

[132] *CClR*, 18-19 Ed. II (1324-25), pp. 219, 501.

[133] *CPatR*, 8-9 Ed. II (1314-16), pp. 184-85, 214, 374, 466, 478. Cf. *CClR*, 15-16 Ed. II (1322), pp. 442, 595-96; *ibid.*, 18-19 Ed. II (1325-26), pp. 290, 391-92, 462; DuPuy, no. 122.

[134] Cf. *CClR*, 8-9 Ed. II (1314-16), pp. 184-85, 374, 466; *ibid.*, 12-15 Ed. II (1318-22), pp. 25, 438.

[135] *CPatR*, 8-9 Ed. II (1315-16), pp. 214, 374, 466; Bain, *op. cit.*, III, no. 428; *CClR*, 8-10 Ed. III (1334-35), pp. 202, 422, 638.

[136] *Reg. Clem. V*, nos. 7885, 7886; Rymer, II, 167-68.

[137] *Roman Roll*, 12 Ed. II (1319), m. 11 — cited by Perkins, "History of the Knights Templars in England," *op. cit.*, p. 197, n. 5.

[138] Register of Archbishop Reynolds, fol. 70b (Lambeth MS) — cited by Perkins, "The Wealth of the Templars in England," *op. cit.*, p. 260, n. 53.

[139] Rymer, II, 487-88.

[140] *CClR*, 17 Ed. II (1324), p. 91.

[141] *Ibid.*, p. 111.

[142] *Ibid.*

[143] *Ibid.*, p. 117.

[144] *Ibid.*, 17-18 Ed. II (1324), pp. 126, 203.

[145] *Ibid.*, 18-19 Ed. II (1325), pp. 301, 392, 437-38 *et passim; ibid.*, 1 Ed. III (1327), p. 153; *ibid.*, 6 Ed. III (1332), p. 514; *ibid.*, 7-8 Ed. III (1333-34), pp. 303-04; *CPatR*, 18 Ed. II (1325), p. 134.

[146] Cf. *ibid.*, 1-2 Ed. III (1327-28), pp. 84, 147, 152, 192, 227, 340, 354; *ibid.*, 9-10 Ed. III (1335-36), pp. 59, 60, 199, 314; *ibid.*, 20 Ed. III (1346), p. 52; *CClR*, 1-2 Ed. III (1327-28), pp. 102, 156, 286; *ibid.*, 6 Ed. III (1332), p. 444; *ibid.*, 7 Ed. III (1333), pp. 6-7. These cases frequently suggest a definite reluctance on the part of the holder to deliver the lands to the Hospitallers.

[147] *Op. cit.*, p. 217.

[148] Cf. Perkins, "The Wealth of the Templars in England," *op. cit.*, p. 262.

[149] See above, n. 113.

[150] Cf. Rymer, II, 567; *Rot. Parl.*, 3 Ric. II (1379-80), III, 78b; and *CPatR*, 3 Ric. II (1380), p. 444. The last two entries refer to a charter issued by Thomas Larcher, Prior of the Hospitallers, dated Aug. 19, 1325, granting to the king, in fee simple, the manors of Temple Hirst, Temple Newsam, Faxfleet, Denney, and Strood which were formerly Templar possessions.

[151] *CPatR*, 9 Ed. III (1335), pp. 204-05; *ibid.*, 13 Ed. III (1339), p. 304; *ibid.*, 14 Ed. III (1340), p. 39; *CClR*, 1 Ed. III (1327), pp. 13-14, 86; *ibid.*, 4 Ed. III (1330), pp 11-12, 211, 531.

[152] Cf. *CPatR*, 19 Ed. II (1325), pp. 187-88; *CClR*, 15 Ed. II (1322), p. 442; *Hosp. Rpt.*, pp. 56, 116, 143, 153, 161, 182, 184-86, 203-04, 210-11.

[153] *CClR*, 6 Ed. III (1332), pp. 496, 514; *ibid.*, 7 Ed. III (1333), p. 149.

[154] *CPatR*, 9 Ed. III (1335), p. 100.

[155] Knowles and Hadcock (*op. cit.*, pp. 235-39) include a survey of most of the Templar possessions handed over to the Hospitallers and make the rather high estimate (p. 28) that about half of the Templar property went to the king and magnates and the other half was obtained by the Hospitallers.

[156] Cf. *CClR*, 12 Ed. III (1339), p. 593; *ibid.*, 14 Ed. III (1340), pp. 470-71.

[157] Lea, *op. cit.*, III, 332-34; DuPuy, nos. 127-36.

[158] Lea, *op. cit.*, III, 329-30.

[159] Wilkins, II, 388-91.

[160] *Ibid.*, 390-93; Rymer, III, 327, 472; *Flores Historiarum*, RS, III, 334. See above, n. 37, for the authorization of payments by the king.

[161] Walsingham, *Historia Anglicana*, RS, I, 128; Wilkins, II, 400; DuPuy, nos. 106C, 109 XII. For the form of confession used at York, see Walter of Hemingburg, *op. cit.*, II, 292.

[162] DuPuy, nos. 109 IV and XII.

[163] Cf. *CClR*, 6 Ed. II (1313), p. 508.

[164] Wilkins, II, 393; *CClR*, 6 Ed. II (1313), pp. 523, 533.

[165] Bain, *op. cit.*, III, no. 103; Wilkins, II, 380; DuPuy, no. 104B. Inquisitors were sent into Scotland with guarantees of royal protection (Rymer, II, 94). Cf. also, *Records of Anthony Bek*, no. 128. There are two articles of value on the Templars in Scotland: Robert Aitken, "The Knights Templars in Scotland," *Scottish Review*, XXXII (1898), 1-36; and John Edwards, "The Templars in Scotland in the Thirteenth Century," *Scottish Historical Review*, V (1907), 13-25.

[166] DuPuy, no. 140D. Cf. *Decretum*, X, 2, 20, 14 on limiting lay testimony.

[167] Rymer, II, 94; DuPuy, no. 140C; *CPatR*, 3 Ed. II (1308), p. 192; *ibid.*, 4 Ed. II (1311), p. 267; *CClR*, 3 Ed. II (1309), p. 179; *Annals of Ireland*, in *Chartularies of St. Mary's Abbey, Dublin*, RS, II, 336; Herbert Wood, "The Knights Templars in Ireland," *Proceedings of the Royal Irish Academy*, XXVI (1907), 327-77, at pp. 348, 353-54. Wood remarks that it cannot be determined whether or not torture was used or if the report of the inquisitors was favorable or unfavorable. The papal inquisitor for England (*Records of Anthony Bek*, no. 128), in accordance with Clement's mandate ordered an inquiry in Ireland to be made.

[168] *Ibid.*, p. 354; DuPuy, no. 140C.

[169] Perkins, "The Knights Templars in the British Isles," *op. cit.*, p. 229.

[170] Most modern historians subscribe to the view that the Templars were not guilty of the charges brought against them: Lea, *op. cit.*, III, 276; Schottmüller, *op. cit.*, II, 532; Finke, *op. cit.*, p. 344; Addison, *op. cit.*, p. 408 *et passim*; Campbell, *op. cit.*, p. 349; Perkins, "History of the Knights Templars in England," *op. cit.*, p. 176; and Julius Gmelin, *Schuld oder Unschuld des Templerordens* (Stuttgart, 1893), p. 508. DuPuy (p. viii) is convinced of their guilt. Two historians, E. Boutaric ("Clement V, Philippe le Bel, et les Templiers," *op. cit.*, pp. 301-40) and J. Delaville le Roulx ("La Suppression des Templiers," *op. cit.*, pp. 29-61) are inclined toward thinking the order, and some of the members definitely, guilty. Charles V. Langlois ("Le Procès des Templiers," *op. cit.*, pp. 382-421) is inclined toward thinking the order innocent.

[171] Wilkins, II, 338: *"propter stultitiam."*

[172] Lea (*op. cit.*, III, 301-17), Schottmüller (*op. cit.*, pp. 408-57), and Prutz (*op. cit.*, pp. 208-19) give brief but informative accounts with extensive references to such materials as exist for each of the areas mentioned here.

[173] DuPuy, no. 105.

[174] See Chap. V below.

[175] DuPuy, no. 137. Cf. n. 21 above.

[176] See above, pp. 88-89.

[177] "The Knights Templars in the British Isles," *op. cit.*, p. 227.

[178] "Tres filias illas jam maritavi; primam et primaevam, scilicet Superbiam, Templariis; secundum vero, scilicet Luxuriam, nigris monachis; tertiam et ultimam, scilicet Cupiditatem, albis monachis." Gerald of Wales, *Speculum Ecclesiae*, ed. J. S. Brewer, in *Giraldi Cambrensis Opera* (RS, No. 21; 8 vols.; London, 1861-91), IV, 54 and *Itinerarium Kambriae et Descriptio Kambriae*, ed. James F. Dimock, *ibid.*, VI, 44; *Flores Historiarum*, RS, II, 116-17; Roger of Hoveden, *op. cit.*, RS, IV, 76-77.

[179] DuPuy, no. 29.

[180] Paris, *Chronica Majora*, RS, IV, 302.

[181] Inner Temple Library, Petyt MS 538, xvii, 400 — cited by Perkins, "History of the Knights Templars in England," *op. cit.*, p. 91, n. 2.

[182] *Op. cit., Lib.* xii, *cap.* 7.

[183] Paris, *Chronica Majora*, RS, II, 145; Roger of Wendover, *op. cit.*, RS, II, 195-

96. Both authors have taken William of Tyre's comment and elaborated upon it.

[184] *De nugis curialium*, tr. Frederick Tupper and Marbury B. Ogle (London, 1924), Bk. I, chap. xx.

[185] *Op. cit.*, III, 243-44.

[186] Rymer, I, 258; DuPuy, no. 32.

[187] *Ibid.*, no. 30; August Potthast (ed.), *Regesta pontificum Romanorum inde ab anno post Christum natum MCXCVIII and annum MCCCIV* (Berlin, 1875), nos. 3226, 4203, 4552.

[188] *Op. cit.*, Bk. I, chap. xxiii. Interestingly enough, in his censure of the military orders, Mapes is even more critical of the Hospitallers than of the Templars.

[189] *Op. cit.*, RS, V, 745-46.

[190] *Ibid.*, 364-65.

[191] See bull of Clement cited by Prutz, *op. cit.*, p. 276. Cf. also, other bulls of the same pope (*ibid.*, pp. 276-78) issued in the same year (1265); and Lea, *op. cit.*, III, 242.

[192] Letter no. 673, *Materials for the History of Thomas Becket*, RS, VII, 310: "Nolite ergo sperare in iniquitate, nec Templariis illis credite qui non ambulant in simplicitate, sed, regis potius quam vestram voluntatem essequi cupientes, vobis nihil aliud quam mendacia de rege ex patre mendacii afferunt ut decipiant."

[193] *Op. cit.*, RS, IV, 291.

[194] *Ibid.*

[195] *Ibid.*, p. 525.

[196] *Ibid.*, V, 148-49. (Tr. J. A. Giles, *Matthew Paris' English History from the years 1235 to 1263* [2 vols.; London, 1852-53], II, 149.)

[197] *Op. cit.*, IV, 168.

[198] *CChR*, 9 Ed. I (1280), p. 237; no. 404, "Sandford Cartulary," *op. cit.*, pp. 267-68. Cf. *Rot. Hund.*, I, 131.

[199] *CChR*, 16 Hen. III (1232), pp. 158, 267; *ClR*, 13 Hen. III (1228), p. 131; *ibid.*, 15 Hen. III (1231), p. 548; *ibid.*, 18 Hen. III (1234), p. 404; *Cal. Doc. rel. to Ire.*, II, no. 120. Cf. remarks on Templar privileges in Chap. II above where Templar exemptions are discussed in detail and where repeated pleas for maintenance of their privileges and exemptions are cited. The frequency of Templar pleas suggests not only non-compliance but envy and hostility as well.

[200] *ClR*, 15 Hen. III (1231), p. 532; *Records of Parliament holden at Westminster . . . (A.D. 1305)*, ed. Frederick W. Maitland (RS, No. 98; London, 1893), p. 135. Cf. *ClR*, 13 Hen. III (1228), p. 131; *ibid.*, 15 Hen. III (1231), p. 548.

[201] Cf. *Rot. Hund.*, I, 244, 255, 278, 282, 286, 291, 292, 387 (Lincolnshire); I, 106, 109, 110, 114, 115, 122 (Yorkshire); I, 210, 238, 370 and II, 59, 60, 80, 225, 570, 722 (for various other counties).

[202] *CChR*, 9 Ed. I (1280), p. 238; *Rot. Hund.* II, 228; Henry de Bracton, *De legibus et consuetudinibus Angliae*, ed. George E. Woodbine ("Yale Historical Publications," No. 3; 4 vols.; New Haven, 1915-42), IV, 280.

[203] *Cal. Doc. rel. to Ire.*, II, nos. 1447, 1448, 1493, 1495, 1539, 1647, 1811; III, nos. 20, 30, 33, 34, 57, 558, 565, 666, 778. Cf. remarks of Wood, "The Knights Templars in Ireland," *op. cit.*, p. 341.

[204] *Rot. Hund.*, I, 129 (Yorkshire).

[205] *Ibid.*, I, 117 (Yorkshire); II, 226 (Warwickshire).

[206] *Ibid.*, II, 27 (Nottinghamshire), 228 (Warwickshire).

[207] *Ibid.*, I, 401 (Grimesby, Lincolnshire).

[208] *Pipe R*, 16 Hen. II (1169-70), pp. 149-50.

[209] Cf. *Register of Malmesbury Abbey*, RS, I, 106.

[210] See above, pp. 34-39.

[211] *Op. cit.*, Lib. xii, cap. 7: "Possessiones autem tam ultra quam citra mare adeo dicuntur immensas habere, ut jam non sit in orbe Christiano provincia, quae

praedictis fratribus bonorum suorum portionem non contulerint; et regiis opulentis pares hodie dicantur habere copias."

[212] *Op. cit.,* RS, II, 145 copies William of Tyre almost verbatim. Also, *ibid.,* IV, 291: *"Habent insuper Templarii in Christanitate novem milia maneriorum, Hospitalarii vero novendecim, praeter emolumenta et varios proventus ex fraternitatibus et praedicationibus provenientes, et per privilegia sua accrescentes."* It would be unwise to take the figure 9,000 too literally.

[213] *Op. cit.,* p. 34: " . . . the defenders of Christendom loaded them with immense wealth . . . ; " and " . . . nowhere but in Jerusalem are they in poverty."

[214] Cited by Edward J. Martin, *The Trial of the Knights Templars* (London, 1928), p. 20.

[215] *Op. Cit., Lib.* XVIII, *cap.* 9. Cf. also Mapes, *op. cit.,* Bk. I, chap. xxi.

[216] *Op. cit.,* RS, IV, 291.

[217] *L'estoire de Eracles empereur et la conqueste de la terre d'outremer* [continuation of the History of William of Tyre], *Lib.* xxv, *cap.* 22-27; xxvi, 7, 9, 11, 12; xxviii, 5. Cf. Lea, *op. cit.,* III, 240; Runciman, *op. cit.,* III, 58, 66-67; Grousset, *op. cit.,* III, 47-49, 97. For details on Richard's conquest of the island, see *Itinerarium . . . Ricardi,* RS, I, 177-204; William of Newburgh, *op. cit.,* RS, I, 350-54; Richard of Devizes, *De rebus gestis Ricardi Primi,* in *Chronicles of the Reigns of Stephen, Henry II, and Richard I,* ed. Richard Howlett (RS, No. 82; 4 vols.; London, 1884-89), III, 423-26; and Benedict of Peterborough, *op. cit.,* RS, II, 163-67, 172-73.

[218] Wilkins, II, 381; DuPuy, no. 140D.

[219] *Ibid.,* 140C; Wilkins, II, 381.

[220] *Quo War.,* 164, 293, 356, 684-85, 786; Shirley, *op. cit.,* RS, I, 181-83 (Letters nos. 158-59). Cf. *Rot. Parl.,* I, 49. Fines for seizure were repeatedly imposed on the Templars: cf. *CPatR,* 18-20 Ed. I (1290-92), pp. 343-44, 436, 507; *ibid.,* 21-28 Ed. I (1293-1300), pp. 26, 504, 542; *ibid.,* 31-33 Ed. I (1303-05), pp. 134, 291, 301, 322, 340.

[221] *Ibid.,* 12-20 Ed. I (1284-92), pp. 120, 243, 343, 436, 486, 507; *ibid.,* 28-29 Ed. I (1300-01), pp. 504, 592, 608.

[222] See above, p. 23.

[223] John Edwards, "The Templars in Scotland in the Thirteenth Century," *op. cit.,* pp. 18-19.

[224] *Ibid.,* p. 14.

[225] *Ibid.,* p. 21; Wilkins, II, 382; Dupuy, no. 140D.

[226] Wilkins, II, 382.

[227] *Op. cit.,* p. 39. In the same passage he commented: "By — let me not say frauds, but — pleasantries of law they evade simony . . . "

[228] Dugdale, VI, 846 (arts. 77-78); Rymer, II, 55.

[229] *ClR,* 15 Hen. III (1231), p. 548; *Rot. Hund.,* I, 110; II, 65; *Reg. of Malmesbury,* RS, I, 98-99.

[230] *CPatR,* 35 Ed. I (1307), p. 548; *Rot. Hund.,* I, 200, 287, 291-92, 381, 391, 402, 405, 417; II, 29, 484, 713.

[231] Cf. Vitry, *op. cit.,* Bk. II, pp. 117-18; Tyre, *op. cit., Lib.* XII, *cap.* 7; Mapes, *op. cit.,* Bk. I, chaps. xviii, xx, xxii; Paris, *Chronica Majora,* RS, II, 144, 159, 327; III, 47, 405-06; V, 154, 158, 655; VI, 160. Generally speaking, Tyre and Paris tend to be quite unfavorable to the Templars.

[232] See above, n. 169.

[233] Many critical statements are made regarding clerics and others, especially against the Cistercians, in the *Latin Poems commonly attributed to Walter Mapes* (ed. Thomas Wright, "Camden Society Publications," No. 16 [London, 1841]); but there are no direct references to the Templars. In the *Carmina Burana* (ed. J. A. Schmeller [Stuttgart, 1847], poem no. 26, p. 30), two passing references, involving neither praise nor censure, are made to the Templars fighting in the Holy Land. Nigellus in his *Speculum Stultorum* (*Anglo-Latin Satirical Poets and Epigrammatists of the Twelfth Century,* ed. Thomas Wright

[RS, No. 59; 2 vols.; London, 1872], I, 82) has Brunellus propose to devote himself to God's service and maybe even to go to Tyre and serve under the Templars. There seems to be no criticism involved in this passage. The "Song against Monks" (*Political Poems and Songs relating to English History from the Accession of Edward III to that of Richard III,* ed. Thomas Wright [RS, No. 14; 2 vols.; London, 1859-61], I, 267) expatiates on the evils of the friars and warns them they may suffer the same fate as the Templars. The song on "The Order of Fair-Ease" (*Political Songs of England from the Reign of John to that of Edward II,* ed. Thomas Wright, "Camden Society Publications," No. 7 [London, 1839], pp. 137-48) criticizes the Hospitallers, Cistercians, Dominicans, Franciscans and others; but significantly, no specific mention is made of the Templars. Nothing can be found against the Templars in *Anecdota literaria, a Collection of Short Poems in English, Latin, and French, illustrative of the Literature and History of England in the Thirteenth Century* (ed. Thomas Wright [London, 1844]) or in Gerald R. Owst's *Literature and Pulpit in Medieval England* (Cambridge, 1933).

[234] *CClR,* 32 Ed. I (1304), p. 208.

[235] Cf. above, n. 39.

[236] Repeatedly the Templars are referred to jointly with other religious and privileged groups, especially the Hospitallers.

[237] The clerical group, of course, had had its conclusion made for it by Pope Clement V and also stood to profit, at least indirectly, from the abolition of the Templar order.

Chapter Five

[1] DuPuy, no. 40B.

[2] For information on the houses and properties of the various religious orders, see Knowles and Hadcock, *op. cit., passim,* and the appropriate volumes of the *Victoria History of the Counties of England, passim.* Cf. also, remarks in Chap. II above.

[3] Gmelin, *op. cit.,* p. 507.

[4] DuPuy, no. 134. Cf. Lea, *op. cit.,* III, 317.

[5] Addison, *op. cit.,* p. 550.

[6] *Ibid.,* p. 562.

[7] Douglas Knoop and G. P. Jones, *A Short History of Freemasonry to 1730* (Manchester, 1940).

Bibliography and Index

𝕭𝖎𝖇𝖑𝖎𝖔𝖌𝖗𝖆𝖕𝖍𝖞

𝕻𝖗𝖎𝖒𝖆𝖗𝖞 𝕾𝖔𝖚𝖗𝖈𝖊𝖘

Collections of Sources

Beugnot, A. and LeProvost, A. (eds.). *Recueil des Historiens des Croisades: les Historiens Occidentaux.* "Académie imperiale des Inscriptions et Belles-Lettres." 5 vols. Paris, 1884-95.

Blancard, Louis (ed.). *Documents inédits sur le commerce de Marseille au moyen age: contrats commerciaux du xiiiᵉ siècle.* 2 vols. Marseille, 1884-85.

Doehaerd, Renée (ed.). *Les relations commerciales entre Gênes, la Beligique et l'Outremont d'après les archives notariales génoises aux xiiiᵉ et xivᵉ siècles,* "Institut belge de Rome, Etudes d'histoire économique et sociale." Vols. II-IV. Brussels, 1941.

Dugdale, William. *Monasticon Anglicanum.* New edition by John Caley, Henry Ellis, and Bulkeley Bandinel. 8 vols. London, 1846.

Lopez, Robert S. and Raymond, Irving W. (eds.). *Medieval Trade in the Mediterranean World: Illustrative Documents.* "Records of Civilization," No. 52. New York, 1955.

Mansi, John D. *Sacrorum conciliorum nova et amplissima collectio.* New edition by P. Labbeus, G. Cossartius, and N. Coleti. Vol. XXI. Venice, 1767.

Migne, Jacques P. (ed.). *Patrologiae cursus completus ... series Latina.* 221 vols. Paris, 1878-90.

Patetta, Federico and Chiandano, Mario (eds.). *Documenti e studi per la storia del commercio e del diritto commerciale italiano.* Turin, 1933.

Rymer, Thomas and Sanderson, Robert (eds.). *Foedera, conventiones, litterae et cujuscunque generis acta publica inter reges Angliae et alios quovis imperatores, reges, pontifices, principes, vel communitates.* Revised edition. Vols. I-II. London, 1816.

Wilkins, D. (eds.). *Concilia Magnae Britanniae et Hiberniae, A. D. 446-1718.* Vols. I-II, London, 1737.

Cartularies, Chronicles, Letters, etc.

Adam of Eynsham. *Magna vita santi Hugonis episcopi Lincolniensis.* Edited by James F. Dimock. Rolls Series, No. 37. London. 1864.

Adam of Murimuth. *Continuatio chronicarum.* Edited by E. Maunde Thompson. Rolls Series, No. 93. London, 1889.

The Anglo-Saxon Chronicle. Edited and translated by Charles Plummer. 2 vols. Oxford, 1892-99.

Annales Monastici. Edited by Henry R. Luard. Rolls Series, No. 36. 5 vols. London, 1864-69.

Bartholomew de Cotton. *Historia Anglicana.* Edited by Henry R. Luard. Rolls Series, No. 16. London, 1859.

Benedict of Peterborough. *Chronicle of the Reigns of Henry II and Richard I, A. D. 1169-1192.* Edited by William Stubbs. Rolls Series, No. 49, 2 vols.

Bracton, Henry de. *De legibus et consuetudinibus Angliae.* Edited by George E. Woodbine. "Yale Historical Publication," No. 3. 4 vols. New Haven, 1915-42.

Capgrave, John. *The Chronicle of England.* Edited by Francis C. Hingeston. Rolls Series, No. 1. London, 1858.

———. *De illustribus Henricis.* Edited by Francis C. Hingeston. Rolls Series, No. 7. London, 1858.

Carmina burana. Edited by J. A. Schmeller. Stuttgart, 1847.

Cartulaire général de l'ordre du Temple, 1119-1150: Receuil des chartres et des bulles relatives à l'ordre du Temple. Edited by Guignes A. M. J. d'Albon. Paris, 1913.

Chartularies of St. Mary's Abbey, Dublin: with the Register of its House at Dunbrody, and Annals of Ireland. Edited by John T. Gilbert. Rolls Series, No. 80. 2 vols. London, 1884.

Chronica monasterii sancti Albani. Edited by Henry T. Riley. Rolls Series, No. 28. 12 vols. London, 1863-76.

Chronicles and Memorials of the Reign of Richard I. Edited by William Stubbs. Rolls Series, No. 38. 2 vols. London, 1864-65.

Chronicles of London. Edited by Charles L. Kingsford. Oxford, 1905.

The Chronicles of London from 44 Hen. III to 17 Edw. III. Translated by Edmund Goldsmid. Edinburgh, 1885.

Chronicles of the Mayors and Sheriffs of London, A. D. 1188 to A. D. 1274. Translated by Henry T. Riley. London, 1863.

Chronicles of the Reigns of Edward I and Edward II. Edited by William Stubbs. Rolls Series, No. 76. 2 vols. London, 1882-83.

Chronicles of the Reigns of Stephen, Henry II, and Richard I. Edited by Richard Howlett. Rolls Series, No. 82. 4 vols. London, 1884-89.

Chronicon Abbatiae de Evesham ad annum 1418. Edited by William D. Macray. Rolls Series, No. 29. London, 1863.

Chronicon Abbatiae Rameseiensis a saec. X usque ad an. circitur 1200. Edited by W. Dunn Macray. Rolls Series, No. 83. London, 1886.

Chronicon Henrici Knighton, vel Cnitthon, monachi Leycestrensis. Edited by Joseph R. Lumby. Rolls Series, No. 92. London, 1889.

Chronicon monasterii de Abingdon. Edited by Joseph Stevenson. Rolls Series, No. 2. 2 vols. London, 1858.

Chroniques de London depuis l'an 44 Hen. III jusqu'à l'an 17 Edw. III. Edited by George J. Aungier. "Publications of the Camden Society," Vol. XXVIII. London, 1844.

Corpus Juris Canonici. Edited by Aemilius Friedberg. 2 vols. Leipzig, 1879.

Curzon, Henri de (ed.). *La Règle du Temple.* Paris, 1886.

Delaville le Roulx, J. (ed.). *Documents concernant les Templiers; extraits des archives de Malte.* Paris, 1882.

Delisle, Léopold (ed.). *Recueil des actes de Henry II, roi d'Angleterre et duc de Normandie, concernant les provinces françaises et les affaires de France.* 3 vols. Paris, 1916-27.

DuBois, Pierre. *The Recovery of the Holy Land.* Translated by Walther I. Brandt. "Records of Civilization," No. 51. New York, 1956.

DuPuy, Pierre. *Historie de l'ordre militaire des Templiers, ou Chevaliers du Temple de Jérusalem, depuis son établissement jusqu'à sa décadence et sa suppression.* Brussels, 1751.

Eracles. *L'estoire de Eracles empereur et la conqueste de la terre d'outremer.* [Continuation of the History of William of Tyre] in *Recueil des historiens des Croisades: les historiens occidentaux.* Vol. II, Paris, 1859.

Eulogium (Historiarum sive temporis): Chronicon ab orbe condito usque ad annum Domini M.CCC.LXVI. a monacho quodam Malmesburiensi exaratum. Edited by Frank S. Haydon. Rolls Series, No. 9. 3 vols. London, 1858-63.

Fitzneale, Richard. *De necessariis observatiis scaccarii dialogus qui vulge dicitur Dialogus de Scacario.* Edited and translated by Charles Johnson. London, [1950].

Fleta. Edited and translated by H. G. Richardson and G. O. Sayles. "Publications of the Selden Society," Vol. LXXII. London, 1955.

Florence of Worchester. *Chronicon ex chronicis.* Edited by Benjamin Thorpe. London, 1848-49.

Flores Historiarum. Edited by Henry R. Luard. Rolls Series, No. 95. 3 vols. London, 1890.

Foucher (Fulcher) of Chartes. *Historia Iherosalymitana gesta Francorum Iherusalem peregrinantium* in *Recueil des historiens des Croisades: les historiens occidentaux*. Vol. III. Paris, 1866.

The French Chronicle of London A. D. 1259 to A. D. 1343. Edited by Henry T. Riley. London, 1863.

Gervase of Canterbury. *Historical Works*. Edited by William Stubbs. Rolls Series, No. 73. 2 vols. London, 1879-80.

Giraldus Cambrensis. *Opera*. Edited by J. S. Brewer, James F. Dimock, and George F. Warner. Rolls Series, No. 21. Vols. IV-VIII. London, 1861-91.

Henry of Huntington. *The History of the English from A. D. 55 to A. D. 1154.* Edited by Thomas Arnold. Rolls Series, No. 74. London, 1879.

Historia et Cartularium monasterii sancti Petri Gloucestriae. Edited by William H. Hart. Rolls Series, No. 33. 3 vols. London, 1863-67.

The Historians of the Church of York and its Archbishops. Edited by James Raine. Rolls Series, No. 71. 2 vols. London, 1886.

Historic and Municipal Documents of Ireland, A.D. 1172-1320, from the Archives of the City of Dublin. Edited by J. T. Gilbert. Rolls Series, No. 53, London, 1870.

Historical Papers and Letters from the Northern Registers. Edited by James Raine. Rolls Series, No. 61. London, 1873.

Jaffé, Philipp, and Wattenbach, William (eds.). *Regesta pontificum Romanorum ab condita ecclesia ad annum post Christum natum MCXCVIII.* 2d edition. 2 vols. Leipzig, 1885-88.

Joinville, Jean Sire de. *Histoire de Saint Louis*. Edited by Natalis de Wailly. Paris, 1868.

Larking, Lambert B. (ed.). *The Knights Hospitallers in England: Being the Report of Prior Philip de Thame to the Grand Master Elyan de Villanova for A.D. 1338.* "Publications of the Camden Society," Vol. LXV. London, 1857.

Leclerq, J. "Un document sur les débuts des Templiers," *Revue d'histoire ecclésiastique*, LII (1957), 81-91.

Lees, Beatrice A. (ed.). *Records of the Templars in England in the Twelfth Century: The Inquest of 1185, with illustrative Charters and Documents.* "Records of the Social and Economic History of England and Wales," Vol. IX. London, 1935.

Lizerand, Georges (ed.). *Le Dossier de l'affaire des Templiers*. Paris, 1923.

Mapes, Walter. *De nugis curialium*. Translated by Frederick Tupper and Marbury B. Ogle. London, 1924.

Materials for the History of Thomas Becket, Archbishop of Canterbury. Edited by James C. Robertson and J. Brigstocke Sheppard. Rolls Series, No. 67. Vols. IV-VII. London, 1879-85.

Memorials of London and London Life in the Thirteenth, Fourteenth, and Fifteenth Centuries. Selected, edited, and translated by Henry T. Riley. London, 1868.

Michelet, M. (ed.). *Le Procès des Templiers*. 2 vols. Paris, 1841-51.

Munimenta Gildhallae Londoniensis: Liber Albus, Liber Custumarum, et Liber Horn. Edited by Henry T. Riley. Rolls Series, No. 12. 3 vols. London, 1859-62.

Odericus Vitalis. *Historia ecclesiastica*. Edited by Auguste le Prevost. 2 vols. Paris, 1838-40.

"Original Documents relating to the Knights Templars," *The Gentleman's Magazine and Historical Review*, III N.S. (1857), 273-80, 519-26.

Oxenedes, Johannes de. *Chronica*. Edited by Henry Ellis. Rolls Series, No. 13. London, 1859.

Paris, Matthew. *Chronica Majora*. Edited by Henry R. Luard. Rolls Series, No. 57. 7 vols. London, 1872-83.

——. *Historia Anglorum sive historia minor.* Edited by Frederic Madden. Rolls Series, No. 44. 3 vols. London, 1866-69.

Potthast, August. (ed.). *Regesta pontificum Romanorum inde ab anno post Christum natum MCXCVIII ad annum MCCCIV.* Berlin, 1874-75.

Ralph of Coggeshall. *Chronicon Anglicanum.* Edited by Joseph Stevenson. Rolls Series No. 66. London, 1875.

Ralph of Diceto. *Opera historica.* Edited by William Stubbs. Rolls Series, No. 68. 2 vols. London, 1876.

Raynouard, François J. M. (ed.). *Monumens historiques, relatifs à la condamnation des Chevaliers du Temple, et à l'abolition de leur ordre.* Paris, 1813.

Records of Anthony Bek, Bishop and Patriarch, 1283-1311. Edited by C. M. Fraser. "Publications of the Surtees Society," Vol. CLXII. London, 1947.

Regestum Clementis Papae V ex Vaticanis archetypis. Edited by the Monks of St. Benedict. 8 vols. Rome, 1884-92.

The Register of Malmesbury Abbey. Edited by J. S. Brewer. Rolls Series No. 72. London, 1879.

The Register of Richard de Kellawe, Lord Palatine and Bishop of Durham, 1311-1316. Edited by Thomas D. Hardy. Rolls Series No. 62. 2 vols. London, 1873-74.

The Register of William Greenfield, Lord Archbishop of York, 1306-1315. "Publications of the Surtees Society," Vols. CXLV, CLII, CLIII. London, 1931-38.

Les registres d'Alexandre IV: Recueil des bulles de ce pape publiées ou analysées d'après les manuscrits originaux du Vatican. Edited by C. Bourel de la Roncière, J. de Loye, and A. Coulon. 2 vols. Paris, 1902-53.

Les registres de Grégoire IX: Recueil des bulles de ce pape publiées ou analysées d'après les manuscrits originaux du Vatican. Edited by Lucien Auvray. 3 vols. Paris, 1896-1908.

Les registres d'Innocent IV publiès ou analysés d'apres les manuscrits originaux du Vatican et de la Bibliothèque nationale. Edited by Elie Berger. 3 vols. Paris, 1884-97.

Registrum epistolarum fratris Johannis Peckham, Archiepiscopi Cantuariensis. Edited by Charles T. Martin. Rolls Series, No. 77. 3 vols. London, 1882-85.

Richard, Canon of St. Trinity, London. *Itinerarium peregrinorum et gesta regis Ricardi* in *Chronicles and Memorials of the Reign of Richard I.* Edited by William Stubbs. Rolls Series, No. 38. Vol. I. London, 1864.

Rishanger, William. *Chronica et annales regnantibus Henrico Tertio et Edwardo Primo, A.D. 1259-1307.* Edited by Henry T. Riley. Rolls Series, No. 28. 2 vols. London, 1865.

Roger of Hovedon. *Chronica.* Edited by William Stubbs. Rolls Series. No. 51. 4 vols. London, 1868-71.

Roger of Wendover. *Chronica sive Flores Historiarum.* Edited by Henry G. Hewlett. Rolls Series, No. 84. 3 vols. London, 1886-89.

The Rolls and Register of Bishop Oliver Sutton, 1280-1299. Edited by Rosalind M. T. Hill. "Publications of the Lincoln Record Society," Vols. XLII-XLIII. Hereford, 1948-50.

Sancti Bernardi, Abbatis primi Claraevallensis, opera genuina. Edited by the Monks of St. Benedict. 3 vols. Paris, 1854.

"The Sanford Cartulary," *The Oxfordshire Record Society,* XIX (1937), 1-177; XXII (1940), 179-328. Edited by Agnes M. Leys.

Selected Letters of Pope Innocent III concerning England (1198-1216). Edited by C. R. Cheney and W. H. Semple. London, 1953.

Stubbs, William and Spelman, Henry (eds.). *Councils and ecclesiastical Documents relating to Great Britain and Ireland.* 3 vols. Oxford, 1869-78.

Stubbs, William (ed.). *Select Charters and other Illustrations of English Constitutional History to the Reign of Edward I.* 9th edition revised. Oxford, 1870.

Shirley, Walter W. (ed.). *Royal and other Historical Letters illustrative of the Reign of Henry III.* Rolls Series, No. 27. 2 vols. London, 1862-66.

Thomas de Burton. *Chronica monasterii de Melsa.* Edited by Edward A. Bond. Rolls Series No. 43. 3 vols. London, 1866-68.

Thomas of Elmham. *Historia monasterii S. Augustini Cantuariensis.* Edited by Charles Hardwick. Rolls Series, No. 8. London, 1858.

Vitry, Jacques de. *Histoire des Croisades.* Edited by F. P. G. Guizot. "Collection des Mémoires relatifs à l'histoire de France," Vol. XXII. Paris, 1825.

———. *The History of Jerusalem.* Translated by Aubrey Stewart. "Palestine Pilgrims' Text Society," Vol. XI, No. 2. London, 1896.

Walsingham, Thomas. *Historia Anglicana (1272-1422)* in *Chronica monasterii sancti Albani.* Edited by Ilenry T. Rilcy. Rolls Series, No. 28. Vols. I-II. London, 1863-64.

———. *Ypodigma Neustriae* in *Chronica monasterii sancti Albani.* Edited by Henry T. Riley. Rolls Series, No. 28. Vol. VII. London, 1876.

Walter of Coventry. *Historical Collections.* Edited by William Stubbs. Roll Series, No. 58, 2 vols. London, 1872-73.

Walter of Guisborough. *The Chronicle of Walter of Guiseborough previously edited as the Chronicle of Walter of Hemingford or Hemingburgh.* Edited by Harry Rothwell. "Publications of the Camden Society," Vol. LXXXIX. London, 1957.

Walter of Hemingburg. *Chronicon . . . de gestis regum Angliae.* Edited by Hans C. Hamilton. 2 vols. London, 1848-49.

William of Malmesbury. *De gestis regum Anglorum et historia novellae.* Edited by William Stubbs. Rolls Series, No. 90. 2 vols. London, 1887-89.

William of Newburgh. *Histoire rerum Anglicarum* in *Chronicles of the Reigns of Stephen, Henry II, and Richard I.* Edited by Richard Howlett. Rolls Series, No. 82. Vols. I-II. London, 1884-85.

William of Tyre. *Historia rerum in partibus transmarinis gestarum.* "Recueil des historiens des Croisades: historiens occidenteaux," Vol. I, Part I. Edited by A. Beugnot and A. LeProvost. Paris, 1844.

William [Guilelmus] of Tyre. *A History of Deeds done beyond the Sea.* Translated by Emily A. Babcock and August C. Krey. "Records of Civilization," No. 35. 2 vols. New York, 1943.

Wright, Thomas (ed.). *Anecdota literaria: a Collection of short Poems in English, Latin, and French, illustrative of the Literature and History of England in the Thirteenth Century, and more especially of the Condition and Manners of the different Classes of Society.* London, 1844.

———. *The Anglo-Latin Satirical Poets and Epigrammatists of the Twelfth Century.* Rolls Series, No. 59. 2 vols. London, 1872.

———. *The Latin Poems commonly attributed to Walter Mapes.* "Publications of the Camden Society," Vol. XVI. London, 1841.

———.. *Political Poems and Songs relating to English History from the Accession of Edward III to that of Richard III.* Rolls Series, No. 14. 2 vols. London, 1859-61..

———. *The Political Songs of England from the Reign of John to that of Edward II.* "Publications of the Camden Society," Vol. VI. London, 1839.

Public Records

Ancient Charters, royal and private, prior to A.D. 1200. Edited by John H. Round. "Publications of the Pipe Roll Society," Vol. X. London, 1888.

Calendar of Charters and Rolls preserved in the Bodleian Library. Edited by William H. Turner. Oxford, 1878.

Calendar of Entries in the Papal Registers relating to Great Britain and Ireland. Edited by William H. Bliss. Vols. I-II. London, 1893-95.

The Cartae Antiquae, Rolls 1-10. Edited by Lionel Landon. "Publications of the Pipe Roll Society," Vol. XVII N.S. London, 1939.

The Chancellor's Roll for the eighth Year of the Reign of King Richard the First, Michaelmas 1196. Edited by Doris M. Stenton. "Publications of the Pipe Roll Society," Vol. VII N.S. London, 1930.

Cole, Henry (ed.). *Documents illustrative of English History in the Thirteenth and Fourteenth Centuries, selected from the Records of the Department of Remembrancer of the Exchequer.* London, 1844.

Feet of Fines for the County of Lincoln for the Reign of King John, 1199-1216. Edited by Margaret S. Walker. "Publications of the Pipe Roll Society," Vol. XXIX N.S. London, 1954.

Feet of Fines of the Reigns of Henry II and Richard I, A.D. 1182-1199. Edited under the direction of the Council of the Pipe Roll Society. "Publications of the Pipe Roll Society," Vols. XVII, XX, XXIII-IV. London, 1894-1900.

Great Britain, Public Record Office. *The Book of Fees commonly called Testa de Nevill.* Prepared under the superintendence of the Deputy Keeper of the Records. 3 vols. London, 1920-31.

———. *Calendar of Chancery Warrants preserved in the Public Record Office, A.D. 1244-1326.* Prepared under the superintendence of the Deputy Keeper of the Records. Vol. I. London, 1927.

———. *Calendar of the Charter Rolls preserved in the Public Record Office, A.D. 1226-1326.* Prepared under the superintendence of the Deputy Keeper of the Records. 3 vols. London, 1903-09.

———. *Calendar of the Close Rolls preserved in the Public Record Office, Edward I, 1272-1307.* Prepared under the superintendence of the Deputy Keeper of the Records. 5 vols. London, 1900-08.

———. *Calendar of the Close Rolls preserved in the Public Record Office, Edward II, 1307-27.* Prepared under the superintendence of the Deputy Keeper of the Records. 4 vols. London, 1892-98.

———. *Calendar of the Close Rolls preserved in the Public Record Office, Edward III, 1327-77.* Prepared under the superintendence of the Deputy Keeper of the Records. 14 vols. London, 1896-1913.

———. *Calendar of Documents preserved in France illustrative of the History of Great Britain and Ireland.* Edited by J. Horace Round. Vol. I. London, 1899.

———. *Calendar of Documents relating to Ireland preserved in Her Majesty's Public Record Office, London, 1171-1307.* Edited by H. S. Sweetman, 5 vols. London, 1875-86.

———. *Calendar of Documents relating to Scotland preserved in Her Majesty's Public Record Office, London.* Edited by Joseph Bain. Vols. I-III. Edinburgh, 1881-88.

———. *Calendar of Fine Rolls preserved in the Public Record Office.* Edited by A. E. Bland. Vols. I-II. London, 1911-12.

———. *Calendar of Inquisitions post mortem and other analagous Documents.* Prepared under the superintendence of the Deputy Keeper of the Records. Vols. II-III. London, 1906-12.

———. *Calendar of the Liberate Rolls preserved in the Public Record Office, 1226-60.* Prepared under the superintendence of the Deputy Keeper of the Records. 4 vols. London, 1916-59.

———. *Calendar of the Patent Rolls preserved in the Public Record Office, Edward I, 1272-1307.* Prepared under the superintendence of the Deputy Keeper of the Records. 4 vols. London, 1893-1901.

———. *Calendar of the Patent Rolls preserved in the Public Record Office, Edward II, 1307-27.* Prepared under the superintendence of the Deputy Keeper of the Records. 5 vols. London, 1894-1904.

———. *Calendar of the Patent Rolls preserved in the Public Record Office, Ed-*

ward III, 1327-77. Prepared under the superintendence of the Deputy Keeper of the Records. 16 vols. London, 1891-1916.

———. *Calendar of the Patent Rolls preserved in the Public Record Office, Henry III, 1216-72.* Prepared under the superintendence of the Deputy Keeper of the Records. 6 vols. London, 1901-13.

———. *The Close Rolls of the Reign of Henry III preserved in the Public Record Office.* Prepared under the superintendence of the Deputy Keeper of the Records. 14 vols. London, 1902-38.

———. *Curia Regis Rolls of the Reigns of Richard I, John, and Henry III preserved in the Public Record Office, A.D. 1189-1230.* Edited by C. T. Fowler *et al.* 13 vols. London, 1922-59.

———. *A descriptive Catalogue of Ancient Deeds in the Public Record Office.* Prepared under the superintendence of the Deputy Keeper of the Records. 6 vols. London, 1890-1915.

———. *Issues of the Exchequer; being a Collection of Payments made out of His Majesty's Revenue from King Henry III to King Henry VI inclusive.* Edited and translated by Frederick Devon. Vol. III. London, 1837.

———. *Patent Rolls of the Reign of Henry III, A.D. 1225-32.* Prepared under the superintendence of the Deputy Keeper of the Records. London, 1903.

———. *Treaty Rolls preserved in the Public Record Office.* Printed under the superintendence of the Deputy Keeper of the Records. Vol. I: 1234-1325. Edited by Pierre Chaplais. London, 1955.

The Great Roll of the Pipe for the fifth through the thirty-fourth Years of the Reign of King Henry II (1158-1188). Edited under the direction of the Council of the Pipe Roll Society. "Publications of the Pipe Roll Society," Vols. I-II, IV-IX, XI-XIII, XVIII-XIX, XXI-XXII, XXV-XXXIV, XXXVI-XXXVIII. London, 1884-1925.

The Great Roll of the Pipe for the First Year of the Reign of King Richard the First, A.D. 1189-1190. Edited under the direction of Joseph Hunter. London, 1844.

The Great Roll of the Pipe for the Reigns of King Richard I and John and for the Fourteenth Year of the Reign of King Henry III. Edited by Doris M. Stenton *et al.* "Publications of the Pipe Roll Society," Vols. I-III, V-VI, VIII-X XII, XIV-XVI, XVIII-XX, XXII-XXIV, XXVII, XXVIII, XXX N.S. London, 1925-55.

The Great Roll of the Pipe for the second, third, and fourth Years of the Reign of King Henry the Second, 1155-1158. Edited under the direction of Joseph Hunter. London, 1844.

The Great Roll of the Pipe for the twenty-sixth Year of the Reign of King Henry III (A.D. 1241-42). New Haven, 1918.

The Memoranda Roll for the Michaelmas Term of the first Year of the Reign of King John (1199-1200). Edited by H. G. Richardson. "Publications of the Pipe Roll Society," Vol. XXI N.S. London, 1943.

The Memoranda Roll of the King's Remembrancer for Michaelmas 1230 - Trinity 1231. Edited by Chalfant Robinson. "Publications of the Pipe Roll Society," Vol. XI. Princeton, 1933.

The Parliamentary Writs and Writs of Military Summons. Edited by Francis Palgrave. Vols. I-II. London, 1827-30.

The Pipe Roll for 1292, Surrey Membrane. Edited by H. M. Mills. "Publications of the Surrey Record Society," Vol. XXI. Guilford, 1924.

The Pipe Roll of the Bishopric of Winchester for the fourth Year of the Pontificate of Peter des Roches, 1208-1209. Edited under the supervision of Hubert Hall. "Studies in Economic and Political Science," Vol. XI. London, 1903.

The Pipe Roll of 31 Henry I, Michelmas, 1130. Edited by Joseph Hunter. London, 1929.

Placita de Quo Warranto temporibus Edw. I, II & III in curia receptae scaccarij Westm. asservata. London, 1818.

Records of Parliament holden at Westminister on the twenty-eighth day of February, in the thirty-third Year of the Reign of King Edward the First (A. D. 1305). Edited by Frederic W. Maitland. Rolls Series, No. 98. London, 1893.

Rotuli curiae regis: Rolls and Records of the Court held before the King's Justiciars or Justices, from the sixth Year of King Richard I to the Accession of King John. Edited by Francis Palgrave. 2 vols. [London], 1835.

Rotuli de oblatis et finibus in Turri Londinensi asservati, tempore regis Johannis. Edited by Thomas D. Hardy. [London], 1835.

Rotuli hundredorum temp. Hen. III & Edw. I in Turr' Lon' et in curia receptae scaccarij Westm. asservati. Edited by W. Illingworth. 2 vols. London, 1812-18.

Rotuli litterarum clausarum in Turri Londinensi asservati. Edited by Thomas D. Hardy. 2 vols. London, 1833-44.

Rotuli litterarum patentium in Turri Londinensi asservati. Edited by Thomas D. Hardy. [London], 1835.

Rotuli Parliamentorum; ut et petitiones et placita in Parliamento tempore Edwardi R. I. Vol. I. [London], 1767.

Taxatio ecclesiastica Angliae et Walliae auctoritate P. Nicholai IV, circa A. D. 1291. [London], 1802.

Three Rolls of the King's Court in the Reign of King Richard the First, A. D. 1194-1195. Edited under the direction of the Council of the Pipe Roll Society. "Publications of the Pipe Roll Society," Vol. XIV. London, 1891.

Secondary Sources

Books

Addison, Charles G. *The Knights Templars.* American edition. New York, 1874.

Ashley, W. J. *Early History of the English Woollen Industry.* "Publications of the American Economic Association," Vol. II, No. 4. Baltimore, 1887.

———. *An Introduction to English Economic History and Theory.* Vol. I, 4th edition. London, 1923.

Baldwin, John M. *Medieval Theories of Just Price; Romanists, Canonists, and Theologians in the Twelfth and Thirteenth Centuries.* "Transactions of the American Philosophical Society," Vol. XLIX, Part 4. Philadelphia, 1959.

Bedford, William K. R. and Holbeche, Richard. *The Order of the Hospital of St. John of Jerusalem, being a History of the English Hospitallers of St. John, their Rise and Fall.* London, 1902.

Bellott, Hugh H. L. *The Inner and Middle Temple.* London, 1902.

Bretano, Robert. *York Metropolitan Jurisdiction and Papal Judges Delegate (1279-1296).* "University of California Publications in History." Vol. LVIII. Berkeley, 1959.

Bridrey, Emile. *La condition juridique des croisés et la privilège de la croix.* Paris, 1950.

The Cambridge Economic History. Vol. I: *The Agrarian Life of the Middle Ages.* Edited by J. Clapham and Eileen Power. Vol. II: *Trade and Industry in the Middle Ages.* Edited by M. Postan and E. E. Rich. Cambridge, 1941-52.

Campbell, G. A. *The Knights Templars, their Rise and Fall.* London, [1937].

Cheney, Christopher R. *From Beckett to Langton; English Church Government, 1170-1213.* Manchester, 1956.

Chrimes, S. B. *An Introduction to the Administrative History of Medieval England.* Oxford, 1952.

Cipolla, Carlo M. *Money, Prices, and Civilization in the Mediterranean World from the Fifth to the Seventeenth Centuries.* Princeton, 1956.

Coke, Sir Edward. *The Second Part of the Institutes of the Laws of England.* Vol. II. London, 1797.

Cunningham, W. *The Growth of English Industry and Commerce during the Early and Middle Ages.* 5th edition. Vol. I. Cambridge, 1910.

Darby, H. C. (ed.). *An historical Geography of England before A. D. 1800.* Cambridge, 1936.

Delisle, Léopold. *Mémoire sur les opérations financières des Templiers.* "Académie des Inscriptions et Belles Lettres, Mémoires," Vol. XXXIII. Paris, 1889.

Denholm-Young, N. *Seignorial Administration in England.* Oxford, 1937.

DeRoover, Raymond A. *L'Evolution de la lettre de change, xive-xviiie siècles.* Paris, 1953.

———. *Money, Banking, and Credit in medieval Bruges: Italian Merchant-Bankers, Lombards, and Money Changers: a Study in the Origins of Banking.* "Publications of the Medieval Academy of America," No. 51. Cambridge, 1948.

DuPuy, Pierre. *Traittez concernant l'histoire de France: sçavoir la condamnation des Templiers.* Paris, 1654.

Easson, David E. *Medieval Religious Houses, Scotland.* London, 1957.

Erdmann, Karl. *Die Entstehung des Kreuzzugsgedanken.* Stuttgart, 1935.

Eyton, Robert W. *Court, Household, and Itinerary of Henry II.* London, 1878.

Finke, Heinrich. *Papsttum und Untergang des Templerordens.* Münster, 1907.

Fuller, Thomas. *Historie of the Holy Warre.* London, 1840.

Gmelin, Julius. *Die Regel des Templerordens.* Innsbruck, 1893.

———. *Schuld oder Unschuld des Templerordens.* Stuttgart, 1893.

Gras, Norman S. B. *The Evolution of the English Corn Market from the Twelfth to the Eighteenth Century.* "Harvard Economic Studies," Vol. XIII. Cambridge, 1915.

Grousset, René. *Histoire des croisades et du royaume franc de Jérusalem.* 3 vols. Paris, 1939.

Gürtler, Nicolaus. *Historia Templariorum observationibus ecclesiasticis aucta.* Amsterdam, 1691.

Heaton, Herbert. *Economic History of Europe.* Revised edition. New York, 1948.

———. *The Yorkshire Woollen and Worsted Industries from the earliest Times up to the Industrial Revolution.* Oxford, 1920.

Heyd, Wilhelm. *Histoire du commerce du Levant au moyen-âge.* 2 vols. Leipzig, 1885-86.

Hülsen, Hans von. *Tragödie der Ritterorden; Templer, Deutsche Herren, Malteser.* München, 1948.

King, Edward J. *The Grand Priory of the Order of the Hospital of St. John of Jerusalem in England.* London, 1924.

Knoop, Douglas and Jones, G. P. *An Introduction to Freemasonry.* Manchester, 1940.

Knowles, David. *The Religious Orders in England.* Vols. I-II. Cambridge, 1950-55.

———, and Hadcock, R. Neville. *Medieval Religious Houses, England and Wales.* London, 1953.

Kosminsky, E. A. *Studies in the Agrarian History of England in the Thirteenth Century.* "Studies in Medieval History," Vol. VIII. Translated by Ruth Kisch. Oxford, 1956.

Landon, Lionel. *The Itinerary of King Richard I with Studies on certain Matters of Interest connected with his Reign.* "Publications of the Pipe Roll Society," Vol. XIII. London, 1935.

Lawton, George. *The Religious Houses of Yorkshire.* London, 1853.

Lea, Henry C. *A History of the Inquisition of the Middle Ages.* 3 vols. New York, 1888.

Lipson, E. *History of the Woollen and Worsted Industries.* London, 1921.

———. *An Introduction to the Economic History of England.* Vol. I: *The Middle Ages.* London, 1915.

Lizerand, Georges. *Clement V et Philippe IV le Bel.* Paris, 1910.

Lunt, William E. *The Financial Relations of the Papacy with England to 1327.* Vol. I of Studies in Anglo-Papal Relations during the Middle Ages. "Publications of the Medieval Academy of America," No. XXXIII. Cambridge, 1939.

———. *Papal Revenues in the Middle Ages.* 2 vols. New York, 1934.

Martin, Edward J. *The Trial of the Templars.* London, 1928.

McKechnie, William S. *Magna Carta: a Commentary on the Great Charter of King John.* 2d edition, Glasgow, 1914.

Mollat, Guillaume. *Les papes d'Avignon. "Bibliothèque de l'enseignement de l'histoire ecclésiastique,"* Vol. XV. Paris, 1920.

Nelson, Benjamin N. *The Idea of Usury: from tribal Brotherhood to universal Otherhood.* "History of Ideas Series," No. 3. Princeton, 1949.

Nicolai, Christoph. *Versuch über die beschuldigingen welche dem Tempelherrenorden gemacht worden, und über dessen Geheimniss; nebst einem Anhange über das Entstehen der Freymauergesellschaft.* Berlin, 1782.

Noonan, John T. *The Scholastic Analysis of Usury.* Cambridge, Mass., 1957.

Norgate, Kate. *Richard the Lion Heart.* London, 1924.

Oman, Charles W. *A History of the Art of War in the Middle Ages.* London, 1898.

Owst, Gerald R. *Literature and Pulpit in medieval England.* Cambridge, 1933.

———. *Preaching in medieval England.* 2 vols. Cambridge, 1926.

Oxford Essays in Medieval History presented to Herbert Edward Salter. Introduction by F. M. Powicke. Oxford, 1934.

Piquet, Jules. *Les Templiers: étude de leurs opérations financières.* Paris, 1939.

Power, Eileen. *The Wool Trade in English Medieval History.* London, 1942.

Powicke, F. M. *Handbook of British Chronology.* London, 1939.

———. *King Henry III and the Lord Edward.* 2 vols. Oxford, 1947.

Prutz, Hans. *Entwicklung und Untergang des Tempelherrenordens.* Berlin, 1888.

———. *Die geistlichen Ritterorden: ihre Stellung zur kirchlichen, politischen, gesellschaftlichen, und wirtschaftlichen Entwicklung des Mittelalters.* Berlin, 1908.

Ramsey, James A. *A History of the Revenues of the Kings of England, 1066-1399.* 2 vols. Oxford, 1925.

Rastoul, Amand. *Les Templiers, 1118-1312.* 4th edition. Paris, 1908.

Raynouard, François J. M. *Les Templiers, tragédie . . . précédée d'un précis historque sur les Templiers.* Paris, 1805.

Rees, William. *A History of the Order of St. John of Jerusalem in Wales and on the Welsh Border including an Account of the Templars.* Cardiff, 1947.

Renouard, Yves. *Les hommes d'affaires italiens du moyen âge.* Paris, 1949.

Rogers, J. E. T. *A History of Agriculture and Prices in England.* Vol. I. Oxford, 1866.

Ruding, Rogers. *Annals of the Coinage of Great Britain and Its Dependencies from the earliest Period of authentic History to the Reign of Queen Victoria.* 3d ed. Vol. I. London, 1840.

Runciman, Steven. *A History of the Crusades.* 3 vols. Cambridge, 1951-54.

Salzman, L. *English Industry of the Middle Ages.* Oxford, 1910.

———. *English Trade in the Middle Ages.* Oxford, 1913.

Sayous, André E. *Les banques de dépôt, les banques de credit, et les sociétés financières.* Paris, 1901.

Schottmüller, Konrad. *Der Untergang des Templer-ordens.* Berlin, 1887.

Setton, Kenneth M. (ed.). *A History of the Crusades.* Vol. I: *The First Hundred Years.* Edited by Marshall W. Baldwin. Philadelphia, 1955.

Siedschlag, Beatrice N. *English Participation in the Crusades, 1150-1220.* Menasha, [Wis.], 1939.

Simon, André. *History of the Wine Trade in England.* 3 vols. London, 1906-09.

Simon, Edith. *The Piebald Standard: A Biography of the Knights Templars.* Boston, 1959.

Smail, Richard C. *Crusading Warfare.* Edited by M. D. Knowles. "Cambridge Studies in Medieval Life and Thought," Vol. III N. S. Cambridge, 1956.

Tanner, John. *Notitia monastica or an Account of all the Abbies, Priories, and House of Friars, heretofore in England and Wales.* London, 1744.

Throop, Palmer A. *Criticism of the Crusade: a Study of Public Opinion and Crusade Propaganda.* Amsterdam, 1940.

Tout, Thomas F. *Chapters in the Administrative History of Medieval England.* "University of Manchester Publications," No. CXXVII. Vols. I-II. Manchester, 1920.

Usher, Abbott P. *The Early History of Deposit Banking in Mediterranean Europe.* "Harvard Economic Studies," Vol. LXXV. Cambridge, 1943.

The Victoria History of the County of Bedford. Edited by H. Arthur Doubleday and William Page. "The Victoria History of the Counties of England." 3 vols. London, 1904-12.

The Victoria History of the County of Berkshire. Edited by P. A. Ditchfield and William Page. "The Victoria History of the Counties of England." 4 vols. London, 1907-24.

The Victoria History of the County of Buckingham. Edited by William Page. "The Victoria History of the Counties of England." Vols. I, III-IV. London, 1905-27.

The Victoria History of the County of Cambridge and the Isle of Ely. Edited by L. F. Salzman. "The Victoria History of the Counties of England." Vol. II. London, 1948.

The Victoria History of the County of Essex. Edited by William Page and J. Horace Round. "The Victoria History of the Counties of England." Vol. II. London, 1907.

The Victoria History of the County of Gloucester. Edited by William Page. "The Victoria History of the Counties of England." Vol. II. London, 1907.

The Victoria History of the County of Hampshire and the Isle of Wight. Edited by H. Arthur Doubleday and William Page. "The Victoria History of the Counties of England." Vols. II, III, V. London, 1903-12.

The Victoria History of the County of Hertford. Edited by William Page. "The Victoria History of the Counties of England." Vols. II-IV. London, 1908-14.

The Victoria History of the County of Huntingdon. Edited by William Page, Granville Proby and S. Inskip Ladds. "The Victoria History of the Counties of England." Vols. II-III. London, 1932-36.

The Victoria History of the County of Kent. Edited by William Page. "The Victoria History of the Counties of England." Vol. II. London, 1926.

The Victoria History of the County of Lancaster. Edited by William Farrer and J. Brownbill. "The Victoria History of the Counties of England." Vol. II. London, 1908.

The Victoria History of the County of Leicester. Edited by W. G. Hoskins. "The Victoria History of the Counties of England." Vol. II. London, 1954.

The Victoria History of the County of Lincoln. Edited by William Page. "The Victoria History of the Counties of England." Vol. II. London, 1906.

The Victoria History of the County of Northampton. Edited by R. M. Serjeantson and W. 'R. D. Adkins. "The Victoria History of the Counties of England." Vol. II. London, 1906.

The Victoria History of the County of Oxford. Edited by H. E. Salter and Mary D. Lobel. "The Victoria History of the Counties of England." Vol. II. London, 1907.

The Victoria History of the County of Somerset. Edited by William Page. "The Victoria History of the Counties of England." Vol. II. London, 1911.

The Victoria History of the County of Suffolk. Edited by William Page. "The Victoria History of the Counties of England." Vol. II. London, 1911.

The Victoria History of the County of Surrey. Edited by H. E. Malden. "The Victoria History of the Counties of England." Vols. III-IX. Westminster, 1902-12.

The Victoria History of the County of Sussex. Edited by William Page. "The Victoria History of the Counties of England." Vol. II. London, 1907.

The Victoria History of the County of Warwick. Edited by L. F. Salzmann. "The Victoria History of the Counties of England." Vols. III-VI. London, 1904-51.

The Victoria History of the County of Worcester. Edited by William Page. "The Victoria History of the Counties of England." Vols. III-IV. London, 1913-24.

The Victoria History of the County of York. Edited by William Page. "The Victoria History of the Counties of England." Vols. II-III. London, 1912-13.

The Victoria History of the County of York, North Riding. Edited by William Page. "The Victoria History of the Counties of England." Vols. I-II. London, 1914-23.

Waas, Adolf. *Geschichte der Kreuzzüge.* 2 vols. Freiburg, 1956.

Williamson, J. Bruce. *The History of the Temple, London, from the Institution of the Order of the Knights of the Temple to the Close of the Stuart Period.* London, 1924.

Woodhouse, F. C. *The military and religious Orders of the Middle Ages.* London, 1879.

Articles

Aitken, Robert. "The Knights Templars in Scotland," *Scottish Review,* XXXII (1898), 1-36.

Beveridge, W. H. "The Yield and Price of Corn in the Middle Ages," *Economic History,* I (1927), 155-67.

Boutaric, E. "Clement V, Philippe le Bel et les Templiers," *Revue des questions historiques,* X (1871), 301-42; XI (1872), 5-40.

Brett, Alfred. "The Manor of Wetherby and Lands within the Manor," *Yorkshire Archaeological Journal,* XXX (1931), 261-73.

Bromberg, Benjamin. "The Financial and Administrative Importance of the Knights Hospitallers to the English Crown," *Economic History,* IV (1940), 307-11.

Carus-Wilson, Eleanor A. "The English Cloth Industry in the late Twelfth and early Thirteenth Centuries," *Economic History Review,* XIV (1944), 32-50.

——— "An Industrial Revolution of the Thirteenth Century," *Economic History Review,* XI (1941), 39-60.

Cate, James L. "The Church and Market Reform in England during the Reign of Henry III," *Medieval and Historiographical Essays in Honor of James Westfall Thompson,* edited by James L. Cate and Eugene N. Anderson (Chicago, 1938), pp. 27-65.

Chetwynd-Stapylton, H. E. "The Templars at Templehurst," *Yorkshire Archaeological and Topographical Journal,* X (1889), 276-86, 431-43.

Delaville le Roulx, J. "La suppression des Templiers," *Revue des questions historiques,* XLVIII (1890), 29-61.

DeRoover, Raymond A. "New Interpretations of the History of Banking," *Journal of World History,* II (1954), 38-76.

Dibbon, L. B. "Chancellor and Keeper of the Seal under Henry III," *English Historical Review,* XXVII (1912), 39-51.

Edwards, John. "The Templars in Scotland in the Thirteenth Century," *Scottish Historical Review,* V (1907), 13-25.

Farmer, D. L. "Some Grain Price Movements in Thirteenth Century England," *Economic History Review,* X (1957-58), 3rd S, 207-20.

Ferris, Eleanor. "The Financial Relations of the Knights Templars to the English Crown," *"American Historical Review,"* VIII (1902), 1-17.

Flahiff, G. B. "The Use of Prohibitions by Clerics against Ecclesiastical Courts in England," *Medieval Studies,* III (1941), 101-16.

———. "The Writ of Prohibition to Court Christian in the Thirteenth Century," *Medieval Studies,* VI (1954), 261-313.

Grange, Amy. "The Fall of the Knights of the Temple," *Dublin Review,* CXVII (1895), 329-46.

Gras, Norman S. B. "Bill of Exchange," *Encyclopedia of the Social Sciences,* II (1932), 539-40.

Graves, Coburn. "The Economic Activities of the Cistercians in medieval England," *Annalecta Sacri Ordinis Cisterciensis,* XIII (1957), fascicles 1-2.

Hall, Margaret W. "Early Bankers in the Genoese Notarial Records," *Economic History Review,* VI (1935), 73-79.

Hammer-Purgstall, Joseph von. "Die Schuld der Templer," *Denkschriften der Kaiserlichen Academie der Wissenschaft, Philosophisch-historische Classe,* VI (1885), 175-210.

Hawtrey, R. G. "Credit," *Encyclopedia of the Social Sciences,* IV (1931), 545-50.

Hope, W. H. St. John. "The Round Church of the Knights Templars in Temple Bruer, Lincolnshire," *Archaeologia,* LXI (1908), 177-98.

Knight, Frank H. "Historical and Theoretical Issues in the Problem of Modern Capitalism," *Journal of Economic and Business History,* I (1928), 119-36.

———. "Interest," *Encyclopedia of the Social Sciences,* VIII (1932), 131-44.

Kosminsky, E. A. "Services and Money Rents in the Thirteenth Century," *Economic History Review,* V (1935), 24-45.

Krey, August C. "William of Tyre: the Making of an Historian in the Middle Ages," *Speculum,* XVI (1941), 149-66.

Landmann, Julius. "History of Commercial Banking to the Close of the Eighteenth Century," *Encyclopedia of the Social Sciences,* II (1930), 423-31.

Langlois, Charles V. "L'Affaire des Templiers," *Journal des Savants,* VI N.S. (1908), 417-35.

———. "Le Procès des Templiers," *Revue des deux mondes,* CIII (1891), 382-421.

Lea, Henry C. "The Absolution Formula of the Templars," *Papers of the American Society of Church History,* V (1893), 37-58.

LeBras, G. "L'usure: la doctrine ecclésiatique de l'usure a l'époque classique (xiie-xve siècle)," *Dictionnaire de Théologie Catholique,* ed. A. Vacant, E. Mangenot, and E. Amann, XV (1950), cols. 2335-72.

Lecestre, Léon. "La Règle du Temple," *Revue des questions historiques,* XL (1886), 577-83.

Leys, Agnes M. "The Forfeiture of the Lands of the Templars in England," *Oxford Essays in Medieval History presented to Herbert Edward Salter,* edited by F. M. Powicke (Oxford, 1934), pp. 155-63.

Lunt, William E. "A Papal Tenth levied in the British Isles from 1274 to 1280," *English Historical Review,* XXXII (1917), 49-89.

Martin, E. J. "The Templars in Yorkshire," *The Yorkshire Archaeological Journal,* XXIX (1930), 366-85; XXX (1931), 135-56.

McLaughlin, T. P. "The Teaching of the Canonists on Usury (XII, XIII, and XIV centuries)", *Medieval Studies,* I (1939), 81-147; II (1940), 1-22.

Minos, P. J. Oliver. "The Knights Templars' Chapel at Garway," *The Reliquary and Illustrated Archaeologist,* V. N.S. (1899), 193-98.

Perkins, Clarence. "The Knights Hospitallers in England after the Fall of the Order of the Temple," *English Historical Review,* XLV (1930), 285-89.

———. "The Knights Templars in the British Isles," *English Historical Review,* XXV (1910), 209-30.

———. "The Trial of the Knights Templars in England," *English Historical Review,* XXIV (1909), 432-47.

———. "The Wealth of the Knights Templars in England," *American Historical Review,* XV (1909), 252-63.

Postan, M. M. "Credit in Medieval Trade," *Economic History Review,* I (1928), 234-61.

―――. "Private financial Instruments in Medieval England," *Vierteljahrschrift für Social- und Wirtschaftsgeschichte,* XXIII (1930), 39-90.

Reynolds, Robert L. "A Business Affair in Genoa in the Year 1200, Banking, Bookkeeping, a Broker (?), and a Lawsuit," *Studi di storia e diritto in onore di Enrico Besta,* (Milan, 1939), II, 167-81.

Salin, Edgar. "Usury," *Encyclopedia of the Social Sciences,* XV (1935), 193-97.

Sandys, Agnes. "The Financial and Administrative Importance of the London Temple in the Thirteenth Century," *Essays in Medieval History presented to Thomas Frederick Tout,* edited by A. G. Little and F. M. Powicke (Manchester, 1925), pp. 147-62.

Sayles, G. "A Dealer in Wardrobe Bills," *Economic History Review,* III (1931), 268-73.

Sayous, André E. "Le capitalisme commercial et financier dans les pays chrétiens de la Méditerranée occidentale depuis la première croisade jusqu'à la fin du moyen âge." *Vierteljahrschrift für Social- und Wirtschaftsgeschichte,* XXIX (1936), 270-95.

Schaube, A. "Die Wollausfuhr Englands vom Jahre 1273," *Vierteljahrschrift für Social- und Wirtschaftsgeschichte,* VI (1908), 39-72, 159-85.

Shannon, Albert C. "The Secrecy of Witnesses in Inquisitorial Tribunals and in Contemporary Secular Criminal Trials," *Essays in Medieval Life and Thought presented in Honor of Austin Patterson Evans,* edited by John H. Mundy et al. (New York, 1955), pp. 59-70.

Strieder, Jacob. "Origin and Evolution of early European Capitalism," *Journal of Economic and Business History,* II (1929), 1-19.

Taylor, R. V. "Ribston and the Knights Templars," *Yorkshire Archaeological and Topographical Journal,* VII (1882), 429-52; VIII (1884), 259-99; IX (1886), 71-98.

Trudon des Ormes, A. "Liste des maisons et de quelques dignitaires de l'ordre du Temple en Syrie, en Chypre, et en France d'après les pièces du procès," *Revue de l'Orient Latin,* V (1897), 389-459.

Usher, Abbott P. "The Origins of Banking: the Primitive Bank of Deposit," *Economic History Review,* IV (1934), 399-428.

Viollet, Paul M. "Les interrogatoires de Jacques de Molai, Grand Maître du Temple; conjectures," *Mémoires de l'Institut national de France, Académie des inscriptions et belles-lettres,* XXXVIII (1911), Part II, 121-36.

Whitwell, Robert J. "Italian Bankers and the English Crown," *Transactions of the Royal Historical Society,* XVII N.S. (1903), 175-233.

―――. "English Monasteries and the Wool Trade in the Thirteenth Century," *Vierteljahrschrift für Social- und Wirtschaftsgeschichte,* II (1904), 1-33.

Wood, Herbert. "The Knights Templars in Ireland," *Proceedings of the Royal Irish Academy.* XXVI (1907), 327-77.

Unpublished Material

Perkins, Clarence. "The History of the Knights Templars in England." Unpublished Ph.D. dissertation, Department of History, Harvard University, 1908.

Index

The text of *The Knights Templars in England* was set by Morneau Typographers in Times Roman with chapter titles in Engraver's Old English. The book was printed by Tyler Printing Company on S. D. Warren's sixty-pound University Eggshell textstock. Arizona Trade Bindery bound the volume in Joanna parchment coral mist vellum. The dust jacket is printed on Hamilton Andorra textstock, the jacket design and drawings are by Beau Williams.